Credit Risk of Financial Instruments

Dedication

To my parents, Robert and Gunta Banks, for 27 years of magnificent support, opportunities and advice.

Credit Risk of Financial Instruments

Erik Banks

MACMILLAN

First published in the United Kingdom by
MACMILLAN PUBLISHERS LTD, 1993
Distributed by Globe Book Services Ltd
Brunel Road, Houndmills,
Basingstoke, Hants RG21 2XS, England

Reprinted 1994, 1995

ISBN 0-333-59593-9

A catalogue record for this book is available from The British Library.

Printed in Great Britain by
Antony Rowe Ltd, Chippenham, Wiltshire

Contents

Dedication ii
Acknowledgements ix

PART I: RISK AND DECISION-MAKING 1

1 Risk in a Changing Environment 3
The historical perspective 3
Risk 7
Regulators in a changing environment 13

2 A General Risk Management Framework 19
Developing the framework 19
Using the framework 21

3 Elements of the Credit Decision 25
The optimal credit decision 25
Element 1: counterparty risk 26
Element 2: risk exposure 30
Element 3: return on a transaction 33
Element 4: maturity considerations 41
Element 5: transaction motivation 43
Element 6: enhancement and risk reduction 48

PART II: CLASSIFICATION AND RISK EQUIVALENCY 53

4 Classification of Risk 55
General risks facing financial institutions 55
Product risk 56
The effects of product risk 57
Market risk, counterparty risk and loss levels 64

5 Risk Equivalency 67
The purpose of risk equivalency 68
Risk equivalency calculations 68

6 **Quantifying the Risk Equivalency Process** 73
Derivation of the risk factor 73

PART III: FINANCIAL INSTRUMENT RISK ANALYSIS 83

7 **Repurchase/Reverse Repurchase Agreements** 85
Definition 85
General credit considerations 89
Risk quantification 90
Risk factors 96

8 **Treasury Securities and Treasury Derivatives** 98
Definition 98
General credit considerations 101
Risk quantification 104
Risk factors 112

9 **Mortgage-back Securities and Associated Derivatives** 115
Definition 115
General credit considerations 123
Risk quantification 125
Risk factors 133

10 **Money Market Instruments** 134
Description 134
General credit considerations 142
Risk quantification 143
Risk factors 153
A final note on registration requirements 153

11 **Bonds** 155
Description 155
General credit considerations 161
Risk quantification 163
Risk factors 168

12 **Foreign Exchange and Currency Derivatives** 169
Definition 169
General credit considerations 174
Risk quantification 176
Netting foreign exchange exposures 190
Risk factors 192

13 Swaps and Swap Derivatives 193
Definition 193
General credit considerations 203
Risk quantification 206
Risk factors 242

Appendix 1: Alternative Method for Computation of Calculated Replacement Cost and Discounted Replacement Cost 244
Introduction 244
Definitions 244
Derivation of the alternative method 245
Numerical examples 246
Further remarks 247

Appendix 2: Graphical Representation of Swap Replacement Costs 249

Appendix 3: Tabular Representations of Swap Replacement Costs 252

Appendix 4: Sample Risk Factors at Various Volatility Levels 259

References 261

Index 265

Acknowledgements

Many credit and financial product professionals at various firms have provided me with instruction and guidance over the past few years; though I cannot list each by name in this section, I owe my thanks and appreciation to all of them.

I would like to specifically thank William Lyman at Merrill Lynch for several years of valuable direction, opportunities and education; without his efforts this book would not have been possible. I would also like to thank Alexander Yablonsky for his thoughtful encouragement and commentary over the past 12 months. Finally, I would like to thank my wife Milena for her enthusiastic support of everything I undertake.

E.B.
Tokyo
November 1992

Part I
Risk and Decision-making

1: Risk in a Changing Environment

THE HISTORICAL PERSPECTIVE

In the decades preceding the 1970s banking was a relatively ordinary and well understood business. Banks were at the same time intermediaries between suppliers and users of funds and managers (and sometimes takers) of risk. Profitability was good, risks were acceptable, competition, though present, was not especially intense and innovation was generally slow. The clear division in countries such as the US and Japan between commercial banking and investment banking, with no real encroachment on one another's territory, added to the relatively comfortable worlds of each business. Even in European countries, where the concept of 'universal banking' was already widely practised (where an institution could have a presence in retail, institutional and investment banking), a few dominant banks controlled the market and were not under pressure to innovate, change or compete.

The 1970s and 1980s witnessed a change in the *status quo* in the banking field. Many external factors played a role in altering the nature, the scope and, most especially, the risks of banking. For the purposes of this discussion, we can reduce the main causes to two factors, increased market volatility and increased competitive pressures. The root causes of both bear some general review before we discuss how the two have altered the state of banking.

Market Volatility

From 1944 to the early 1970s one key financial measure, the foreign currency exchange rate, was governed by the so-called Bretton Woods Agreement, which essentially called for a regime of fixed, though periodically adjustable, exchange rates. Although gold was ostensibly the absolute standard, in practice the US dollar acted as the benchmark currency. Foreign currency values were based on the dollar, which was itself exchangeable for gold at \$35/oz. The US bought and sold gold at \$35/oz, so foreign currencies were effectively convertible into gold *via* the dollar. Monetary authorities of individual countries adjusted their currencies periodically in relation to the US dollar, within a band of about 1 per cent.

The system worked reasonably well until approximately 1967. From that year on, a series of US balance of payment deficits began placing pressure on the dollar. Devaluation of the dollar was thought to be difficult, since all currencies were tied to it. The US favoured a revaluation of the currencies of countries with balance of payments surpluses, such as Japan and Germany, while those countries favoured a reduction of the US balance of payments deficit. The *impasse* began to weaken the adjustable rate mechanism and in August 1971 the US added a further blow by temporarily suspending dollar convertibility into gold. At that point, foreign governments elected not to intervene to support currency values against the dollar, since convertibility was no longer possible and the future value of the dollar was uncertain. This effectively spelled the end of the fixed exchange rate framework.

A last ditch effort to save the system was made in December 1971 through the Smithsonian Agreement, which called for revaluation of the Deutschmark and the yen against the dollar (by 13.5 per cent and 17 per cent respectively), an increase in the fluctuation band from 1 per cent to 2.25 per cent and an increase in the price of gold to $38/oz, even though convertibility had not been reinstated by the US. These efforts, however, were not enough to prevent what many felt was inevitable: fully floating exchange rates. Just six months after the Smithsonian Agreement, sterling was floated against the dollar (and all other currencies). Most other major currencies followed suit by March 1973, signalling an end to the Bretton Woods Agreement and to nearly 30 years of fixed exchange rates.

From a risk perspective, the collapse of the Bretton Woods Agreement was (and remains) significant. As will be explored below, the relationship between spot and forward foreign exchange rates is tied to interest rates and interest rate differentials between countries. With a system of freely floating exchange rates, one would expect much greater movement in underlying interest rates. The shift from a fixed to a floating rate regime has increased market movements in both currencies and interest rates to levels previously unknown in banking. The magnitude of this volatility has, in turn, led to greater opportunities for banks to take risks and to engage in risk management and has accelerated the overall pace of product innovation. These aspects will be considered further in a later section.

Competition

Although a discussion of competition within the banking business can be extremely broad (and may well include factors not relevant here), there are at least four principal reasons for the unprecedented levels of competition in both commercial and investment banking since the 1970s.

First, there has been a gradual blurring of the distinction between commercial and investment banking as a result of deregulation in many markets over the past two decades. In certain countries, such as Japan and the US, barriers to competition between the two fields are governed by law. Article 65 of the Securities and Exchange Law in Japan prevents commercial banks from engaging in the trust and securities business and investment banks from engaging in commercial banking business. In the US the same distinction is enforced by the Glass-Steagall Act of 1933. In countries such as the UK and the Netherlands the division between the two lines of banking has been one of market practice, not legal prohibition. For example, the major UK clearing banks were historically not involved in the securities business (leaving that to the discount houses and the merchant banks) and did not effectively start participating in the securities business until the 'Big Bang' of October 1986. The major Dutch banks concentrated their efforts on commercial banking (leaving securities activities to the more specialised merchant banks).

Gradual deregulation in US markets has meant that commercial banks in particular can offer more services, and participate in more markets, than before. Some of the deregulation was spurred by a loosening of interest rate controls in the early 1980s. This had the effect of allowing banks to offer more competitive rates on a variety of new savings products. In 1987 the Federal Reserve also increased the number of markets in which commercial banks could be involved by allowing them to underwrite, and deal in, securities. Underwriting of and dealing in commercial paper, mortgage-backed and asset-backed securities and certain municipal bonds is also permitted, providing such business is conducted through an affiliate of a bank holding company. In 1989 these affiliates were allowed to underwrite and deal in corporate bonds and in 1990 JP Morgan's subsidiary was permitted to underwrite equities, an act which would have been unthinkable under the original Glass-Steagall framework.

Much the same is happening in Japan. While Article 65 still remains in force, recent legislative changes enacted by the Parliament will allow commercial banks to own and operate trust banks and securities firms and will allow securities firms to own and operate commercial banks. Although certain areas will still be off limits to commercial banks (eg equity underwriting and pension fund management), there will be much greater participation by these institutions in areas such as corporate bond underwriting and dealing. The overall pattern seems to be gradually following events in the US markets.

In the major European countries most large commercial banks now have separate securities subsidiaries engaged in a range of investment banking products or have incorporated some or all aspects of the business into their main banking operations. The concept of universal banking has been embraced by banks throughout the European Community (with the exception of Belgium, which still restricts participation in the two businesses).

The trend throughout the world has become clear. The erosion of barriers between the two types of banking has meant that both groups are active in swaps, mortgage-backed securities, futures, options, foreign exchange, municipal and public sector bonds, repurchase agreements and so on, heightening the level of competition.

The second reason for increased competition is found in a concept known as disintermediation. In its simplest form disintermediation can be thought of as the process of excluding banks and securities firms from their traditional roles as direct financiers. As borrowers, savers and investors have become more sophisticated and more knowledgeable about markets, instruments and opportunities, they have elected to become direct participants in the financing process, effectively removing financial institutions from their traditional function as intermediaries or 'middle men'. This process, which has been increasingly apparent during the past decade, has caused many financial institutions to be squeezed out of their traditional markets. This, in turn, has led to loss of profits and revenues from transactions which were once virtually guaranteed business.

The ultimate result of the disintermediation process and the ensuing pressure on profitability has been a search for new markets. Specifically, institutions which have been forced out of their customary markets have attempted to find new business in more complex and generally riskier products and markets, which carry higher margins and require a level of expertise not readily available within institutional customers. The most promising areas for participation have been asset-backed securitisation, off-balance sheet derivatives, lease financing, debt and equity underwriting, corporate finance and advisory work and other structured financings. The result is that there has been a marked increase in competition in all of these areas, as more institutions are driven from one market to another by disintermediation.

The third primary reason for increased competition is relatively straightforward: the lure of profitability. Many of the areas just mentioned are enormously profitable for institutions to be in. Many generate fee income and thus do not use a bank's balance sheet. That has the effect of boosting performance measures and utilising little or no capital (or using a larger amount of capital for only a short period of time). As one might expect, when profitability is very high (and barriers to entry are surmountable), the level of participation and competition grows.

The fourth and final reason for increased competition is related to the global nature of the financial markets. Although this phrase has been somewhat overworked during the 1980s and 1990s, the reality is that markets for many products are truly global, with financial instruments traded or transacted 24 hours a day. The mere fact that there are markets active (with revenues and profits being generated) at any point in time means that participation is high and competition is strong. Instantaneous information and trading technologies and highly interdependent financial systems and economies have translated into a series of larger, more important and more liquid markets, in which most financial institutions need to participate to remain major players. Institutions have dropped out of particular market segments for profitability reasons and because, they claim, they cannot be everything to everyone (as witnessed in the US commercial paper and Eurocommercial paper markets, the gilts market and several regional equity markets). However, most banks realise the need to be active in many of the major markets and product areas around the clock, which has undoubtedly led to increased competition.

RISK

Our original premise stated that market volatility and *competition* have each played a significant role in altering the state of banking in the past 20 years. Although the changes to banking as a whole have been numerous, perhaps the most important has been an increase in risk. Risk, though it can be defined in many ways and can take many forms (which we shall explore in detail later), is central to the banking business. During the 1980s and 1990s, however, banks have been exposed to new types of risk, with different characteristics and magnitudes from those dealt with in the earlier days of banking. Some of these risks have come from the markets themselves, as banks have attempted to manage risk resulting from volatility. Others have been fuelled by competition. In a drive to be the best and the most profitable, banks have entered markets once foreign to them or have created new products or instruments whose value, use and characteristics may or may not be fully understood. The central point is that volatility and competition have forced banks to assume risks which they have not previously assumed. The form, substance, measurement and management of these risks are a central topic of this book.

The 'by-products' of increased risk for financial institutions have been various. Banks have become more active risk takers and managers, they have become more astute product innovators and, on the negative side, they have occasionally made unwise business decisions for the sake of earnings, market penetration, reputation and so on. This has led to their being exposed to defaults (and losses) on a variety of instruments and markets.

Of necessity, banks involved in the financial markets today have adapted themselves to take and to manage risk. Although this has traditionally been a part of the role of the banker, there is no doubt that the risks facing banks today are significantly greater and more complex and far more destructive if not fully understood. Banks are often called on to take risks directly. These are hedged or eliminated so far as is possible but in many instances this cannot be achieved. Two examples serve to illustrate this. A bank may be called on to provide bridge financing for a particular deal and will do so in anticipation of a successful underwriting of securities for the borrower at some future point, which will serve to repay the bridging loan. Until the securities have been issued and the loan has been repaid, the bank has taken on an enormous amount of risk (in this case counterparty risk, which, as we shall see, cannot be hedged or reduced). As a second example, consider a bank transacting a very complex swap, with a distant final maturity, which does not lend itself to satisfactory hedging. Until the opposing side of the swap can be established to offset the flows (if indeed this is possible, by no means a certainty given the esoteric nature of the deal), the bank is exposed at the least to counterparty risk and market risk (both to be covered in detail later).

Banks are also more active risk managers. As a result of market volatility and the need to understand and deal with new risks brought on by the markets, banks have become adept at managing their own businesses in a generally conservative and prudent fashion. Most institutions active in the financial markets have explicit and focused internal policies for dealing with risk, such that at any point in time they are not excessively exposed to those instruments or markets which might cause financial damage. The internal risk management function created by banks also offers their clients the opportunity to benefit from a given institution's risk management skills (for a fee).

Product innovation has developed alongside the risk management function. On encountering new and increased risks in a given market, banks have, over the past few years, generally been quick to innovate. This may be the result of a bank's need to reduce, eliminate or diversify its own risks or it may simply be a response to the needs of a client who requires protection of a special nature because of its exposure in a given market. It may also stem from a desire to take advantage of profit opportunities in a given market or to raise funds in a new and cheaper fashion. Whatever the reason, banks have been at the forefront of the development of new instruments to cope with changing markets. These products include currency and interest rate swaps, swap derivatives, medium-term notes, high yield bonds, bonds with warrants, index warrants, forward rate agreements and collateralised mortgage obligations. Most of them have given banks and their clients the ability to manage risks, to finance themselves in new ways or to take an outright view on a given market.

Another by-product of increased risk is a tendency by some institutions to make unwise business decisions, to transact the wrong types of business for the wrong reasons. Specifically, as a bank moves into new markets and new products in an attempt to increase revenues, earnings and market share and to improve league table positions, it is possible that difficulties may ensue in the future. In the past, some institutions involved in particularly competitive situations have expanded into businesses they may not fully comprehend and would not ordinarily participate in, for the sake of earnings, market penetration and reputation. Risk management directives, credit standards and other internal operating guidelines may be sacrificed in such cases. Thus, while we have already mentioned that risk can bring out the skill and expertise in a bank by allowing it to demonstrate its ability to take and to manage risk and to create new products, it can also force an institution to turn against its natural skills and standard operating policies (which normally allow it to operate as a prudent institution), for the sake of market participation and potential profits.

The topics we have just covered would mean little unless banks suffered losses as a result of risk. The fourth by-product of risk demonstrates how risks have translated into actual defaults over time. With these practical results the theoretical discussion on risk becomes more firmly grounded in the real practice of banking.

Although defaults and losses have occurred in banking since the beginning of the industry, the 1980s and 1990s have seen more than their fair share of difficulties. Before discussing these difficulties, it is helpful to recall that a default occurs when an issuer or a counterparty ceases, for any reason, to perform on a contractual obligation. Most defaults occur as a result of continued or sudden financial deterioration leading to forced or voluntary bankruptcy. In certain cases defaults may also occur because a counterparty wilfully elects to cease performance under a contract. It should be noted that a default scenario represents counterparty risk at its maximum. Losses, in contrast, are the end result of defaults. They represent the sum which a bank has to subtract from earnings that represents income or funds which can no longer be claimed because the source can no longer provide them. Our discussion will centre largely on defaults, as these are based on information which is publicly available. Actual losses are based on information which may or may not be part of the public record. We know, however, that in a worst case scenario defaults will equal losses. Only if some security is available or if value is recovered in a bankruptcy court will losses be less than defaults.

US Commercial Paper

After the watershed Penn Central US commercial paper (USCP) default in 1970 (which we shall discuss in Chapter 10) there was only one other instance of default in the USCP markets until 1989. In 1982 Manville Corporation defaulted with $15m outstanding. With the exception of Manville, no other rated issuers ceased to perform on their CP programmes, reflecting a very low default rate over the course of 19 years. At the time of default Manville paper accounted for under 0.01 per cent of total CP outstanding. The picture in 1989 and beyond, however, is rather different. In just three years five issuers defaulted on over $720m of CP. These issuers were Integrated Resources ($213m in June 1989), Colorado Ute ($19m in August 1989), Equitable Lomas Leasing ($53m in September 1989), Mortgage and Realty Trust ($167m in March 1990) and Columbia Gas ($268m in June 1991). Defaults represented nearly 0.1 per cent of outstandings in 1989 alone, a tenfold rise since 1982 and a very substantial sum given the growth in total outstandings during those seven years. In the defaults mentioned above losses were sustained by investors and dealers alike. The actual reasons for the defaults were various but all were ultimately attributable to financial difficulties of the issuers.

Eurocommercial Paper

The Eurocommercial paper (ECP) market, in common with the USCP market, saw no problems among rated issuers until 1989, when four issuers defaulted in rapid succession. Integrated Resources failed on $63m of ECP in June 1989 (at the time of its USCP default), Wang Labs failed on $96m in August 1989, Lomas Financial on $17m in September 1989 and the Development Finance Corporation of New Zealand (DFC) on $270m in October 1989. Although DFC also had a USCP programme in place at the time of the ECP default, there were no current outstandings. In addition, Polly Peck International failed on $91m in the sterling CP market in October 1990. Losses were once again borne by both investors and dealers and the reasons for default were related to counterparty failure.

Bonds

The experience of the bond market has been even worse than that of the USCP and ECP markets. The two principal reasons for this are the level of corporate restructurings and the issuance of high yield debt. Mergers, acquisitions, divestitures, leveraged buyouts and management buyouts have left many bond issuers in a weakened financial state as a result of increased debt loads, high interest costs, forced asset sales and so on. Such restructurings have left issuers unable to service their bond obligations. The second problem is often a consequence of the first, with higher risk, higher yield junk bonds being employed by many companies, sometimes as a result of restructurings, in other cases as the only source of funds available, given a company's questionable credit quality. The default rate on junk issuers is significantly higher than that for investment grade issuers. (In 1991 the default rate on speculative credits was 9.5 per cent)

According to a 1992 report by the US rating agency Moody's, total defaults in the public debt markets totalled $8.4b between 1970 and 1988. In contrast, total defaults between 1989 and 1991 reached a staggering $55.4b. In 1991 alone a total of $20.3b in defaults occurred, including Executive Life ($1.85b) EII Holdings ($1.24b), Memorex Telex NV ($1b), TWA ($947m), Bank of New England ($914m) and Columbia Gas ($1.34b).

The pattern of defaults in the bond market is also revealing; in terms of the number of issuers defaulting on public debt, 1983 was the lowest point with only 14 failures. By the time the excesses of the 1980s were over, the number of counterparties defaulting had increased substantially, with 70 in 1989, 96 in 1990 and 94 in 1991. The expectation by many bankers and rating agencies is that this number will remain high until more companies fail from excess debt or are 're-equitised' in the markets. As with the money market instruments discussed above, the losers in bond defaults have been both investors and dealers.

Swaps

Swap defaults have not yet occurred in the same fashion or magnitude as defaults involving money market instruments or bonds. At least part of the reason is that swaps are generally transacted with higher quality counterparties which are less apt to fail. It is also conceivable that the short time that swaps have been in existence has not been sufficient to give these contracts the opportunity to display any default characteristics.

A 1992 survey by the US accounting firm Arthur Andersen (in which banks and dealers accounting for 70 per cent of the market were covered) revealed total defaults (net of recoveries) of $358m. Approximately 50 per cent of the defaults (and the resulting losses) are attributable to the UK local authorities case (discussed below). A further $95m is attributable to defaults by non-financial corporations, $20m by US savings and loan institutions, $63m by diverse financial institutions and $3m by government authorities. Losses to date as a percentage of notional swaps outstanding are 0.0001 per cent. However, since the notional principal in swaps is not at risk, a more accurate measure is losses to gross mark-to-market exposure (which we shall explore in Chapter 13). This gives a figure of approximately 0.5 per cent, based on gross mark-to-market exposure of $77.5b.

A major case of default arose through swap transactions entered into throughout the second half of the 1980s by various local authorities in the UK. Although these were initially aimed at hedging interest rates, later contracts were ultimately determined to be speculative. The rapid rise in UK interest rates from 1988 onwards made the contracts unprofitable for the local authorities, which elected not to pay. Since the UK courts found the local authorities to be acting *ultra vires*, or outside the scope of their powers, the courts determined the contracts to be unenforceable (the key case is *Hazell* v *Hammersmith and Fulham London Borough Council [1991] 2 WLR 372*). As a result, banks suffered losses estimated initially at approximately $178m and it is likely that the final figure will be higher still, since not all banks with exposure have resolved legal proceedings. Since that landmark case, many participants in the swap markets have taken steps to ensure that they conduct swaps not only with clients which are creditworthy but also with those which are legally empowered to transact.

There have also been instances where counterparties have filed for bankruptcy with swaps outstanding. In such cases regulators and bankruptcy receivers have acted quickly to transfer portfolios of swaps to other parties to ensure a continued stream of payments. Examples of this can be found in the failures of the Bank of New England (BNE), Drexel Burnham Lambert, British and Commonwealth plc and the Development Finance Corporation of New Zealand. All had swap portfolios which were in the money and which were effectively transferred with no loss to the underlying parties. At the time of writing there is some question as to the ultimate fate of banks with swaps outstanding to the Canadian developer Olympia & York, which has sought bankruptcy protection in the UK and Canada (though not in the US). Several banks have swap exposures to the developer and how the situation will be resolved remains to be seen.

Although the swap market has up to now generally functioned smoothly in the face of potential difficulties, there is concern among regulators and participants that a large default (or a series of defaults) could have a broader, 'domino' effect on a portion of the market. Should that occur, swap defaults and losses could affect numerous institutions. If one bank is expecting performance on a swap from another bank which fails, the first bank may in turn be unable to perform on an associated swap to a third counterparty and so on down the line. This is one reason why banks in the swap market tend to transact primarily with higher credit quality counterparties. Since swaps represent term exposure, the opportunity for default is clearly much greater and deserves more attention.

We have demonstrated very briefly that defaults can, and do, occur. The above are only representative examples for certain products; we shall mention others in chapters relating to specific products. At this point, however, it is vital to stress that the risk of dealing with financial instruments is very real. Many institutions and investors have lost billions of dollars as counterparties have ceased to perform as expected. In light of this it is essential to emphasise the importance of risk and of building a risk management framework. By doing so, an institution will have greater success in handling involvement with credits which are likely to default in the future.

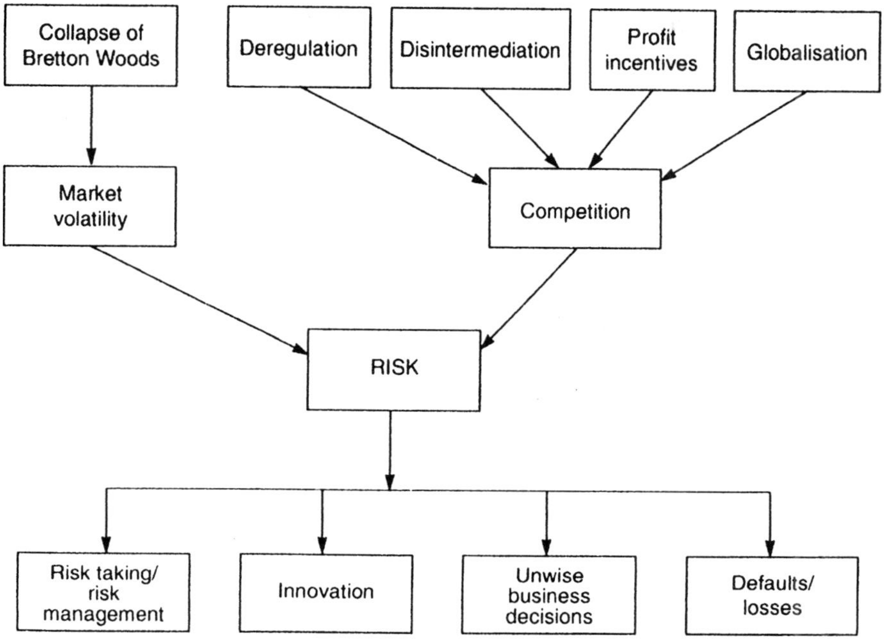

Figure 1.1. Risk in a Changing Environment.

From an illustrative standpoint, we can encapsulate much of our discussion in Figure 1.1 above.

REGULATORS IN A CHANGING ENVIRONMENT

While risk has affected many of the institutions active in today's markets, regulators have also been required to make changes to enforce oversight of products and institutions in their respective areas. The main regulators in each country are charged with overseeing the activities of financial institutions operating in their local markets. The major regulators in select countries include:

- Federal Reserve: oversees state-chartered member banks and single/multiple bank holding companies in the US;
- Office of the Comptroller of the Currency (OCC): oversees national banks in the US;
- Securities and Exchange Commission (SEC): oversees broker-dealers and securities firms in the US;
- Bank of England: oversees financial institutions in the UK;

- Deutsche Bundesbank: oversees financial institutions in Germany in conjunction with the Federal Banking Supervisory Office;
- Banque de France: oversees financial institutions in France through four associated Commissions;
- Bank of Japan and Ministry of Finance: oversee financial institutions in Japan;
- Reserve Bank of Australia: oversees financial institutions in Australia;
- Nederlandsche Bank: oversees financial institutions in the Netherlands.

In addition, the Bank for International Settlements (BIS), located in Basle, Switzerland, functions as the central banker to the world's central banks. Although the BIS has no formal regulatory powers over other OECD banks, it is very often a focal point for coordinating action among members. In this capacity the BIS served very effectively in coordinating the capital adequacy framework adopted by the Group of 10 countries in 1988.

Part of the challenge facing regulators in attempting to deal with new financial products and increasingly volatile markets is the diversity of regulatory arrangements among countries. A recent study by the OECD (*Systemic Risks in Securities Markets*, OECD, 1992) reveals a remarkable disparity in the regulatory authorities involved in monitoring different sectors of any country's financial system; when the comparison is made between different countries, even greater divergence appears. A few illustrations are given below.

- A bank's on-balance sheet securities activities in Europe, the US and New Zealand are monitored by the respective banking supervisors.
- Securities firms owned by banks in Europe (except Spain) are regulated by the banking supervisors.
- Securities firms owned by banks in Canada are monitored by the provincial securities regulators and certain self-regulatory associations, while in the US they are monitored by the SEC. In the UK they are monitored by the securities regulators but the group as a whole receives additional oversight from the Bank of England.
- In Austria, Ireland and the Netherlands securities firms with no affiliates are regulated by the stock exchanges.
- In Australia, Canada, Belgium, Spain and the US securities firms with no affiliates are regulated by the equivalent securities commission regulators.
- In Japan securities firms with no affiliates are monitored by the securities bureau within the Ministry of Finance; non-bank financial institutions involved in a range of securities transactions are monitored by the Ministry for International Trade and Industry (MITI).
- In the US the SEC monitors stocks and stock indices but the Commodities and Futures Trading Commission (CFTC) monitors stock index futures.
- The Federal Reserve monitors single and multiple bank holding compa-

nies and state-chartered member banks in the US, while the OCC monitors national banks. State regulators are also involved in the regulation of state banks.
- The Federal Reserve interprets and enforces the Glass-Steagall Act, while the SEC interprets and enforces the Securities Act and the Securities Exchange Act. Both Acts affect banks, bank holding companies, securities companies and securities affiliates of bank holding companies.

The above arrangements are bound to lead to a certain level of confusion. In addition, the level of regulation of markets and products varies considerably. While certain markets are heavily regulated, others are not regulated at all and still others are in the process of being evaluated by regulatory bodies.

Examples of areas which are tightly monitored include the US corporate bond and equity markets, participation in which has, until very recently, been limited to securities firms. A select number of commercial affiliates are now allowed to underwrite and deal in corporate bonds and equities, though the market as a whole still remains closed to most commercial banks. The USCP market is very strictly regulated by the SEC, which places restrictions on both dealers and issuers. The US municipal bond market is also tightly controlled, with participation limited to securities firms (except in general obligation bonds, which are open to commercial banks). Primary dealings in the US Government bond and bill markets are limited to the select group of primary dealers; oversight is provided by the Federal Reserve, although it has no statutory authority to regulate these dealers. In Japan commercial banks are still excluded by the Bank of Japan and the Ministry of Finance from participating in the yen-denominated corporate bond and equity markets and are allowed to deal only in certain public sector debt issues.

Among the areas which are not regulated to any substantial degree are the Eurobond and Eurocommercial paper markets. Participation in both of these markets by commercial banks, investment banks, issuers and investors is broad. Although the UK Financial Services Act of 1986 has increased reporting requirements for Eurobond issues, the general requirements are not onerous (and are far less than the requirements for issues in the domestic sterling market for example). In addition, certain issuers elect to list their Eurobonds on the Luxembourg Stock Exchange, which is free from regulation. The global foreign exchange market is largely unregulated as well (although certain regulators place a maximum level on the amount of open foreign currency exposure a given institution can have at any point in time). Ongoing secondary trading of US Government securities can, in certain instances, be exempt from regulation of substance. To the extent that an institution deals only in exempt securities (US Government bonds, agencies, Certificates of Deposit, Bankers' Acceptances and CP) it is free from the

SEC's oversight. In addition, if a dealer in non-exempt securities (corporate bonds) places all US Government dealing through a so-called Government Securities Inc. (GSI) subsidiary, the GSI will be free from regulation.

Two key areas receiving the scrutiny of regulators at the moment are the interest and currency swap markets and the equity-linked and equity derivatives markets. These areas remain essentially unregulated; they are profitable, they are growing rapidly and, in certain instances, they are risky. Certain regulators have stated publicly that the level of sophistication in these markets is so complex, and the pace of innovation so rapid, that regulators are being left behind (see Farrant and Lagayette). This is not to suggest that formal regulation of these products is or is not required. The important point is to ensure that regulators have understood, analysed and reviewed these instruments and have addressed the possible risks faced by financial institutions and systems in their respective jurisdictions as a result of dealing in them. Part of the regulators' decision-making process will inevitably rely on a risk management framework such as the one we present in Chapter 2.

Much of the regulators' time has been devoted to dealing with insolvencies of financial institutions in their jurisdictions. In the US there has been substantial press coverage of the savings and loan crisis and the facts need not be repeated here. Suffice it to say that the various regulatory agencies have spent considerable time and money in attempting to resolve the financial failures of hundreds of institutions. In addition to these difficulties, US regulators have been involved in the winding up of several high profile failures, including BNE, Drexel Burnham Lambert and Franklin Savings, all victims of different types of risk (in BNE's case bad commercial and property loans eventually forced the bank down, in Drexel's case failure was ultimately caused by its massive, illiquid junk bond positions and loss of confidence in the dealer over insider trading and fraud charges and in Franklin Savings' case substantial unrealised losses from complex hedging strategies involving futures, options and swaps drove regulators to close the institution down).

The Bank of England has also been involved in several difficult situations, including the failures of British and Commonwealth and the Bank of Credit and Commerce International (BCCI). In Japan the Bank of Japan and the Ministry of Finance have been occupied in orchestrating rescue operations for banks, such as the recent Toyo Shinkin affair. Regulators in Norway and Finland have all been involved in large recapitalisation programmes for key financial institutions in each country (Den norske Bank, Christiania Bank, Skopbank).

There is little doubt that regulators around the world find themselves strapped for time and money in dealing with crises within their own financial systems. While many of the causes of these failures are primarily attributable to economic factors or to outright fraud and mismanagement, at least a portion of the problems can be traced back to our original premise: risk has increased in the financial sector over the past 20 years and financial institutions have become victims of this increase.

Regulators have also achieved successes. Chief among these is the 1988 BIS capital adequacy agreement, agreed to by regulators from the Group of 10 countries. The arrangement, documented in the *International Convergence of Capital Measurement and Capital Standards* (which will be referred to throughout this text), calls for two distinct elements.

The first requirement is a minimum level of 8 per cent equity to risk-adjusted assets. At least half of this must be Tier 1 (or core) equity, defined as paid-in capital and disclosed reserves. The remainder may be Tier 2 (or supplementary) equity, defined as undisclosed reserves, asset revaluations, general provisions, hybrid capital instruments and subordinated long-term debt.

The second element is a common risk weighting of assets, from 0 per cent in the case of cash to 100 per cent in the case of commercial and industrial loans and certain derivatives.

Although we shall discuss the individual weightings and their implications in the next chapter, the important point to stress is that the BIS agreement is an attempt by regulators to comprehend the function and risk of traditional and new products and to ensure that all institutions in the various countries are playing on a 'level field'. While this is an effective first step, other work remains to be done. As an example, the BIS agreement is applicable only to commercial banking institutions and not to securities firms, insurance companies or other non-bank financial institutions. These sectors of the industry are active participants in many of the same instruments and products, with the result that capital requirements and risk weighting are not applicable to a significant portion of all participants in these markets.

The International Organisation of Securities Commissions (IOSCO), in conjunction with the Basle Committee, is attempting to introduce minimum capital standards for securities firms, following the general pattern set by the BIS guidelines. There are currently broad differences between securities firms in different countries in the monitoring of risks in transactions and in setting aside capital in support of such transactions. The arrangement will initially focus on debt and equity positions and on definitions of eligible capital.

It is clear that financial institutions are active in a number of new markets and instruments as a response to the changing risk environment around them. Such activities are very different from those which bankers and regulators have undertaken in the past and there is a need to understand the nature of these activities. To quote a senior official at the BIS,

> The proliferation of financial instruments and off-balance sheet operations has made our system less, rather than more, transparent . . . The growing importance of off-balance sheet business . . . makes it increasingly difficult to assess the direct

> credit, liquidity and interest rate risks assumed by any individual financial firm (Farrant).

Swary and Topf, in their 1992 volume *Global Financial Deregulation*, echo many of the above sentiments.

> Financial innovation, however defined or measured, has recently been accelerating in pace and scope. In addition to fundamentally altering the financial environment, the resultant changes have raised serious concerns regarding . . . the safety and soundness of the financial system and the stability of individual financial institutions and whole classes of financial firms.

This text seeks to explore the qualitative and quantitative aspects of risks attributable to financial instruments in today's markets, which are so much a part of the banking business throughout the world.

2: A General Risk Management Framework

DEVELOPING THE FRAMEWORK

Understanding from our previous discussion that increased market volatility and competition have led, among other things, to an increased level of risk for most participants in banking, it is useful to adopt a general risk management framework for treating the subject. Risk management can be defined generally as the management of events that cannot be predicted. Since many of the by-products of increased risk cannot be predicted and are potentially damaging to an institution if not handled properly, an organised and methodical approach to the management of risks is warranted.

To place the issues in perspective it is helpful to refer to a broadly based risk management structure applicable to many fields of risk, including insurance and reinsurance, actuarial science and portfolio management. In such frameworks risk management traditionally focuses on pure risk and speculative risk. Pure risk is defined as risk where the outcomes are zero or negative. This type of risk is most often linked with insurance, where one of two events can happen: either a claim is made, resulting in a loss to the insurer, or no claim is made, resulting in no loss or gain to the insurer (once premium income has been received). Speculative risk is defined as risk where the outcomes can be positive or negative. The risks we cover in this text fall into the speculative category. A bank will gain from transacting a certain instrument with a given counterparty if the transaction is properly managed; if not, the bank will suffer a loss.

The risk management process is initially divided into three separate stages, identification, measurement and management.

Identification

In the initial phase of our framework risks must be identified. This seems obvious but can often be very difficult, since it is important to recognise and classify all risks likely to be encountered. Any risk which is wrongly identified or not identified at all will lead to incomplete or, worse, negative results. It is during this stage that the less obvious, and hidden, risks must be captured. By accurately identifying risks and categorising them by type or dominant characteristic, a bank will be in an excellent position to undertake the second phase of the process. Chapter 4 identifies and classifies different types of risk found in the financial markets.

Measurement

Once identified, risks must be measured. This is also often a challenging task and any mismeasurement of identified risks can lead to negative results. Measurement can be especially difficult when dealing with a stochastic (ever-changing) environment. Much of the business of banking requires risk measurement in stochastic conditions and this can lead to complications when dealing with the future value of volatile variables such as interest rates or exchange rates.

It is during the measurement phase that a bank is required to develop risk measurement techniques and equations and to apply them to its portfolio. Some of the measurement techniques are intuitive in nature and very easily understood. Others are much more complex, relying on mathematical and/or statistical equations and certain underlying assumptions which are subject to change. The most important goal of the measurement process is to develop a measure conservative enough to ensure that a bank is able to have a reasonably certain idea of the risks it is assuming but not so conservative that potentially good business is driven away. Measurement must therefore be accurate, without overstating or understating risk. Chapter 5 focuses on the theoretical aspects of quantifying the risk of different products and Chapter 6 is devoted to developing a practical working model to quantify certain types of risk. Such a model will be utilised throughout the book in discussions of individual products.

Management

Phase three of the framework is initially centred on a basic decision. Once risks have been identified and measured, an institution will have to elect whether or not it wants to engage in a particular transaction with a particular client (or, in a larger perspective, whether or not it wants to engage in a particular line of banking generally). Since risks will have been identified and measured at this stage, the bank is in a position to make this decision. In a banking environment such a decision is generally based on a number of elements, including credit quality, amount of risk, return on the transaction, maturity of the transaction, motivation for the transaction and whether any enhancement is available or required (these items will be covered at length in

Chapter 3). If a bank chooses not to transact business with a particular client, there is no further work to be done, since no risk will be assumed by the bank.

However, more frequently the decision will lead to the bank's transacting business with a client. At this stage we need to focus on the management of exposures, since risk will be assumed in executing the transaction. This portion of the process is multidimensional and will depend on a variety of external factors: the bank's view of the risk, its view of the underlying client, its return on the transaction, its capital constraints, its business priorities and so on. The management of risk broadly falls into three categories.

Retention

Risk is retained on the bank's books. If the bank feels the risk levels are acceptable based on the strength of the client and/or the return on the transaction, the business (and the associated risk) can be kept as a standard transaction. In practice, one would expect most risks to fall into this category, as that is the general business of a bank.

Reduction

If a bank feels the overall level of risk is unacceptably high and/or the return on the transaction does not fully compensate for risks taken, then a reduction is likely to be in order. Risk reduction is possible through a number of mechanisms, including partial collateralisation or product restructuring (both discussed at length in later chapters).

Transference

If the risks of transacting are unacceptably high and/or the transaction return is completely insufficient to cover perceived or actual risks, the entire risk can be transferred. The transference process can be accomplished *via* complete collateralisation, intermediation or a third party enhancement. Again, all three techniques are discussed in later chapters.

Figure 2.1 shows the framework in the form of a flow chart.

USING THE FRAMEWORK

With a risk management framework in place, an institution is in a position to deal with the by-products generated by an increased level of risk. If the management structure is effective, a bank should be in a position to take and manage risk, to create new products and to enter markets once foreign to it, without experiencing losses created by counterparty default. Managing speculative risks enables a bank to minimise losses and maximise profits, maximising the value of the bank.

We now analyse the four possible results of the decision as to whether or not to do business.

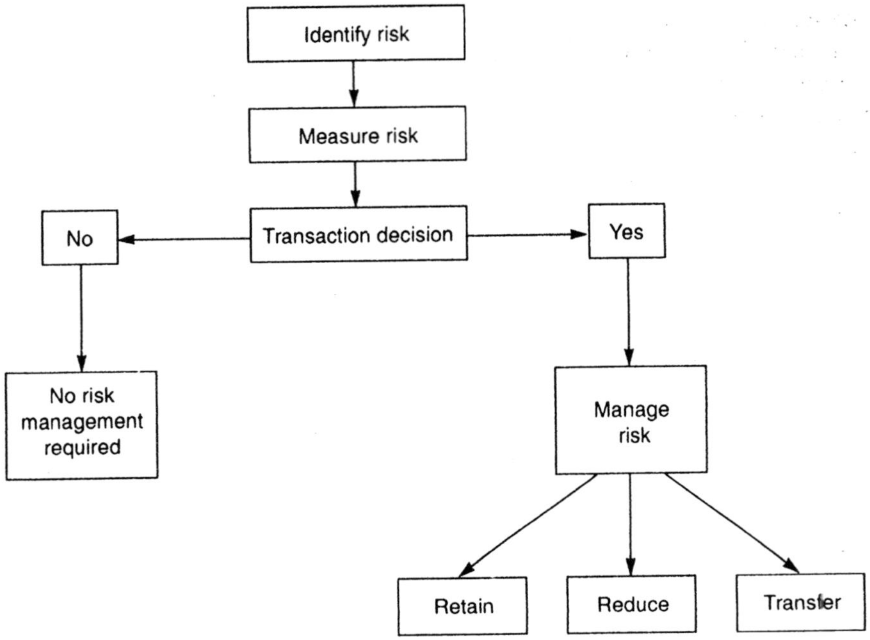

Figure 2.1. A General Risk Management Framework.

Assume that a bank, having identified and measured risk and weighed the elements of the credit decision, elects not to transact business. If this is a correct decision, the bank will preserve its capital through not being exposed to a counterparty which ultimately defaults; this maximises value. If the decision is incorrect, the bank will lose revenue as a result of forfeiting business which ultimately would have been successful; this does not maximise value.

Now assume that the bank, having identified and measured risk and weighed the elements of the credit decision, elects to transact business. If this is a correct decision, the bank will preserve (and ultimately increase) its capital and will generate revenues from the business (depending upon how the risk is managed, i.e. retained, reduced or transferred); this maximises value. If the decision is incorrect, the bank may suffer a loss of capital as a result of having exposure to a counterparty which ultimately defaults (again, the loss of capital will depend on the management of the exposure); this may maximise value (if risk was transferred) or it may partially or totally reduce value (if risk was not transferred).

Figure 2.2 shows the entire process in the form of a flow chart.

Two of the four paths within the framework will maximise value, by

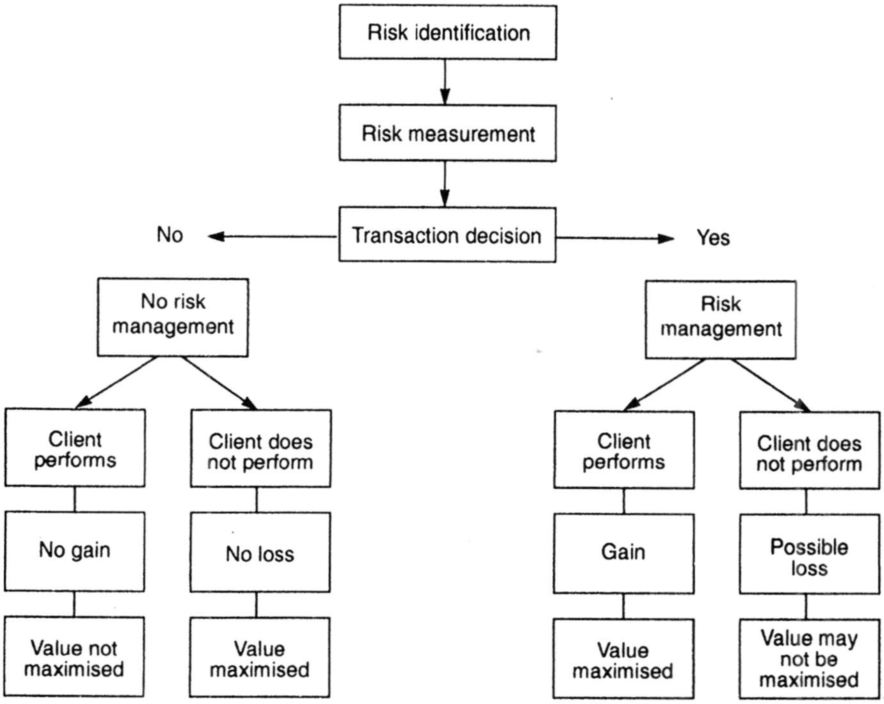

Figure 2.2. Risk Management Goals.

avoiding losses and capturing gains. A third path may maximise value if handled correctly but may detract from value if handled incorrectly: an exposure which is transferred and which subsequently becomes a loss will maximise value (since the loss will effectively have been avoided); an exposure which is reduced or retained and which subsequently ceases to perform will cause partial or total reduction in value. A fourth path will not allow value to be maximised: business which ultimately performs but is not transacted will be value sacrificed.

From a credit standpoint, a bank is interested primarily in ensuring that the risk management framework avoids outright losses or manages exposures in such a way that subsequent losses do not damage the institution. From a business standpoint, the risk management system should allow it to transact business so that profits are maximised. The combination of these two goals must always be considered to arrive at the correct decision. If either viewpoint dominates within a risk management system, the bank will never maximise value. If an institution is so risk averse that it does not assume any risk, it will sacrifice business and if it is so business conscious that it will transact despite risk, it will face certain losses.

Summary Note

As indicated above, for the reader's information, the items covered in this chapter will be discussed as follows during the course of the book: risk identification and classification in Chapters 4 and 5, risk measurement in Chapters 5 and 6 (and in greater detail in each product chapter) and the transaction decision and risk management techniques in Chapter 3 (and, where relevant, in individual product chapters).

3: Elements of the Credit Decision

THE OPTIMAL CREDIT DECISION

As we have seen above, exposure to a given counterparty will not be incurred if an institution elects not to transact business. If, however, a decision to transact is taken, management of the exposure becomes a necessity. In order for a bank to arrive at the decision of whether or not to transact, it must consider a series of factors: counterparty credit quality, risk, return, maturity, motivation and enhancement. In considering these elements, the bank will arrive at a decision; we term this the credit decision. If affirmative, the decision will commit a bank to a given transaction in a certain structure; if negative, it will avoid commitment to the transaction.

In this discussion we focus on description of the above factors in the decision-making process and discuss how each functions and interacts with the others. Before doing so, it is helpful to define in a general equation how one theoretically arrives at the optimal credit decision. We can do so through the following:

$$\text{Optimal Credit Decision} = f(CR, RE, Ret, Mat, Mot, Enc)$$

where CR is a counterparty's risk, represented by its credit quality,
RE is the level of risk exposure present in the transaction,
Ret is the return on the transaction,
Mat is the maturity of the transaction,
Mot is the motivation for the transaction,
Enc is enhancement on the transaction.

We interpret the statement as saying that the optimal credit decision is a function of several variables, all of which must be considered in order for the correct decision to be taken. The specific variables which must be considered are the counterparty's credit quality, the level of risk attributable to the transaction, the return attributable to the transaction, the maximum maturity of the transaction, the counterparty's motivation for executing the transaction and whether credit enhancement of any sort is required or available in the transaction.

ELEMENT 1: COUNTERPARTY RISK

Counterparty risk (also known as credit risk) is defined simply as the risk that a bank's counterparty will fail to perform during the life of the transaction. The failure in most instances will be due to financial deterioration or collapse, although failure may also be wilful.

Consideration of counterparty risk is the primary task of a credit officer or credit committee. Bank credit officers receive specialised training in the credit analysis of potential clients and are generally vested with certain approval authorities which they are required to use in the best interests of the bank. The review process generally involves the following steps:

- a formal and rigorous financial analysis of the client's audited financial statements, including balance sheet, income statement and statement of changes in financial position; it may also include ratio analysis and projections of future performance under varying assumptions;
- a review of the client's performance against its competition to detect strengths and weaknesses;
- a study of the client's industry in general, including current and future outlook, perhaps including a review of rating agency reports, industry literature and so on;
- a discussion with the client's management (in certain instances) to help clarify or explain particular issues.

A seemingly obvious, though occasionally misunderstood and neglected, requirement is to ensure that the analyst has reviewed the financial statements of the precise legal counterparty which will ultimately be the bank's client. Many potential counterparties have non-guaranteed onshore or offshore subsidiaries through which they transact, primarily for tax purposes. Clear differentiation between the parent and the subsidiary is particularly vital, as trading desks and other business units may assume that an entity with a similar name as the parent company carries the same credit risk as the parent.

If a bank were asked to consider a credit facility for XYZ and assumed the business unit was referring to XYZ Co, the parent, only to discover after the transaction was booked that it was facing XYZ Ltd Cayman, an offshore subsidiary without the benefit of a parent guarantee, it would be legally obliged to continue the deal. An onshore or offshore subsidiary, in virtually all instances, is of poorer credit quality than the parent itself. Without a guarantee or some other form of support a bank may be unwilling to take on the counterparty risk of the smaller, less creditworthy entity.

A further, related point to consider in the analysis process is that it is incumbent upon the analyst to ensure that the risk to an entire legal group be considered in totality. A bank may have extended credit to the parent XYZ and may also have analysed and recommended approval of exposure to two other group companies, XYZ Europe Ltd and XYZ Canada Ltd. Although each of these companies is legally separate and should have the independent financial strength to support a given facility, an analyst must take into account group creditworthiness and total exposure to the group.

Comfort can be taken from the fact that, despite their relationship, the collapse of XYZ Europe would not affect the financial performance of XYZ and XYZ Canada. If the financial strength of one unit is dependent on the activities of one or more of the other units, this must be factored into the credit analysis and subsequent credit recommendation. Likewise, group exposures, though booked with separate legal entities, should be considered in total. If XYZ Europe files for bankruptcy, a bank may lose money on its exposure to that company. It should not, however, lose money on exposures extended to other group companies so long as they remain solvent. In a worst case scenario, however, if there is a high degree of interdependency between the various units, the entire amount of exposure to the group could be at risk.

At the conclusion of the analysis process and after considering the above points, the credit officer should be in a position to assign a certain credit quality 'label', 'rating' or 'score' to the client. Some institutions employ a numerical rating scale to help identify varying degrees of creditworthiness; others confine themselves to broader descriptive categories. For the purposes of this text, we choose the latter, for ease of use. It should be understood, however, that various gradations of credit quality may fall within a given descriptive band.

With a rating or quality assignment, an analyst is able to begin identifying which transactions or facilities under consideration are appropriate and which are not. As we add different variables to the decision-making process, it will become clear that one of the keys to the entire framework is the level of a client's creditworthiness, since it is ultimately a client's ability to perform which dictates the success or failure of a transaction. For this reason we compare the various decision-making variables against counterparties determined to be of high, medium or low credit quality.

Although the central topic of this book is not credit analysis or the specific determination of the credit quality of a given company, it is useful for reference purposes to define generally what makes a counterparty a high, medium or low quality credit.

High Quality

These are institutions which exhibit excellent financial strength from a credit perspective. Although the ways of defining financial strength are varied, we can think of institutions in this category as having:

- excellent liquidity: substantial cash resources on hand to meet obligations in a timely fashion; those with sufficient cash on hand can also expand and invest in capital equipment without raising additional external funds;

- low leverage: low debt levels and/or high equity levels, in addition to providing a larger capital cushion, will translate into lower interest expense;
- strong earnings: strong and growing revenues, operating income and net income, not artificially buoyed by one-off earnings or extraordinary items;
- substantial cash flow: sound income levels after adding back non-cash expenses such as depreciation; this is a true measure of a company's ability to generate cash from operations;
- performance measures which are well above average: solid financial ratios such as interest coverage (how many times earnings before interest and taxes cover a company's interest expense), the current ratio (current assets to current liabilities, a liquidity measure), operating margin (operating income compared with total revenues, indicating earnings efficiency), net margin (net income compared with total revenues, indicating net earnings efficiency), leverage (debt to equity) and so on.

A consistent track record in the above measures adds legitimacy to the claim that a company is of high credit quality. A dominant market share, performance above the peer group average and a good reputation and management team also play a role in making a credit high quality. These counterparties would be considered 'investment grade' by analysts and rating agencies.

Medium Quality

These are institutions which exhibit good financial strength in most areas but compare somewhat unfavourably in one or more areas against the high quality credits. By and large one would expect the following:

- good liquidity: a sufficient amount of cash resources on hand to meet obligations in a timely fashion;
- moderate leverage: although debt levels may be higher than the best credits, they remain reasonable; interest expense will logically be somewhat higher, detracting from earnings;
- sound earnings: healthy and stable or increasing revenues, operating income and net income;
- ample cash flow: sufficient cash from operations after adding back depreciation;
- performance measures which are approximately average: satisfactory financial ratios as detailed above.

Again, a certain amount of consistency in financial performance would be characteristic of a medium quality company. These counterparties may also have strong management teams, good market shares and positive images and reputations. Medium quality counterparties would generally be considered 'investment grade'.

Low Quality

These are credits where financial composition and performance are decidedly weak. This will be reflected in specific vulnerabilities on the balance sheet and income statement, as well as in poor comparison with peers or competitors. Low quality credits may be characterised by:

- tight liquidity: a barely sufficient (or perhaps ultimately insufficient) amount of cash resources on hand to meet obligations in a timely fashion;
- high leverage: debt levels which are very high, perhaps to the point of being constraining, with interest expense consuming a large portion of current earnings;
- poor earnings: stagnant or declining revenues, operating income and net income; earnings may be boosted by asset sales and other extraordinary gains as a stop-gap measure;
- inadequate cash flow: insufficient cash after operations after adding back depreciation;
- performance measures which are well below average: unsatisfactory financial ratios as detailed above.

Low quality credits may be held in low regard in the market. Management may be deemed ineffective and market shares may be eroding. It should be pointed out that low quality credits may also be in a recovery phase, which could have positive implications for the future. Low quality counterparties are considered 'sub-investment grade' entities.

The above definitions are broadly based and are intended only to give the reader a general feel for the factors that make a given counterparty high, medium or low quality. As mentioned, varying degrees of refinement can be applied to the process.

Counterparty risk analysis should ultimately be able to tell us, with a reasonably high degree of certainty if we have completed the task correctly, whether or not a given company will continue to perform on its credit obligations. If a counterparty fails, it does not necessarily mean a bank will sustain a loss, as we shall explore in Chapter 4. However, if a counterparty does fail and the credit analysis has been performed correctly, a bank should have either no exposure or exposure which is structured or enhanced so as to prevent any loss from occurring.

Table 3.1. Credit Quality and Risk Exposure

Credit quality	High risk	Transaction risk Medium risk	Low risk
High quality	Likely	Yes	Yes
Medium quality	Not likely	Yes	Yes
Low quality	No	Not likely	Likely

As a final note it should be mentioned that counterparty risk is a risk which is not hedgeable. With market risk, for example, an institution may well be able to hedge away interest rate or currency rate movements through offsetting positions in futures, options, swaps, forwards and so on. There is, however, no equivalent offsetting position which can be taken when dealing with counterparty risk, as an institution facing a certain client can only rely on that client to perform. Thus, an institution entering into a transaction will, at a minimum, always face counterparty risk.

ELEMENT 2: RISK EXPOSURE

Risk exposure is defined as the amount of risk a given transaction or product carries with it; it represents the amount a bank could lose if its counterparty defaults. Depending on the exact product under consideration and the precise risk being considered, there is a variety of ways in which to value exposure, both initially and on an ongoing basis. In this section we use the term generically in order to place the concept in a decision-making framework. In later chapters we shall analyse the specific exposures encountered when dealing with certain products. These will be categorised as having market risk, settlement risk, inventory risk or provisional risk.

From a practical standpoint, we know that a bank considering extending credit limits to sub-investment grade or weak companies should be prudent and limit total risk to a very modest amount (if any at all). Conversely, the strongest AAA-rated companies should be the recipients of the largest portion of risk exposure. In between, there are varying degrees of credit quality and risk exposure trade-offs, which combine to form the 'grey area' familiar in different disciplines. To illustrate, a grid can be prepared (see Table 3.1) indicating the likelihood of whether a bank or financial institution would execute a given transaction with a given counterparty.

While the grid vastly oversimplifies the range of decisions which can be made, it illustrates a very fundamental point: we want, and need, to limit the types of transaction we execute with low quality counterparties to those with low amounts of risk. Alternatively, we can consider restructuring a high risk transaction so that is assumes the characteristics of a low risk product. Any number of ways exist to reduce risk, including delivery *versus* payment, upfront collateral, periodic mark-to-market, option to terminate and so on, depending on the specific product we are considering. This subject is treated at length later in this chapter and in the individual product chapters. Using low risk transactions to limit exposure to lower quality institutions is simply a prudent course of action, reinforced every time a sub-investment grade company is unable to perform on a credit obligation.

While we need to limit the range of products we are willing to transact with low quality clients, the same constraints begin to disappear as we move up the credit quality spectrum. Once we arrive at our strongest AAA clients, the range of products we are willing to transact widens significantly, the options we previously had to consider to reduce risk for lower quality clients are largely eliminated and, indeed, our appetite for exposure increases dramatically. The last point is important in that many of the high risk transactions we are prepared to consider booking with such institutions carry the greatest amount of credit exposure.

Perhaps the most difficult area to deal with from a decision-making standpoint is the medium quality band for which the range of acceptable transactions is still potentially quite large. The difficulties are for two reasons.

First, a company which is perceived by a credit analyst to be of average quality can, on occasion, slip in to a non-investment grade category fairly swiftly. While a strong AAA company can certainly deteriorate over a period of time, that deterioration tends to be visible to a credit officer and is usually reported by the financial press. An institution granting a credit limit to such a company would generally have sufficient time to terminate or restructure the credit relationship. Conversely, with a non-investment grade company, the relationship should already be limited to low risk transactions (with relatively low credit exposure as well).

With an average company, however, deterioration can be fast and unpredictable and the bank may still be exposed to some medium or high risk transactions. Although there are various warning signs (which are a central topic of many of the credit analysis books available) to identify some of this rapid financial decay, there are times when no such warnings exist or when they arrive too late for action. In those instances an institution extending a credit facility can be left in an untenable position. Part of the correct credit decision presumes confidence in analysis of the counterparty, an ability to focus on any warning signals which may exist and the knowledge that middle quality credits can swiftly become sub-investment grade credits.

The second difficulty with medium quality credits relates to product suitability. There is a broad range of products which an analyst would normally consider acceptable for an average, investment grade company. Higher risk transactions with longer maturities are often booked with such companies and they are generally appropriate. Most transactions with this client base will reach maturity with no difficulties or loss to the bank. However, if there is a problem, it can be costly, since these transactions tend by definition to carry higher levels of risk exposure.

An example can put this concept in perspective. An industry average, investment grade credit for a five-year swap transaction is proposed to a bank credit committee by the swap desk. The deal is a straightforward, plain vanilla interest rate swap, fixed *versus* floating, with net payments made on a matched basis. The credit analyst, having performed the analysis, recommends approval of the transaction and the committee signs off.

One year later the company begins to suffer for any of a number of reasons. The analyst calls up the swap desk to find out the status of the swap exposure. As luck (and interest rates) would have it, the mark-to-market value of the swap is in the company's favour. Therefore the bank booking the deal has no credit exposure to the company; the company is expecting the bank to perform on its obligation and therefore has exposure to the bank. Having determined this, the analyst decides to monitor the company over the next quarter and then review its latest financial results. This is not unreasonable, particularly given the current value of the swap. Next quarter the analyst will decide whether the credit relationship should be terminated, restructured or maintained.

Two months later the company files for bankruptcy. The analyst is stunned, since a company which appeared to be reasonably sound (albeit on a downtrend) is close to disappearing. The collapse of a middle quality company in a relatively short period, particularly during difficult economic times, is not a novelty. Also of note is that during the two-month period interest rates moved sufficiently to turn the mark-to-market slightly in the bank's favour. The bank is therefore exposed to the company and is now forced to become an unsecured creditor and to go through legal proceedings in the hope of recovering what it is owed. In addition, it must go into the market to replace the swap transaction.

This scenario is neither unlikely nor implausible; it has happened in the past and it will continue to happen. Recent, well documented occurrences include the failures of Mortgage and Realty Trust, Columbia Gas, Development Finance Corporation of New Zealand, Polly Peck, Olympia & York and Mountleigh. All were medium quality companies which deteriorated and/or defaulted in a reasonably short period. Many institutions which had extended credit facilities to these companies have suffered losses.

The example above also serves to illustrate the importance of product suitability and that knowledge of products and their associated risk exposures is an essential part of the decision-making process.

Consider the following: what if, instead of a five-year interest rate swap (with net payments on a semi-annual basis), the swap desk had proposed an off-market swap with an upfront payment to the company or a zero coupon swap with annual payments made to the company but none received from it until maturity or a cross-currency swap with full initial and final exchange of principal on a free delivery basis or even a straight interest rate swap with a payment mismatch in the company's favour (ie the bank pays quarterly but the company pays only annually)? Most of the above structures (to be treated in Chapter 13) would be considered high risk transactions and would in many cases be deemed inappropriate for many medium quality companies. Knowledge of the risk and risk exposure in various products and their derivative structures obviously plays a crucial role in arriving at the correct credit decision.

ELEMENT 3: RETURN ON A TRANSACTION

One of the most important topics being addressed by many financial institutions focuses on risk as it relates to return. It is no longer sufficient for a bank to look at only one side of the equation, ie the risks it might face in dealing with a given product or instrument. It is increasingly vital that the returns derived from such risks be appropriately measured and considered. This is particularly true for an institution facing the scrutiny of shareholders and the requirements of regulators. An appropriate time to consider these issues is when evaluating the entire credit decision.

The classic trade-off in finance has always been one of risk for return. Investors willing to hold riskier securities (whether the securities are more volatile, less creditworthy or less liquid) can expect a higher return (*via* a higher coupon or a larger capital gain). The same concept can, and should, apply to an institution considering a new or additional financial transaction. A transaction which carries the highest risk to a bank should bring with it the greatest return. While a bank entering into a transaction will face other risks in addition to counterparty risk, the most important consideration in a standard transaction is the quality of the counterparty. The bank needs to know whether it will perform its side of the obligation; this is the essence of credit risk and the most vital risk component in the pricing mechanism. As one might expect, a transaction executed with an AAA-rated institution will carry a very small credit risk premium, while one executed with a BBB-rated institution will carry a significantly higher premium. The trade-offs are summarised in Table 3.2.

The decisions should be read as the return required given transaction parameters of credit quality and risk. Table 3.2 places in clear terms what should be obvious to those accustomed to a risk/return trade-off.

To the reader, it may seem obvious that a bank which is engaging in an active swap business, for example, would employ an effective framework to deal with credit risk pricing. A 1987 survey of the largest US dealers ('Interest

Table 3.2. Credit Quality and Transaction Risk Against Return on a Transaction

	Transaction risk		
Credit quality	High risk	Medium risk	Low risk
High quality	Medium/high	Low/medium	Low
Medium quality	High	Medium/high	Low
Low quality	High	High	Medium

Rate Swaps: Use, Risk and Prices', *New England Economic Review*, November/December 1987, pages 22–32) concluded otherwise, however. Findings revealed that 20 of the largest 'did not consistently and methodically include a credit risk premium in quotes'. While a bank's swap desk can very effectively market a deal, price the transaction in general terms, hedge it, find a counterparty to lay the risk off and unwind the hedge, all in an orderly and methodical fashion, it may not be able to price credit risk. More than a few institutions elect simply to negotiate a spread while structuring a deal, many times on an *ad hoc* basis. At most a trader may keep in mind the absolute minimum spread required to make the deal profitable (the unit's hurdle rate and its cost of capital). At worst, particularly in a competitive situation, the spread may fall below the hurdle rate and the institution may not even cover its cost of capital requirements, let alone any credit risk requirements. In an effort to win the business, a dealer may find himself sacrificing basis points of profit. At that point any thought or notion of an accurate or methodical way of pricing credit risk into a transaction is not at the forefront.

While certain institutions operate in such a fashion, others are more sophisticated and accurate about utilising a risk/return framework. Certain financial institutions, particularly large commercial banks, have advanced ways of assigning the credit risk premium to a given transaction. At some institutions, for example, a deal cannot be booked unless the appropriate credit spread has been built into overall deal pricing. If a swap dealer attempts to execute a transaction where the credit officer has assigned a credit risk spread of 10 basis points and the deal, for competitive reasons, is being bid by another institution at 5 basis points, the swap dealer is forced to sacrifice the transaction. From a credit officer's point of view (and perhaps from a shareholder's point of view as well) this is the more correct and, ultimately, profitable approach. For the dealer, however, it may represent business lost to another bank. In the long run a more effective use of the risk/reward framework benefits the institution as a whole; marginal deals are turned away and the business in its entirety is compensated for the real risks being assumed. Credit risk is a very real phenomenon and must be priced into a transaction, ideally in a systematic fashion.

As one might expect, there are many ways in which pricing can be incorporated into financial instruments. As indicated above, most measures of profitability must initially include a cost of capital component. The use of capital by a department within a firm is not free to that department: if $1m of the institution's capital is required to support a given transaction, a charge must be levied on the use of that $1m. That charge then becomes part of the deal pricing. Next comes the credit risk component and the greater the actual or perceived credit risk, the higher the profit requirement. After this is a category to capture other miscellaneous risks which may or may not be encountered during the life of a particular transaction. If a transaction is 'standard', with no special liquidity, hedging, legal or operational considerations, no special premia would be required. If, however, any of those risks are present to a significant degree, pricing should be adjusted accordingly. A charge to cover business overhead expenses helps defray an institution's fixed costs and, finally, a spread to reflect a business unit's own hurdle rate considerations is included. That is, if the particular unit is required for internal budget targets to make 3 per cent over and above the cost of capital, it would factor this into the spread. Not all profit for this last component would have to be priced in every transaction; it is conceivable that a few large, particularly profitable transactions could compensate for a normal individual transaction spread. In equation form we can state:

$$\text{Total Spread} = \text{RWCoC} + \text{CS} + \text{ORS} + \text{BOE} + \text{IHR} \tag{3.1}$$

where RWCoC is the risk-weighted cost of capital,
CS is the credit spread,
ORS is the 'other' risk spread,
BOE is the business overhead expense charge,
IHR is the internal hurdle rate.

We refine the basic total spread equation by defining the specific components above:

$$\text{RWCoC} = \text{k} \times \text{CoC} \tag{3.2}$$

where k is the risk-weighted capital attributable to the transaction and is calculated by

$$\text{Capital Ratio} = \frac{\text{k}}{(\text{RW} \times (\text{RF} \times \text{N}))} \tag{3.3}$$

where N is the notional amount of the transaction,
RW is the relevant risk weighting assigned by regulators or the bank for the transaction in question,
RF is a risk factor applied to the transaction (which will be derived in Part II)

and where we solve for k, an unknown given our traditional capital requirement (for a bank it might be 8 per cent or more).

CoC is a standard cost of capital measure, such as

$$CoC = K_d (1 - t_c) \frac{B}{(B + S)} + K_e \frac{S}{(B + S)} \quad (3.4)$$

where K_d is the cost of debt,
K_e is the cost of equity,
t_c is the tax rate,
B is the market value of debt,
S is the market value of equity.

Note that Ke might be estimated through a dividend valuation model or through the capital asset pricing model. Readers interested in the derivation and application of Ke are urged to consult a corporate finance text. Although the above is an important measure (and is one of only a few available), our central concern is not the formula but the end result. For our purposes we can view this measure as a constant which changes when advised by a bank's treasury department.

Our credit spread CS can be calculated in a number of ways. We propose two alternatives:

$$CS = (N \times HV \times \sqrt{T} \times (\text{loan rate}_{\text{client}} - \text{funding rate})) \quad (3.5)$$

where N is the notional amount of the transaction,
HV is the historical volatility associated with the transaction,
$\sqrt{T}$, or time, which we shall explore further in Part II, is the maturity of the transaction,
loan $\text{rate}_{\text{client}}$ is the rate charged to a client of a particular credit quality,
funding rate is the rate the bank must pay on its funds.

or

$$CS = (N \times (RF \times \text{required spread})) \quad (3.6)$$

where N is the notional amount of the transaction,

RF is the risk factor associated with the transaction,
required spread is the spread which must be taken for a client of a particular credit quality.

Note that the two credit spread formulae are essentially duplicates of one another. We shall see in Part II that the risk factor RF is precisely equal to HV times the square root of time T, once HV has been adjusted to the appropriate confidence level. Further note that the funding rate from the first equation could be set to 0 if the transaction is not one which is fully funded (a swap, option or forward). The first equation is more useful when considering a funded transaction. The loan rate client and required spread from these two equations might be established in a standard grid by credit quality and updated on a periodic basis. As an example, a bank might tier its profit requirements as follows:

Rating	*Required spread*
AAA	10 basis points
AA	40 basis points
A	60 basis points
BBB	100 basis points
BB	200 basis points
B	No business

The OSR 'other' spread required is defined as any constant in a transaction which compensates for perceived operational, liquidity, legal or hedging risks. These would be dependent upon any special circumstances surrounding a given deal and would not be encountered in every transaction. To the extent that a given situation is standard or straightforward, follows normal operational and legal parameters and has no special liquidity or hedging considerations, this term should equal zero.

The BOE charge, although important in helping an institution to achieve total profitability, is not a central concern of this text. For our purposes this can be a constant supplied by the treasury or finance departments.

The internal hurdle rate IHR is calculated as:

$$\text{IHR} = \text{k} \times \text{hurdle rate} \tag{3.7}$$

where k as above is capital required to support the transaction,
hurdle rate, a constant, is a business unit's own required profit target (generally a return on equity measure, hence the use of k in the equation).

We can now consider an example of the use of the total spread equation.

Bank X is contemplating a six-month \$50m forward sale of Treasuries to Company Y. Bank X's effective cost of capital is 10 per cent, the internal hurdle rate it requires (over and above its cost of capital) is 5 per cent and it must maintain capital adequacy of 8 per cent. The risk factor for a six-month forward Treasury is 11 per cent and the bank sees no special legal, operational or hedge requirements for the deal; the business overhead charge is estimated at 2 basis points. Company Y is a reasonably weak BBB counterparty; it has had some financial difficulties and the analyst at Bank X considers them to be approximately sub-investment grade. If the bank were extending a loan to the company, it would take a 100 basis point spread every year. With these parameters in mind, the total spread on the deal would be:

$$\text{Total Spread} = \text{RWCoC} + \text{CS} + \text{ORS} + \text{BOE} + \text{IHR}$$

or

$$\$44{,}000 + \$27{,}500 + \$0 + \$10{,}000 + \$22{,}000 = \$103{,}500$$

The total spread of \$103,500 is 21 basis points on \$50m. Several items bear noting at this juncture. First, the Bank for International Settlements (BIS) guidelines assign a risk weighting for capital purposes of 100 per cent on a forward. Secondly, the transaction does not represent a funding commitment on the part of Bank X, so no funding rate need be included. Thirdly, the credit risk spread of \$27,500 represents 30 per cent of the total income earned on the trade. Institutions not pricing credit risk into a transaction in a methodical way are losing profit opportunities. If Bank X's competitor, Bank Z, wanted to execute the transaction at any cost, it could cut the credit risk spread partially or totally. That would cause X to lose the business in a competitive bid situation but would make Z more susceptible to longer-term credit difficulties. If Z routinely neglects to price credit in the transaction, it may well find itself with a great deal of business, much of it from counterparties which are not creditworthy and will default. Pricing credit *via* a spread formula should be no different from including any other pricing element, whether a capital charge, a funding cost or a hurdle rate. Omitting any of them will cause the institution's returns to be misaligned with its risks and its costs.

Credit Spreads

The above formulae display two ways to compute an appropriate credit spread. Items we have termed 'required spread' and 'loan spread client' will obviously vary from bank to bank, depending on their views on a given

Table 3.3. Discounted Returns (per cent)

	Risk factor	2 per cent return	Discounted return
Year 1	3.2	0.064	0.058
Year 2	5.3	0.106	0.087
Year 3	2.0	0.004	0.003
Total		0.174	0.148

client's creditworthiness. Generally speaking, most institutions charge clients of varying credit qualities different percentage fees for a given transaction. As we have shown, higher rated clients pay much thinner credit spreads and lower rated clients pay larger ones. In all cases, regardless of the actual figure used, differentiation must be made if accurate credit pricing is to occur.

A further note should be made: the required return from a given client is always multiplied by the notional amount of the transaction (to put the percentage fee in dollar terms) and adjusted by the level of anticipated or potential risk through the risk factor (adjusted historical volatility multiplied by the square root of time). This is true for virtually all products covered in this text, which are classified as off-balance sheet items. Traditional balance sheet items, such as loans and deposits, are not risk-adjusted as they represent fully funded transactions. This second step is important because it equates the required return with the potential risk of a transaction. As we shall see in Chapters 5 and 6, most derivative transactions in the market today carry risk equal to only a proportion of the notional amount. Required profitability would be severely overstated if credit spread equation were not adjusted for risk. Such an overstatement would, of course, cause customers to undertake transactions with other institutions offering lower (and more accurate) pricing.

The time value of money should also be taken into consideration. In a transaction with a long maturity it is vital that required profits are appropriately discounted. Consider the following three-year interest rate swap, with associated risk factors. If the counterparty is sub-investment grade, a bank might normally require a 2 per cent annual return. We know that the credit spread is derived from a risk-equivalent return, or RF times required spread. This yields a total of 17.5 basis points over the three-year transaction. However, that is what is required in future value terms. If we use a discount rate of 10 per cent to determine the relevant return today, the figure is only 14.8 basis points (see Table 3.3).

Table 3.4. Summary of Key Balance Sheet items

Weight	Category
0 per cent	Cash, OECD central government deposits
0 per cent	Claims collateralised by cash, OECD deposits
20 per cent	Claims on multilateral development banks
20 per cent	Claims on banks in the OECD
50 per cent	Loans secured by residential mortgages
100 per cent	Claims on private sector
100 per cent	Claims on banks outside the OECD
100 per cent	Claims on commercial companies
100 per cent	Real estate, fixed assets, other assets

The BIS Requirements and Profitability

As already discussed, the Basle Committee, under the auspices of the BIS, issued its key paper, *International Convergence of Capital Measurement and Capital Standards*, in July 1988. We have already mentioned that the central point of the BIS agreement was to ensure that banking institutions maintain sufficient (and uniform) capital levels in support of their business.

In order to arrive at an appropriate risk-adjusted capital figure, the BIS set out weighting requirements for different types of asset. Assets carrying greater risks have higher weightings and, appropriately, require more capital to support them. These are summarised in Tables 3.4 and 3.5, drawn from the original paper.

As one might expect, the BIS requirements for capital have placed constraints on a bank's internal profitability requirements. Previously a bank needed to be less attuned to return on capital measures, since a precise amount of capital did not have to be set aside for a given transaction; this is no longer true. Since a specific amount of capital is required in support of a given transaction, that capital will represent a cost to the department within the bank which is utilising it. This cost must be priced into the spread on the transaction.

Some of the instruments that we shall be dealing with later, such as forwards and repurchase agreements, carry a 100 per cent risk weighting. Others, such as swaps and NIF/RUF underwriting commitments, carry only 50 per cent weightings. It might seem that the capital charge on the latter would be lower (translating into a lower spread requirement when pricing a

Table 3.5. Summary of Key Off-balance Sheet Items

Weight	Category
100 per cent	Credit substitutes (guarantees, letters of credit, etc)
50 per cent	Contingent items (standby letters of credit, etc)
20 per cent	Self-liquidating contingencies
100 per cent	Repurchases/reverse repurchases*
100 per cent	Forward asset purchase
50 per cent	Underwriting commitments (NIFs, RUFs)
50 per cent	Derivative transactions**
50 per cent	Other commitments over one year
0 per cent	Commitments which can be cancelled

* in the case of reverse repos where collateral is taken, these are to be viewed as collateralised loans and weighted accordingly (depending on the collateral).
** including interest and currency rate contracts of various types; weighting may be as high as 100 per cent by local choice. If collateral is taken on a swap transaction, the risk weighting is reduced to a minimum level of 20 per cent.

deal). However, the lower risk weighting will in most instances be offset, partially or totally, by the fact that swaps and NIFs carry higher risk factors (see Part III). As such, capital charge spreads will in most cases be no lower than for those instruments with higher risk weightings.

ELEMENT 4: MATURITY CONSIDERATIONS

A fourth element worthy of mention, and one which adds a vital dimension to the credit decision process, is the maturity of the deal being considered. While some might expect a direct, positive correlation between maturity factor and risk, it is more accurate to separate the concepts. In an absolute sense, within a given product category, the longer a transaction, the more risk it will contain. However, in a comparative framework, across products, this is not necessarily the case.

Consider a bank engaged in two transactions. It is extending a one-month, unsecured bridge loan to a company, which expects to replace that short-term financing with other long-term or permanent financing. For the one-month period that transaction is a high risk exposure, particularly as it is unsecured. At the same time the bank is extending a limit for a 12-month repurchase agreement; assuming for discussion purposes that it is not marked-to-

Table 3.6. Credit Quality Against Maturity of the Transaction

Credit quality	Maturity Long-term	 Medium-term	 Short-term
High quality	Yes	Yes	Yes
Medium quality	Likely	Yes	Yes
Low quality	No	Not likely	Likely

market daily, that transaction, though longer in maturity, carries far less risk than the loan because a repurchase agreement represents a secured transaction. Thus, maturities cannot always be compared across products. However, within a given product category it is generally safe to say that the longer a transaction, the greater the risk. A one-month bridge loan can be seen as less risky than one for 24 months and a two-year swap carries less risk than a 10-year swap (assuming all other parameters are equal). Despite our inability to compare maturities across products, the importance of transaction maturity cannot be stressed enough.

Table 3.6 places the above discussion in our grid framework, illustrating the likelihood of approval by an individual or committee with credit authority for a given product range. The maturities are defined as: long-term: five years and beyond; medium-term: from one to five years; short-term: under one year.

It is worth highlighting that the actual maturity structure of a particular product can often be altered by a number of different methods. A 10-year swap can be reduced to, effectively, a three-month exposure by the use of a mark-to-market with quarterly settlement (at which time the mark-to-market value of the swap is settled and the deal is 'rewritten' at then prevailing market rates). Although initial credit exposure in a deal such as this would be calculated using 10-year rates, the mark-to-market allows exposure to be controlled and maturities to be reduced. Similarly, a 10-year swap deal can be structured with an annual option to terminate. Again, initial potential risk would be calculated on 10-year rates but the option to terminate at market every year allows the true exposure to be limited to one year. A repurchase agreement with a 30-day tenor can be kept current with the market by a daily mark-to-market and a call for collateral when the market for the underlying security moves by a specified percentage, thus reducing effective maturities to one day.

It is important to realise that the above devices allow transaction maturity, which at the outset might create the view that a deal cannot be completed, to be restructured, thus allowing a deal to be booked while remaining within prudent credit guidelines. In doing so the credit analyst places an additional burden on the product manager, the operational unit and the legal department (who might all be involved in changing standard operating procedures to accommodate the special requirements of a non-standard maturity). However, apart from the fact that the need for prudent credit protection is vital, the rewards in obtaining additional business are likely to be worth the additional effort.

It should be noted that the above concepts cannot always be negotiated or incorporated into a deal. The reasons may have to do with reluctance on the client's part, legal or operational barriers which cannot be overcome, regulatory difficulties or other problems. Therefore, strategies altering maturity may not always be a viable solution. In situations where deal maturity cannot be shortened the analyst must continue to focus on existing maximum maturity guidelines in arriving at a credit decision.

ELEMENT 5: TRANSACTION MOTIVATION

A fifth fundamental aspect of the decision-making process is transaction motivation. The general premise for this concept centres on certain questions that all credit officers and committees should ask when contemplating credit requests. First, should the client under consideration for a particular transaction be executing that type of transaction? Secondly, taking it a step further, why is the client executing the transaction? The answers to these questions allow the credit analyst to determine whether the transaction as proposed is appropriate for the counterparty. If the motivation for the transaction is unclear (other than profit for the bank or financial institution) or there is doubt as to whether the client should even be involved in such a transaction, a credit analyst must explore the issue further.

As always, a grey area exists because, even though a transaction may not appear to be appropriate or suitable to the analyst, relationship considerations, bank priorities and budgetary requirements may cloud the issue. Nevertheless, the responsible analyst or committee considering a deal where motivation and suitability issues are at the forefront must raise these questions and explore the answers as well as possible and must stand firm where necessary. If a transaction is inappropriate for the client but is still executed and the client subsequently fails, wholly or partly because of the transaction, the bank involved could be affected directly if it is owed money on the deal (or could face legal action if the client suspects pressure or wrongdoing from the bank).

Several simple examples can illustrate how this concept plays out in the markets.

Scenario One

This type of scenario constantly occurs in press reports. A traditional savings and loan wishes to buy junk bonds from a securities firm. Is this transaction appropriate for the client? Unlikely. Savings and loans are in business to take funds from depositors and to make real estate mortgage loans, not to buy speculative grade securities. The inappropriateness of the deal initially, together with the subsequent downturn of the junk bond market and the failure of many junk bond issuers, has financially impaired many savings and loan institutions.

Scenario Two

A food processing company wants to enter into an oil-based swap where the bank would pay the company a fixed price on oil (say $23 per barrel) and the company would pay the bank a floating monthly average based on West Texas Intermediate crude, as traded on the New York Mercantile Exchange. Is this transaction appropriate? No. The company is not a producer of oil and is therefore not seeking to hedge its production. The transaction would appear to be for speculative purposes, which is acceptable only if the company has the financial resources to support a speculative transaction. However, other ways (such as futures) exist to speculate in the oil market, which would generally be more appropriate and more secure for the bank because of the margin provisions posted by the company.

Scenario Three

A small bank in the Midwestern US which makes residential and small commercial loans has bought a Deutschmark-denominated bond. It wishes to enter into a cross-currency swap (paying Deutschmarks and receiving dollars). Is this transaction appropriate? Probably. A small institution with a certain amount of sophistication in financial matters may well want to enhance the yield of its portfolio. If it understands the transaction and the risks involved and can support it from a financial standpoint, the bond/swap strategy is likely to be acceptable.

Scenario Four

A medium-sized mortgage banking operation (which originates conforming mortgages and sells them on to GNMA pools) is considering buying forward GNMA securities equal to its current production. Is this transaction appropriate? No. A traditional mortgage banker is in the business of originating mortgages and should then be hedging its production by selling forward GNMA securities; it should not be buying forward such large amounts of securities as this runs contrary to its business. Note that a small long forward line is sometimes appropriate if the mortgage banker wants to 'pair off' its securities. That is, if it originally sold forward GNMAs but, after further consideration, has decided to sell a portion of its production to FNMA, it would 'pair off' its GNMA and FNMA positions and would require a small long forward line to do so.

Scenario Five

A multinational corporation wishes to engage in foreign exchange trading, with delivery. Is this transaction appropriate? Being a multinational corporation with receipts denominated in various currencies, foreign exchange would be logical (and perhaps even desirable) if the transactions are for hedging purposes.

In the course of asking whether a transaction is appropriate, the difference between hedging, speculating, arbitraging and yield enhancing should be considered. These are discussed below.

Hedging

Hedging occurs when a counterparty enters into a transaction which will limit the downside potential of a deal already on its books (or soon to be on its books). As an example, a company which is selling dollars and buying a Swiss franc asset may enter into a forward contract today to convert its Swiss franc principal back into dollars when the asset matures (ie selling forward Swiss francs for dollars). In that way, it is not exposed to possible fluctuations between the Swiss franc and the dollar over the life of the asset. By hedging, the company has effectively limited its downside potential by locking in a forward rate. Depending on the transaction in question, a number of products exist to hedge a given deal: exchange-traded or over-the-counter (OTC) options, futures, options on futures, treasury bonds, spot and forward foreign exchange, currency options, swaps, swap options, forward mortgage-backed securities and so on.

Speculating

Speculation involves, in one form or another, taking an outright position in a security or a transaction without a hedge in place. The reason for speculation is simply potential profit. A speculator seeks only to maximise potential profit in a deal and, by not having a hedge in place, can generally limit the downside only to the size of the initial investment.

It is possible to speculate with a range of instruments, including bonds, futures, options, foreign exchange, equities, stock indices, swaps and mortgage-backed securities. A typical speculative trade might occur when an institution, believing that the value of sterling will rise, sells dollars for sterling spot and does not cover its position with a forward sale of sterling for dollars. The institution thus has an open position in sterling and can convert back to dollars only through another spot trade or through a subsequent forward trade. However, since the institution elected not to execute its forward trade at the time it took its sterling position, it cannot be assured of getting that same forward rate tomorrow, next week or next month. In taking that speculative position the institution will hope to cover its sterling position at a later date when the value of the currency is higher and it has made its profit.

Arbitraging

Arbitraging is typically defined as a simultaneous purchase and sale which produces a 'riskless' profit. The theory is that, by taking advantage of imperfections in the market, an arbitrage transaction can be executed to capture any price discrepancies which may exist. In the age of electronic information, computerised trading and global markets arbitrage opportunities are exceedingly difficult to capture. However, they do exist and can be used to make profit. As an example, a company may determine that it can exploit certain opportunities by arbitraging discrepancies between the cash and futures markets for a given commodity (perhaps stock indices). It would go long in one market and short in the other in an attempt to lock in some small profit.

More complex arbitrage scenarios can be set up, involving various securities, forwards and so on. Covered interest arbitrage is an arrangement where an institution might take advantage of discrepancies in the forward foreign exchange market. It could sell a dollar-denominated CD for dollars and buy yen spot, while at the same time buying a yen-denominated CD and selling forward yen for dollars to coincide with the maturity of the yen CD. If the arbitrage opportunity truly existed, the institution would make a riskless profit over and above its yield on the dollar CD. This may sound somewhat like hedging; the key difference is that in a hedge an institution is not necessarily locking in a riskless profit, it is merely protecting its downside risk. This type of arbitrage is explored more fully in Chapter 12.

Yield Enhancing

This is another term for obtaining additional profit from a position already on one's books (or soon to be on one's books). It is typically a very low risk transaction, designed to add only a few basis points of profit to total return. Yield enhancement is possible through various instruments. In a very pure sense, one can think of a reverse repurchase agreement as a yield enhancement: available (and idle) cash on the balance sheet can be used to enter into a reverse repurchase agreement which will provide a small return. Another common yield enhancing technique exists where the coupon on a fixed rate security is swapped into floating (or *vice versa*) for a period of time, when rates so dictate, which will provide a slightly higher effective yield to the underlying asset.

In addition to these four motivations, there are pure funding transactions. The motivation for a counterparty to issue two instruments discussed in this book, bonds and money market instruments, is to raise funds. The use of the funds following issuance may fall into one of the categories just described but at the outset they must be viewed only as funding transactions.

This discussion raises several issues related to the motivation for engaging in a transaction. In many instances a credit committee or credit officer will be asked to approve a transaction involving one of the strategies listed above. In determining whether an institution is qualified for a deal, it is worth investigating which of the above strategies is being pursued. Some important considerations should be noted.

A hedging transaction, though potentially risky to the bank extending the credit limit, is typically thought to be a sound strategy for the underlying client because it seeks to eliminate risk from the client's books, not to add to it (although hedges are sometimes imperfect or, given abnormal discrepancies in markets, can actually fail to work). A pure hedging transaction can be viewed as appropriate for the entire range of credit qualities.

Although speculation tends to carry a negative connotation, the reality is that speculators support, and in many instances make possible, activity in a given market. Without speculators it would be difficult, if not impossible, for markets to be as efficient as they are today. However, if a small local company in the US with no foreign currency receipts takes on an unhedged currency position, the analyst would, in the course of deciding whether the transaction is appropriate, determine whether the company had the financial resources to take on such a speculative position. Speculation can be quite acceptable from a credit standpoint if the credit officer has determined that the client, in taking on an outright position, can support the position in a worst case scenario. The downside risk on a speculative position can be substantial. In general, speculative positions should be limited to medium and high quality credits.

Arbitrage schemes are quite acceptable for a broad range of credits if they are truly arbitrage in the classic sense. If the credit officer can determine that the arbitrage is legitimate, then a variety of credit qualities can be considered for the transaction. If the arbitrage does not appear to be as riskless as might be hoped, it must be viewed more in the context of a speculative transaction, with credit quality adjustments as necessary.

A yield enhancement deal is generally thought of as fairly low risk, as it seeks to add only a small, often guaranteed, return to assets already on the books, with little or no risk to the counterparty. Such transactions would generally be acceptable for all counterparties.

As any analyst who has attempted to consider the above issues knows, it can be enormously difficult to attempt to determine a counterparty's motivation in entering a given transaction. Certain products, however, have clearly associated motivations.

Consideration of a Foreign Exchange Line
This will be for hedging if the balance sheet reveals foreign exchange flows and speculation if the balance sheet reveals no such currency flows.

Consideration of a Mortgage-backed Securities Options Line
This will be aimed at yield enhancement, hedging or arbitrage if the balance sheet reveals similar mortgage-backed securities and speculation if not.

Consideration of a Currency Swap
This will be for yield enhancement or hedging if the balance sheet has foreign currency assets or liabilities and speculation if no such foreign currency items are apparent.

There are many instances when an analyst will have insufficient information to associate a given transaction with a given motivation. In such cases it is beneficial to discuss the issue with the trader, salesperson or product manager handling the account. This is especially vital when dealing with the lower tier of credit qualities.

As before, we can summarise the above guidelines in a grid, which shows the likelihood that a deal will be approved by an individual or committee with credit authority (see Table 3.7).

ELEMENT 6: ENHANCEMENT AND RISK REDUCTION

A counterparty will often not be sufficiently strong to support a proposed transaction. In such instances two avenues are open. The exposure can be rejected out of hand, requiring no further action or decision by the bank, or it can be enhanced to reduce the perceived or actual risk.

Table 3.7. Credit Quality Against Motivation for the Transaction

Credit quality	Motivation Hedge	Speculate	Arbitrage	Yield enhance
High quality	Yes	Yes	Yes	Yes
Medium quality	Yes	Likely	Yes	Yes
Low quality	Likely	No	Likely	Likely

If a credit officer elects to restructure a transaction, he has at his disposal a variety of different techniques. In the most obvious instance the counterparty can pledge collateral on its books in support of the transaction, in an amount at least equal to the anticipated exposure. Collateral can take a variety of forms but bankers, for good reason, generally like to limit collateral to cash, the government securities of an OECD country or high quality corporate paper. The main considerations in taking securities are that they be marketable, liquid and able to retain most or all of their value while a given transaction is outstanding. It is also vital that the counterparty pledging the securities as collateral has good title, so that the securities can be transferred to the bank legally. From a legal standpoint, the bank must ensure that it perfects a security interest in the collateral it is receiving.

Securities taken in support of a deal (sufficient to cover the risk) are held until required. If the counterparty defaults, the bank is in a position to liquidate the securities and cover the loss sustained by the default. If no default occurs, the securities are returned at the conclusion of the deal. In the US, transactions such as repurchase agreements and swaps allow a bank to circumvent an automatic 'stay' which would normally prevent assets from being liquidated in the event of bankruptcy. The exemption allows a bank to liquidate collateral to cover its loss immediately (this topic will be discussed further in the individual product chapters).

Other forms of enhancement to reduce risk include third party guarantees, surety bonds, letters of credit and external insurance. In all instances these arrangements have the same effect. The bank is effectively, by means of third party support, taking on the risk of the guarantor or supporter instead of that of the counterparty. Should the counterparty default on the transaction, the supporter is obliged to cover the loss sustained by the bank. This, of course, implies that the third party is taking the risk of the counterparty itself but that is not the concern of the bank. There are many reasons why a third party would be willing to assume the counterparty's risk when the bank will not. There could be some legal ownership tie between the two; there may be some other financing or business relationships at stake; the counterparty might have placed collateral with the third party which is satisfactory to that third party but not to the bank (eg securities or assets which are relatively illiquid); the third party might be willing to take the additional risk for an attractive spread and so on. As with collateral, the bank needs to ensure that any third party arrangement is supported by appropriate legal documentation and follows the legal procedures established by the internal compliance unit.

A custody arrangement can often help to mitigate risk. Under such an arrangement a third party acting for both the bank and the counterparty is employed to hold cash and/or securities on both sides. By employing a custodian, the bank lowers or eliminates certain types of risk, such as settlement risk. Naturally, the bank needs to be comfortable that the party it selects to execute custodial services is of good financial standing, creditworthiness and reputation. Failure by the custody agent could result in a loss to the bank.

Beyond collateral, third party enhancement and custody, a bank may want to consider structural changes to a particular product. A credit officer may suggest a means by which a given transaction be restructured so that elements of risk are reduced or eliminated. Although these alterations will be described in detail in each product chapter as applicable, some of the more obvious ones can be mentioned at this point. Establishing a delivery *versus* payment scheme, where the bank makes no payment of cash or securities until it receives confirmation of receipt from the counterparty, is an effective way to deal with settlement risk. Altering the cash flows on a particular transaction so that a cash buffer is created or the bank makes no payment until the end of the transaction is a reasonable way of dealing with certain term exposures. Incorporating a right to mark a transaction to market or to terminate it after a shorter period than normal market convention for that product has the effect of reducing a bank's term exposure to a given counterparty.

These, and other, risk reducing alterations will be covered in more detail at a later stage.

As one might expect, the primary need for risk enhancing arrangements comes with lower quality counterparties or for transactions where risk is extremely high. Table 3.8 summarises whether a deal with certain risk parameters with a certain quality of counterparty will require risk enhancement.

As one might expect, a bank extending a facility with credit enhancement will command a lower profit spread than if no enhancement is required. This confirms our previous discussion on risk and return: high risk transactions command high returns. Since the inclusion of collateral, third party enhancement and so on lowers the risk to the bank, the corresponding return on the transaction should by definition be lower. In addition, the capital required to support such a transaction will be lower. Compare, for example, an unsecured and a secured swap. The BIS guidelines give an unsecured swap a 50 per cent risk weighting, while a swap collateralised by cash or acceptable

Table 3.8. Credit Quality Against Risk Enhancement

Credit quality	Transaction Risk High risk	Medium risk	Low risk
High quality	Possible	No	No
Medium quality	Possible	Unlikely	No
Low quality	Yes	Yes	Possible

OECD government securities carries a 20 per cent weighting. If the unsecured swap required $50,000 of capital, the secured swap would require only $20,000, lowering a bank's required return from the client.

It should be noted that risk enhancement arrangements represent a component in our risk management framework. If a bank, in evaluating the risk management model, elects to reduce or transfer risk exposure in a given situation, it can use one or more of the methods detailed above.

With these six elements of the credit decision, an analyst or committee considering a transaction should be in a position to make the correct credit decision. By taking the decision, the bank is electing whether or not to transact with a given counterparty. That in turn will determine how it proceeds within the risk management framework presented in Chapter 2.

Although all six elements are vital in the decision-making process, we will turn our attention in the remainder of this book to the second element, risk exposure. More specifically, we will explore risk exposure in its component parts, classification and measurement. Once we have explored these areas we will be in a position to examine specific products, their associated risks and the techniques of managing such risks.

Part II
Risk Classification and Risk Equivalency

4: Classification of Risk

As indicated in our risk management framework in Chapter 2, the accurate classification of risk is a vital first step in the entire risk management process. If a bank is unable correctly to identify and classify the risks it is facing, it will be unable to measure risk exposure properly. This chapter is devoted to a description of the different types of risk a bank is likely to face in the normal course of business.

GENERAL RISKS FACING FINANCIAL INSTITUTIONS

An institution active in the financial markets will, at any time, face a series of risks which it must consider, measure and manage. While this text will concern itself primarily with counterparty risk and product risk, it is worth noting in general terms how and when other risks might be encountered.

Operational Risk

This is the risk that a failure or error in systems and operations technology and/or procedures will result in a loss. As an example, if a bank's operational infrastructure is unable to issue a large margin call on a given transaction because its systems are down or its procedures are at fault and a counterparty fails after funds were due to have been received, the bank has experienced a loss due to operational risk.

Legal or Documentary Risk

There is a risk that a failure in legal procedures or documentation will result in a loss. In a practical sense legal risk can arise in many different forms, some related to perfecting security interests in collateral, others to liabilities faced when dealing with a certain product and so on. As an example, a failure by the legal unit effectively to perfect an interest in a particular instrument to be used as collateral may mean that the bank will lose money if the counterparty defaults and the bank has no legal access to the collateral required to cover its exposure.

Liquidity Risk

The risk that a security or asset held as collateral cannot be liquidated without a loss in market value is known as liquidity risk. If a bank takes a particularly illiquid instrument as collateral and is forced to liquidate in order to cover a default by a counterparty, it may find itself unable to do so at the price it anticipated. This will leave the bank open to all or a portion of the exposure faced with the defaulting counterparty.

Hedging Risk

Imperfect or incorrect hedging of a transaction creates the risk of a loss. As an example, if a swap desk is attempting to hedge a particularly esoteric swap with unique characteristics, it may find itself either unable to do so, resulting in market exposure, or able to do so incorrectly or only partially, again resulting in a degree of market exposure. To the extent that it cannot match up the second side of the swap and unwind the hedge it may be forced to take continuing losses on its position.

Sovereign Risk

In a transaction with a sovereign or government counterparty there is the risk that the counterparty or the relevant regulator will impose restrictions on the transaction, resulting in a loss. For example, a counterparty residing in a country where exchange controls have just been placed on all foreign currency transactions may be unable to source foreign currency to repay or terminate a given transaction and thus be forced to default. This could result in a loss to the bank.

Counterparty Risk

As previously discussed, this is the risk that a counterparty will cease to perform and will default on a transaction, resulting in a loss. If a bank's counterparty deteriorates financially to the point where it can no longer honour its obligations, the bank will sustain a loss on any transactions outstanding.

PRODUCT RISK

The following categories of risk are generally grouped under the term product risk (we used the generic term 'risk exposure' in Chapter 3).

Market Risk

There is a risk that a movement in market rates will cause a temporary or permanent loss of value in a transaction. If rates cause a particular deal to move in a certain direction, market risk will increase. If a counterparty defaults when market risk is positive, the bank will sustain a loss.

Delivery Risk

Temporary loss of control of funds or securities when dealing in different time zones creates the risk of a loss. If a bank's counterparty fails after receiving, but before delivering, foreign exchange for example, the bank will suffer a delivery risk loss.

Position Risk

The financial difficulties of an issuer (or market movements) may cause a temporary or permanent impairment of the value of the bank's position in the issuer's securities. If a bank holds the securities of a particular issuer and is forced to liquidate them as a result of market movements or adverse news regarding the issuer, it will sustain a loss owing to position risk.

Provisional Risk

Provisional risk can take several forms but is essentially the risk that certain actions or events in the future will cause a bank to increase its exposure to a given client is described as provisional risk. If a counterparty defaults once exposure has been increased, a greater loss will ensue.

THE EFFECTS OF PRODUCT RISK

Our discussion is now refined to focus on product risks which add credit exposure to a transaction; we ignore for the present the other general categories of risk previously mentioned. Although different institutions may employ diverse terminology to describe the categories below, the concepts should generally be uniform.

Market Risk

The market risk category encompasses most of the derivative products in the market today: repurchase agreements, foreign exchange, swaps, extended settlements, equity derivatives, futures, options and so on. As we shall see throughout this book, this category has three important characteristics. First, initial and ongoing exposure is determined by original levels and subsequent movements in the interest rates, currency rates or commodity prices affecting the instrument. Such movements will ultimately determine the amount of exposure a bank has in a given transaction. Secondly, the majority of instruments affected by market risk are risk-adjusted to a fraction of the notional amount of the facility (see Chapter 5). Very few market risk products or transactions carry risk exposure equivalent to the notional amount of the facility being extended (the exceptions are centred almost exclusively around zero coupon swaps and deeply in-the-money derivative options). Thirdly, a market risk transaction is not a marketable instrument, although it may be a liquid instrument. While a given transaction with a counterparty has value and can be liquidated, it cannot readily be transferred to another party (or it can be transferred only with extensive negotiations).

Under the umbrella of market risk we need to differentiate between potential market risk and actual market risk.

Potential Market Risk (PMR)

Potential market risk is simply the risk exposure the bank must allocate against a counterparty's credit limit at the inception of a transaction. Potential market risk attempts to account for future market risk movements which may affect the bank's exposure to a counterparty. The PMR allocation comes from using the correct risk factor during the risk equivalency process and is based on a statistical analysis of the movement of prices or rates involving the underlying instrument (ie market risk movements). These issues are covered in detail in Chapters 5 and 6. PMR is necessary to give the analyst or credit committee a starting point in quantifying the risk of the transaction. It can be thought of as a worst case scenario or a conservative measure of risk applied during the life of the transaction. If a counterparty defaults during the transaction, it is very likely that the actual exposure a bank will face will be less than the potential market risk. However, for purposes of decision-making, PMR represents the amount of risk which must be applied to a given counterparty's total risk limits. It is calculated by general formula (5.1) (see Chapter 5).

Actual Market Risk (AMR)

Actual market risk (also known as mark-to-market risk) is defined as the market risk exposure the bank faces with a counterparty on an ongoing basis after having entered into a transaction. Actual market risk is not a function of the risk factor but of current market rates used to value the position. To the extent that rates move in the direction estimated by the risk equivalency process, AMR will tend to approximate PMR. One would expect AMR to fluctuate over the life of the transaction in line with fluctuations in market rates. Should a counterparty default on a transaction, the bank's exposure to that client will depend on the amount of actual market risk at the point of default. If the risk equivalency process and the resulting risk factors have been correctly implemented, actual market risk at the time of default should be less than or equal to potential market risk.

At this point it is relevant to emphasise the difference between potential risk and actual risk. Certain institutions utilise potential risk as their measure of the risk of a given transaction. Others focus strictly on an actual risk calculation. Bishop and Dixon, in their discussion of risk in *The Foreign Exchange Handbook*, further point out that some institutions will, at any point during the life of the transaction, take the larger of 'deemed risk' (which we term potential risk) and mark-to-market risk. That certainly seems to be a reasonable approach. At the inception of a transaction, however, the only relevant figure is potential risk. An analyst has no other method for calculating the level of risk which might be inherent in a given deal prior to inception. The construction of an accurate potential risk framework (which is the subject of Chapter 6), while perhaps conservative, provides a credit analyst with a logical starting point in evaluating risk. It should be stated further that, if the correct procedure has been followed in establishing the initial risk figure, actual risk will be less than or equal to the predicted potential risk figure between 90 per cent and 99 per cent of the time, depending on the particular confidence level being used.

Delivery (or Settlement) Risk

Delivery risk is the second major risk classification; it is known variously as free delivery, split settlement or clean risk. Free delivery is encountered primarily in the settling of foreign exchange and foreign securities transactions and can be defined as the risk a bank faces for a short period of time (typically 24 to 48 hours), when it has delivered on its portion of the transaction but is still awaiting delivery of the sum due to it. During that time the bank has 100 per cent risk on its counterparty, as it has already released its payment and is waiting to receive the counterparty's payment. Should the counterparty fail during that time, the bank will have full exposure on the transaction.

Free deliveries occur because of time zone differences and the need to present currency or securities for payment at specific locations. For example, if a bank has entered into a dollar/Deutschmark foreign exchange trade, paying the Deutschmarks to its German counterparty, it will release them the day prior to value date because of time zone differences (the differences are covered at length in Chapter 12). Thus, the US bank will have pard funds away before receipt of the dollars it is owed. Such delivery risks are counted as 100 per cent risk, albeit for short periods of time. With weaker counterparties delivery risk assumes greater significance and caution must be exercised. Strategies for circumventing delivery risk are discussed at length in Chapter 12 on foreign exchange.

Position (or Inventory) Risk

Inventory risk is encountered when a bank or dealer holds the securities (defined primarily as bonds and money market instruments) of another issuer. In these instances the holder is facing 100 per cent risk on the positions it holds on its books and is concerned primarily with how the counterparty's financial condition may affect its position. It will also be concerned to a lesser extent with the effect of rate movements on the value of the instrument, which is simply a market risk measure. Although market movements can affect the value of inventory positions, the risk attributable to financial deterioration is far greater.

Inventory positions are counted as 100 per cent risk primarily because the bank, in holding the bond or money market security, has essentially extended an uncollateralised loan to the issuer. The issuer has given the bank its paper (representing a promise to pay in the future) and the bank has given the issuer its cash. It is clear that the bank thus has 100 per cent exposure to the issuer in an amount equal to the paper being held or the loan being extended. Only when this paper matures or is otherwise sold into the secondary market can the inventory risk be removed.

A subset of inventory risk, although not always found where an inventory position is taken, is the risk associated with 'hard puts'. Hard puts are simply agreements between the dealer and the investor which allow the investor to 'put' (sell) to the dealer a certain amount of paper at a certain price. If a hard put is exercised by the investor, the dealer is forced to add to its inventory position in that paper. A hard put is typically granted by a dealer when it is attempting to increase liquidity for a given name. The put makes the paper more marketable because the investor has an option to resell it to the dealer. Note that a hard put is distinguished from a 'soft put', described in the section on provisional risk. Inclusion of hard puts as a position risk is conservative, since they are not certain to be exercised. Certain institutions view such obligations as representing a provisional risk, as discussed below.

Returning to our discussion on inventory risk in general, it is easy to see how inventory exposure can affect a bank in a worst case scenario. Assume that Company XYZ has issued $100m of commercial paper through a bank. The bank, being temporarily unable to place the paper with investors, is holding the position on its books; thus, XYZ has $100m of the bank's money and the bank has XYZ's promise to return the cash when the notes mature (together with periodic interest payments). Assume further that XYZ declares bankruptcy one week prior to the maturity of the notes. The bank, holding $100m of unsecured paper, becomes an unsecured creditor of XYZ. It is very likely that on default the value of the commercial paper inventory position will fall from $100m to $30m, $20m or even zero, depending on the value of the company in bankruptcy. Even as a company deteriorates in credit quality, the market value of the paper can be expected to decline. The bank has 100 per cent exposure since it is possible for the $100m position to become completely valueless.

Rate movements may also temporarily or permanently impair the value of the securities, causing a loss for the bank unable to hold until maturity. Thus, the ramifications of market risk extend from market risk products to inventory positions.

As a final point it should be made clear that, since bonds, commercial paper and other money market instruments are in marketable form, readily transferable between dealer and investor and generally quite liquid, a normal inventory position is not strictly equivalent to a market risk transaction, which is not in marketable form, tends to be less liquid and represents only fractional risk.

Provisional Risk

Provisional risks are risks which a bank may face during the life of the transaction should certain events occur. Banks involved in such transactions do not always face certain exposure. Much is ultimately dependent on whether or not a specified event happens; if it does not, the bank will face no additional risk exposure; but if it does, the risks are very real. Thus, a banker or analyst cannot ignore these conditional risks and a separate category is established for them. Provisional risk applies primarily in four different scenarios, as discussed below.

Funding Commitments

A bank may face risk if it is required to perform on a pre-arranged funding commitment. If a bank is involved in a Eurocommercial paper or Euronote programme through a revolving underwriting facility (RUF) or a note issuance facility (NIF) and has agreed to provide a funding commitment, the risk may be said to be provisional. If notes cannot be placed under a NIF or a RUF, the bank is required to take up the excess by providing funds to the issuer. To the extent that this occurs, a bank will assume the role of an unsecured lender. If all notes under a programme are successfully placed, however, the bank will not be required to undertake any type of funding arrangement and will not increase its exposure to the issuer.

Underwriter's Liability

This is the risk (aside from the inventory risk of holding the paper) which a bank faces in the event of default by an issuer on a commercial paper note or, in certain instances, an underwritten security. The concept is explored in greater detail in Chapters 10 and 11 in Part III. Briefly, however, it is the liability the dealer or underwriter may face in selling notes to investors if it does not perform adequate due diligence, fails to disclose a material fact and/or discloses an improper fact.

If an issuer defaults on its commercial paper or bond obligation (resulting in losses to investors) and if any of the three items above is found to be present, investors holding defaulted paper may be able to force the dealer to take back the paper at par or to reimburse them for losses sustained. In this instance the dealer will be paying out 100 per cent of the amount lost but might obtain only a fraction of that from the issuer following bankruptcy court proceedings.

Given that this risk is always present when a dealer sells U.S. commercial paper and may be present when an underwriter sells a bond, it must be accounted for in some fashion. However, unlike market risk or inventory risk, it cannot always be determined beforehand who bears the risk or whether any exposure actually exists. A court, in adjudicating a paper or bond default case, may well find that the dealer performed its due diligence requirement satisfactorily, disclosed all relevant facts correctly to investors and, as such, did not violate any of the requirements set out in the Securities Act of 1933 and/or the Securities Exchange Act of 1934 (which detail the requirements in the US). In this case the investors, not the dealer, would bear the loss. In practice, the liability associated with commercial paper is thought to be much greater than with bonds (particularly after the bonds have been in the market for a period of time); the reasons for this are explored in greater detail in Chapters 10 and 11. Again, in order to account for this potential liability, the exposure is classified as a provisional risk.

Third Party Support

A bank may face risk in the event that a credit support mechanism (letter of credit, guarantee, revolving bank line and so on) is drawn on in support of a money market or bond issue. In this instance provisional risk is present when a default on a commercial paper note triggers a drawing under the letter of credit or other support facility. If an issuer is unable to make a payment on its maturing notes and has letter of credit support from a third party (typically a large, highly rated international bank), the letter of credit provider will pay noteholders the amounts due to them and will then attempt to recover those amounts itself or through the courts if the issuer has filed for bankruptcy.

Thus, if an issuer's supported programme is in default, the dealer expects to be paid by the letter of credit provider and so has inventory exposure to that counterparty, not to the original issuer. Exposure to the credit provider cannot be ignored and should be counted as a provisional risk for credit purposes, particularly in standby situations. If a direct pay support mechanism is used, it is likely that a dealer would attribute the risk directly to the support provider's position limits. In a worst case scenario a dealer holding paper that is supported could face a loss if both the issuer and the support provider default. As one might expect, the chance of such an occurrence is very remote. If the original issuer continues to perform as expected and the support mechanism is not activated, the dealer faces no additional risk to the support provider.

'Soft Puts'

There is a risk of having paper 'put' back to the bank or dealer under a repricing or remarketing mechanism. A soft put can be defined as a potential obligation a bank might have when it is acting as a remarketing or repricing agent on a money market issue or security. For example, in the case of auction market preferred stock or variable rate notes, the bank, as remarketing agent, is charged with establishing a new rate on the security (typically in conjunction with the issuer and in response to the demands of the market). A failure to set the correct rate can leave the remarketing agent with additional inventory on its books. In other words, investors holding paper during the coupon reset date refuse to participate because of dissatisfaction with the new rate. The remarketer must then take the paper onto its own books until either it can sell it out in the secondary market or it resets the coupon at the next reset date.

In assuming the role of remarketing agent, the bank or dealer has essentially sold a put to the investor (which, in option terminology, would allow the investor to exercise the put and sell paper back to the remarketing agent). These puts are considered 'soft' because they are inherent in the product and not specifically written outside it. A prudent credit approach would take account of this potential obligation by categorising it as a provisional risk. Note that the hard puts discussed under the inventory section are sometimes thought to be more provisional in nature, as they may or may not come to pass. Inclusion of such puttable transactions under either position or provisional risk could be considered correct.

The overview of provisional risk should indicate that no risk equivalency is applicable for the category as a whole. If any of the events outlined above occurs (ie a funding commitment under a RUF or NIF is drawn, an issuer defaults on commercial paper or a bond and the dealer is found liable, a support mechanism is called into use or a soft put is exercised), the actual incremental risk to the bank or dealer will be dollar-for-dollar (ie the bank either provides funds, makes the investor 'whole' on the loss, adds to its total exposure to the supporter of an issue or is forced to take back an issuer's paper from an investor). While provisional exposure is more difficult to quantify because it is dependent on events which may or may not take place in the future, it is nevertheless a category of risk which cannot be ignored.

MARKET RISK, COUNTERPARTY RISK AND LOSS LEVELS

Though we have already discussed market risk and counterparty risk in this text, it is worth investigating how these concepts interact when considered in unison. Market risk, as we know, may increase or decrease over time as a result of changes in interest or currency rates. When it increases, it implies additional exposure to a bank extending a credit facility. As it decreases, a bank's exposure is reduced. The vital point to stress is that market risk exposure exists in some form throughout the life of a market risk transaction, although its value may fluctuate (and in some cases may be negative, implying no exposure for the bank).

Counterparty risk, as we have seen, is simply the risk that a client will cease to perform on a contractual obligation. The cessation may be wilful or it may be the result of financial deterioration or collapse. The level of counterparty risk a bank may encounter will be low or minimal if the client is of good credit quality and high if the client is of poor credit quality. In addition, counterparty risk may increase or decrease over the life of the transaction as the underlying creditworthiness of the client changes. This is primarily true in long-term transactions where a company has time to deteriorate or improve financially. As with market risk, counterparty risk will be present in some form throughout the life of a transaction.

Market risk and counterparty risk will each be present during a given transaction with a given counterparty (in varying degrees which may or may not change) but the level and movement of one risk is independent of the level and movement of the other. If market risk increases, counterparty risk will not necessarily intensify and, similarly, if counterparty risk increases, market risk will not necessarily rise (although the two may both move in the same direction for unrelated reasons). There may be an exception to this where an enormous market move in a very large position adversely affects a company's credit; this, however, is very unlikely ever to occur if the analyst has done his or her job correctly by disallowing such large, and potentially volatile, exposures to a company which cannot afford to take the risk.

Although the movement of each type of risk is independent, there is a relationship between the two so far as a credit officer or credit committee is concerned: the amount of market risk which exists when counterparty risk reaches its maximum point (default or failure) is the amount the bank will lose. If market risk is high when default occurs, the loss sustained by the bank will be high. If it is low (or even negative, which is possible for certain market risk transactions), the bank will face a minimal loss (or no loss at all). In this respect the two variables are connected. Let us consider the following equations, where we assume the maximum point of each case to be the extreme: maximum counterparty risk (defined as max CR) is counterparty default and maximum market risk (defined as max MR) is the maximum expected market exposure (or potential market exposure).

$$\text{set of } \{\text{counterparty risk CR, market risk MR}\} \rightarrow \text{resulting loss}$$

$$\{\text{min CR, min} \vee 0 \text{ MR}\} \rightarrow 0 \text{ loss}$$

$$\{\text{min CR, max MR}\} \rightarrow 0 \text{ loss}$$

$$\{\text{max CR, min} \vee 0 \text{ MR}\} \rightarrow \text{min} \vee 0 \text{ loss}$$

$$\{\text{max CR, max MR}\} \rightarrow \text{max loss}$$

It should be noted that we do not apply the same concept directly to a discussion of position risk. While position risk may fluctuate over the life of a transaction as it is affected by movements in rates (just as market risk is), it must be remembered that position risks are susceptible primarily to counterparty deterioration or default. As we shall see when discussing money market instruments and bonds, the value of an inventory position can be adversely affected by the performance of the issuer, ie the bank's counterparty; there is a positive correlation between counterparty risk and position risk.

Having reviewed the major categories of product risk, we can summarise as follows:

I. Market Risk
- A. Potential Market Risk
- B. Actual Market (or Mark-to-Market) Risk

II. Settlement (or Delivery) Risk

III. Inventory (or Position) Risk (including 'Hard Puts')

IV. Provisional Risk
- A. Funding Commitment
- B. Underwriter's Liability
- C. Third Party Support
- D. 'Soft Puts'

As always, different institutions have different ways of classifying risk categories. The preceding presentation is by no means the only way to approach the topic. Certain institutions have broader categories, focusing simply on trading products and inventory positions. Others take a more detailed approach by establishing categories for individual instruments or those with similar characteristics (ie maturity, liquidity, marketability). Regardless of individual risk classification categories, most institutions involved in the financial products discussed in Part III employ some type of risk classification. Such categorisation is especially important when an institution is attempting to implement an effective risk management framework.

5: Risk Equivalency

An integral part of the risk management process, as we have seen, is accurate measurement of risks. In order to measure risks precisely, particularly for those instruments we have termed market risk-based, it is vital to comprehend (and to apply) the risk equivalency process.

Commercial banks have had many years of experience in lending to a variety of counterparties on both a secured and an unsecured basis. These credit decisions tend to be at once simple and difficult. They are simple because the risk in lending is generally straightforward and does not vary much from case to case. A commercial bank extending an unsecured loan has 100 per cent risk exposure; there is no complexity in the calculation. If the lending is being undertaken on a secured basis, the value of the collateral has to be factored in and altered on a periodic basis. However, although a certain amount of adjustment is necessary, the resulting calculation is not difficult and will depend on the amount of funds being lent minus the appraised or estimated value of the collateral. The difficulty in the decision-making process with pure funding transactions arises because the credit being extended represents dollar-for-dollar risk exposure where no security is involved. From a banker's perspective these are difficult decisions to make because the risk is high.

From the perspective of a credit analyst or credit committee at an investment bank (or a commercial bank dealing in derivative products) the approach to valuing risk is rather different, although the decision-making may be equally difficult. The process involves risk equivalency, one of the fundamental concepts of risk analysis (note that it is often referred to by other names, including risk-adjusted loan equivalency, credit risk equivalency and risk-adjusted exposure). In simple terms the risk equivalency process allows an analyst to put the risk of different types of product on an equal footing and to relate the resulting amounts in a common fashion against a single credit line. This approach corresponds to the second step of our risk management framework, the measurement of risks, and is essential to making a sound credit decision. The risk equivalency concept applies solely to those products which are affected by market risk movements.

THE PURPOSE OF RISK EQUIVALENCY

There are at least three reasons why certain transactions must be risk-adjusted: first, products found in the money and capital markets often carry some level of security, collateral or protection. Secondly, transactions may be two-sided, with each institution expecting simultaneous performance of a given act (such as a swap, where flows of interest or currency generally travel in both directions concurrently). Thirdly, most of the products in this market are not funding transactions, where funds are advanced to a counterparty until some point in the future. As a result, the analysis of particular risks in these markets cannot be likened to traditional, unsecured bank lending, where the bank has 100 per cent exposure to the client. As we shall demonstrate, risk exposure is typically only a portion of the notional amount of a given transaction.

While most of the products in the money and capital markets have to be placed on comparable terms to value risk exposure correctly, we have noted above that certain transactions do carry dollar-for-dollar risk (or 100 per cent of the credit extended). These transactions behave and appear more like the traditional unsecured lending mentioned above. Settlement risks, inventory (or position) risks and provisional risks, as described in Chapter 4, cannot be adjusted; only market risks can be adjusted.

RISK EQUIVALENCY CALCULATIONS

The bulk of the new derivative instruments present in the market today are classified as market risk products. They are affected primarily by rate movements and can be extremely volatile. Because of the wide use of these new derivatives, we shall devote some space to the development of a framework to value these risks.

The actual process of risk equivalency involves applying certain risk factors to the notional amount of the facility or deal being considered. The figure obtained by multiplying the two items in equation (5.1) below will yield the relevant risk equivalent exposure for a particular product, putting all products on a comparable risk basis. For the analyst or committee making a decision on a given credit issue this is the figure which must be considered when assessing the exposure the bank will have to a counterparty.

$$\text{REE} = \text{RF} \times \text{N} \tag{5.1}$$

where REE is the risk equivalent exposure in \$,
RF is the relevant risk factor in per cent,
N is the notional amount of the transaction in \$.

The general derivation of RF is explored in Chapter 6 of this book and will be used in each of the individual product chapters in Part III. Note also that the approach employed in this text will be based on a potential exposure framework, not a mark-to-market framework as discussed in Chapter 4. Equation (5.1) represents a general risk equivalency equation; as one might expect, different products and transactions will require certain refinements to the basic equation. Such refinements are discussed in the individual product chapters in Part III.

If we had a potential transaction with Company XYZ and we determined the risk equivalent exposure (REE) to be \$5m (ie a \$100m transaction where a risk factor of 5 per cent was applicable), this figure would represent the potential usage under XYZ's overall credit limits. If the bank had extended internal credit limits of \$50m to XYZ and \$25m was already allocated in the form of an unsecured loan, the transaction above, if approved, would subtract a further \$5m from the remaining \$25m credit limit. Assuming all other parameters associated with the transaction to be in order, the committee would be inclined to approve the transaction.

It should be clear that unfamiliarity with the concept of risk equivalency can lead to a misallocation of risk exposure for a given transaction. Since risk equivalency yields a figure which is substantially lower in virtually all cases than the notional amount of a transaction, ignorance of the concept and process will result in potential deals and transactions being rejected.

In order to demonstrate the notion of risk equivalency, several simple examples are included below.

Example One

A broker-dealer is prepared to extend a credit line for repurchase agreements and reverse repurchase agreements (a repo/reverse line) to a regional commercial bank. The bank is interested in investing its excess cash balances by entering into one-month reverses with the broker-dealer, through which it will add a few basis points of yield to its otherwise idle cash. In a reverse, which can have maturities from overnight to 12 months and beyond, the bank gives the dealer its cash and receives securities in return. Assuming the transaction exchanges two-year Treasury notes for \$50m cash, the analyst evaluating the extension of this credit limit calculates, by means of the risk equivalency process, that the correct risk to apply to the deal is \$3m, based on the underlying security being 'repoed'. The difference in granting credit limits of \$3m and \$50m is obviously substantial.

Why does the analyst apply only a portion of the total notional amount as risk exposure? Because, although the dealer has released \$50.6m of securities (\$50m in securities plus a \$600,000 'haircut', or overcollateralisation level – to be discussed further in Chapter 7), it has also taken \$50m in cash from the bank. It is therefore exposed to \$600,000 in securities plus the \$2.4m risk (obtained through a 4 8 per cent risk factor) of potential market movements which could cause the value of the securities to rise during the life of the transaction. The derivation of the potential market movement is arrived at by looking at the historical volatility of the two-year Treasury note and applying a basic statistical model with appropriate confidence levels to the data (these items are discussed at length in Chapter 6). We summarise the risk as

$$\text{REE} = \text{RF} \times \text{N}$$

or

$$\$2.4\text{m} = 4.8 \text{ per cent of } \$50\text{m}$$

Adding the \$600,000 haircut gives a total of \$3m. The total equation for repos and reverses is covered in Chapter 7.

In general, the longer the maturity on the Treasury security being repoed or reversed, the higher the volatility factor, the greater the risk factor and the larger the risk equivalent exposure. However, before getting into an intricate discussion of the risks of doing repo business, the point to highlight is that the risk of the transaction has been modified and we find that the dealer does not have dollar-for-dollar exposure on the deal. Its risk exposure to the bank is reduced because it has taken some security (in this case cash) in return.

Example Two

A bank wishes to execute an interest rate swap with a major company. The terms of the deal are very straightforward: semi-annual payments between the bank and the company (the former paying floating, the latter paying fixed), always on a net basis (ie the party owing the larger sum makes a net payment to the other party). The notional principal is \$10m, the tenor of the transaction is two years and payment rates are 8 per cent fixed and six-month LIBOR plus 10 basis points floating. Current LIBOR is 8.5 per cent, yielding a total floating payment of 8.60 per cent for the first six months.

The risk of this transaction is not \$10m but only a fraction of \$10m. Once again, the reason for the fractional exposure has to do with the fact that the notional amount of the deal is not being swapped and both the bank and the company stand a chance of making some net payments during the life of the swap. Neither party to the transaction has any additional or off-market payments to make to the other party (which might cause a greater risk). Both parties are paying a coupon every six months, so the only risk for the bank is the cost of replacing the swap in the market should the company default on its payments.

By equation (5.1) exposure is

$$\$160{,}000 \;=\; 1.6 \text{ per cent of } \$10\text{m}$$

In this particular case the appropriate risk equivalent exposure would be $160,000, which is obtained from a 1.6 per cent swap risk factor, based on both the fixed rate payment level and the final maturity (to be explained in greater detail in Chapter 13 on swaps). It is worth noting that the risk of the transaction today is $160,000; the value of that risk will change over time in accordance with movements in rates. The initial risk exposure is, in most instances, the most conservative measure of the risk on a transaction and the maximum amount the bank is likely to face during the life of the deal. Again, this is the figure that a credit committee would focus on in allocating risk to the deal.

Example Three

A company wishes to buy $10m of Treasury bills from a securities firm for settlement in 30 days. Thus no cash or securities will change hands on trade date. If it were releasing the $10m in Treasuries today and not expecting payment for 30 days, then the securities firm would be said to have a 'free delivery', or 'clean risk', situation, where risk exposure would be equal to the full $10m (the securities firm would in essence be making a 30-day unsecured loan to the company). However, since cash and securities will both be exchanged one month from now, the potential risk to the securities firm is $500,000, based on a risk factor of 0.5 per cent. Returning to equation (5.1) we have

$$\$500{,}000 = 0.5 \text{ per cent of } \$10\text{m}$$

This transaction, known as a forward, extended or delayed settlement, exposes the securities firm to the risk of market movement on the underlying securities being sold. Should interest rates rise during the 30-day period in question, the value of the Treasury securities will fall and, if the company fails or otherwise chooses to default on the transaction during the same period, the securities firm may be forced to sell the securities at this lower price. This will result in a loss to the securities firm. The use of a 0.5 per cent risk factor in this instance captures the potential risk exposure the firm faces during the next 30 days.

After reviewing these simple examples it should be clear that not every transaction or product encountered in the financial markets carries risk equal to 100 per cent of the notional amount. Most of the instruments treated in this book (which are among the most common in the financial markets) carry risk equal to only a fraction of their notional amount.

It is important for the credit analyst or product manager to understand the concept of risk equivalency so that there can be an accurate assessment of the risks being undertaken. Also worth stressing is that the approach for dealing with these instruments is very different from that taken for unsecured commercial bank lending. If a commercial banking officer is becoming involved in transactions which need to be modified from a risk perspective, he or she must have a full understanding of the process.

6: Quantifying the Risk Equivalency Process

By now the reader should be aware of the importance of the risk equivalency process in determining product risk and allocating the correct amount of risk exposure to a given transaction; the development of an accurate risk equivalency gauge is an important component in the measurement stage of the risk management process. It is vital at this point to understand thoroughly the basis for the derivation of our risk factor variable RF, discussed in Chapter 5. Remember that the risk equivalency process is applicable only in deriving potential risk equivalent exposure (REE) and is utilised only for those products or transactions which are deemed to add market risk exposure to the bank (inventory and provisional risks require no adjustments).

DERIVATION OF THE RISK FACTOR

The derivation of RF begins with a statistical study of the historical rates governing the instrument or security being transacted; placing these historical rates in a predictive framework provides an indication of where market rates might go in the future. Once we have determined the possible level of future market rates (after incorporating confidence level and maturity parameters, as detailed below), we can quantify the maximum market risk movement we are likely to experience while the transaction is outstanding; this is what RF effectively captures. It should be noted that, in addition to an examination of historical volatilities to derive RF, there are other types of volatility estimates which can be used: kernel estimators, flexible fourier form estimators and other non-parametric measures. In practice, use of historical volatility is the most widely used system for this type of analysis and will be the focus of this chapter.

In order to derive the RF of a Treasury option on a five-year bond, for example, we would begin by looking at the historical movement of the five-year Treasury bond rate. A timeframe of several years should be used to provide a meaningful view of volatility. The 10 years between 1980 and 1990 have provided the economy and the markets with recession, high and low inflation, high and low unemployment, strength and weakness of the dollar, increasing deficits, a bull market in equities and bonds, collapse of the equity and junk markets and so on. In short, the past decade has been very volatile and is able to provide enough market movement to give us confidence that the RF derived from such a period will provide a conservative measure of volatility. Note that data based on a full decade of observations would not typically be required in order to establish a meaningful volatility measure; three to five years is generally sufficient.

As one might expect, to derive the RF on a foreign exchange option we replace the historical view of the Treasury bond with an historical view of the relevant exchange rates. Likewise, the RF on forward GNMA securities would concentrate on the market performance of GNMA rates over the past few years.

Volatility Measurement

The derivation of historical volatilities generally has four stages. First, periodic sample information (rates, prices, etc) based on a closing figure, an average of daily high/low figures or some other representation is gathered. The information may be daily, weekly, or monthly. For our purposes these data points are denoted:

$$p_0, p_1, \ldots, p_n.$$

Most historical volatility analysis tends to focus on historical yields or rates, as opposed to prices, but both are technically correct and either can be utilised. Secondly, the percentage change from one period to the next is calculated. For our purposes this is denoted by the following series:

$$R_1 = \frac{[p_1 - p_0]}{p_0}$$

$$R_1 = \frac{[p_1 - p_0]}{p_1}$$

$$\vdots$$

$$R_n = \frac{[p_n - p_{n-1}]}{p_{n-1}}$$

Thirdly, the standard deviation for the period is calculated by the following formulae:

Mean: $\mu(R_x) = \sum_{z=1}^{n} \left(\frac{R_z}{n}\right)$

Variance: $\sigma^2 = \sum_{z=1}^{n} \frac{(R_z - R_x)^2}{n}$

Standard Deviation: $\sigma = \sqrt{\sigma^2} = \sqrt{\sum_{z=1}^{n} \frac{(R_z - R_x)^2}{n}}$

Fourthly, once the standard deviation is complete, it will equal our period volatility. If daily or monthly price data were used we would translate the standard deviation into an annual figure, as that is a more widely used measure of volatility. This is accomplished by taking the square root of either the relevant trading days or months during which the index is active. For most purposes we can assume a 'rule of thumb' of 250 trading days per year; this likewise translates into about 8.3 months per year.

square root of 250 gives 15.8 for daily data;
square root of 8.3 gives 2.9 for monthly data;
square root of 1 gives 1 for annual data.

Thus, if daily price volatilities were calculated, we should simply multiply the resulting standard deviation by 15.8; if monthly volatilities were used, we should multiply by 2.9. This provides one method of calculating an annual historical volatility measure, summarised as:

$$HV = \sigma \sqrt{x}$$

where x is 250 for daily data, 8.3 for monthly data or 1 for annual data.

A second way in which to calculate historical volatilities is to use the natural log of securities prices (this implies use of the lognormal distribution, discussed at length below. For now we focus on the formula). This method simply takes the natural log of the daily price and compares it with the natural log of the previous day's price. The second step involves taking the difference between the two natural logs, calculating the standard deviation of the difference and multiplying the result by the square root of 250 to obtain an annualised volatility factor. In summary form, we obtain the following:

$$x_1 = \ln(p_0) - \ln(p_1)$$
$$s_1 = \sigma_1(x_1)$$
$$HV = s_1 \sqrt{250}$$

In addition to the two approaches discussed above, there are numerous other ways to calculate volatilities. Use of historical volatility information is one of the central elements found in option pricing models and many option texts cover a variety of volatility calculations.

In order to illustrate use of the first volatility calculation above, we can consider the following daily bond price information for a five-year Treasury note. A limited sample of six points is shown in order to keep the example clear.

price information:

$$
\begin{aligned}
p0 &= 101.5 \\
p1 &= 101 \\
p2 &= 100 \\
p3 &= 101 \\
p4 &= 100.25 \\
p5 &= 99.75
\end{aligned}
$$

percentage change:

$$
\begin{aligned}
R1 &= (101 - 101.5)/101.5 = -0.0049 \\
R2 &= (100 - 101)/101 = -0.0099 \\
R3 &= (101 - 100)/100 = 0.01 \\
R4 &= (100.25 - 101)/101 = -0.0074 \\
R5 &= (99.75 - 100.25)/100.25 = -0.0049
\end{aligned}
$$

mean:

$$
\begin{aligned}
&(-0.0049 + (-0.0099) + 0.01 + (-0.0074) + (-0.0049))/5 \\
&= -0.0034
\end{aligned}
$$

variance:

$$
\begin{aligned}
&((-0.0049 - 0.0034)_2 + (-0.0099 - 0.0034)_2 + (0.01 - 0.0034)_2 \\
&\quad + (-0.0074 - 0.0034)_2 + (-0.0049 - 0.0034)_2)/5 \\
&= (0.0000688 + 0.0001768 + 0.0000435 + 0.0001167 \\
&\quad + 0.0000688)/5 \\
&= (0.0004746)/5 \\
&= 0.0000949
\end{aligned}
$$

standard deviation:

square root of 0.0000949 = 0.0097416

In percentage terms the daily volatility is equal to 0.97416 per cent.

annual historical volatility:

$$\begin{aligned} HV &= 0.97416 \text{ per cent} \times \sqrt{250} \\ &= 0.0097416 \times 15.8 \\ &= 0.1539 \\ &= 15.39 \text{ per cent.} \end{aligned}$$

We can therefore say that, based on the small sample of daily price information on five-year Treasury notes, the annual volatility is 15.39 per cent; that is, past market movements have shown that the Treasury note can move by 15.39 per cent during a given year. Use of this figure against a confidence level and a maturity element helps develop the total picture for the derivation of RF.

It should be noted that statistical theory and sampling techniques dictate that the sample of price information we are taking be as extensive as possible to give an accurate picture of price movements. The above sample of six points would certainly not be enough to let us conclude safely that the annual volatility on Treasury notes is 15.39 per cent.

Confidence Levels

Once the appropriate index and relevant historical data have been identified and gathered and the above statistics have been calculated, the volatility should be adjusted to the appropriate confidence level. We need to create a 'comfort' or 'confidence' level which covers between 90 and 99 per cent of all likely scenarios in order for our risk factors to make a useful contribution to the process. In other words, we need to be certain that our risk factors have been adjusted such that a future observation is less than or equal to our predicted rate at least 90 per cent of the time. Those readers familiar with a normal distribution (ie a standard bell-shaped curve) will recall that one standard deviation on a normal distribution will include 68 per cent of all observations, two standard deviations will include 95 per cent of all observations and three standard deviations will include 99 per cent of all observations.

For the purposes of this study, we will be focusing on a lognormal, rather than a normal, distribution (ie a curve which is skewed slightly to the right). There are two reasons for the use of a lognormal distribution. Intuitively, it makes sense to use such a distribution because we know that there is technically no upper bound to the direction of interest rates, currency rates, bond prices and so on. The lower bound will always be zero but, given that rates or prices can theoretically move towards infinity, a distribution skewed to the right gives a greater degree of accuracy.

Leaving aside the intuitive approach, an examination of much of the work done on the distribution of rates and prices will show that use of a lognormal function is widely accepted. According to M. Ferron and G. Handjinicolaou (*Handbook of Currency and Interest Rate Risk Management*, p. 23), 'a large body of academic research has determined that the behaviour of interest rates in the future is most appropriately modelled by means of a probability distribution function which is lognormal'.

Without spending any further time on that large body of academic research (which is well beyond the scope of this text), the central point is an understanding that use of the lognormal function is accurate for the rate movements affecting the instruments we are considering in this text. In a lognormal curve the likelihood of a value's lying within one standard deviation is 84 per cent and within two standard deviations 98 per cent. The 90 per cent confidence level equates to just over 1.28 standard deviations. For the purposes of this text, a 90 per cent confidence level is deemed sufficient; in practice, many institutions using a risk factor framework will adjust volatility levels between 90 per cent and 99 per cent.

To summarise, the above tells us that, in establishing a range of 1.28 standard deviations about our volatility measure, we can be certain that a future observation (ie a movement in rates) will be less than or equal to our historical volatility measure at least 90 per cent of the time. Our associated risk factor will then be relevant in 90 per cent (or more) of cases, which adds a tremendous degree of comfort to the decision-making process.

Maturity Considerations

As a final element we need to consider the time factor. Since we are attempting to estimate where a price or rate will be at some point in the future (by looking at past volatilities and adjusting them to a certain confidence level), we cannot ignore the maturity of the trade. As one might anticipate, the longer the maturity, the greater the chance for a rate to move and the greater the potential risk to a bank extending a credit line.

Referring once again to Ferron and Handjinicolaou, 'assuming lognormality, the degree of diffusion (the scale of interest rate movements consisting of several periods increases with the number of periods) is a function of the square root of time elapsed' (*op cit*, p. 23). This is also known as the 'square root rule' and is the final item required before setting up a general equation to derive our risk factor RF. (Readers interested in the statistics behind the square root rule may consult one of the many statistics texts on the subject.)

The Risk Factor

With these elements, the general formula for our risk factor becomes:

$$RF = CLF \times HV \times \sqrt{T} \tag{6.1}$$

where CLF is the confidence level factor,
HV is the historical volatility,
T is the cumulative time to maturity.

If a confidence level of 98 per cent is desired, the appropriate CLF would be 2; if 90 per cent is sufficient, the CLF would be 1.28. If the HV is measured on an annual basis, care should be taken that the square root of time is also measured in the same way (eg if the trade is for one year, it should be the square root of 1 not of 250, assuming annualised volatility).

In order to clarify the formula, let us return to the example we touched on earlier. We noted that the annualised HV on a five-year Treasury note was 15.39 per cent. Assume that we want to derive a risk factor on a six-month extended settlement trade of five-year notes, with a 90 per cent confidence level on a lognormal distribution. Referring to equation (6.1) above we would proceed as follows:

CLF = 1.28
HV = 15.39
T = 0.5 (recall that our HV was already adjusted to an annual basis, so that our factor is half a year, or 0.5)

Then,

$$RF = 1.28 \times 15.39 \times \sqrt{0.5}$$
$$RF = 13.92$$

This indicates that, based on historical volatilities, we are at least 90 per cent certain that the value of the five-year note will be no more than 13.92 per cent higher or lower than our starting rate during the six months the extended settlement transaction remains on the books. Assuming that we had contracted to sell the client \$100m for settlement in six months, our risk equivalent exposure would be \$13.9m. We have just put into practice the theoretical risk factor framework developed above.

Once we have determined our confidence level and the historical volatility for a particular instrument, we can create a table of risk factors which contains figures for relevant maturities. The use of such a table enables the credit analyst or lending officer to risk-adjust a given transaction quickly, without spending time memorising formulae or recalculating frequently used data. As an example, consider the following task.

We want to construct a grid which will reflect risk factors for forward settlement of bills, notes and bonds, adjusted to 90 per cent confidence level for trades of one, three, six and 12 months. We calculate the following annualised historical volatilities from a three-year sample of Treasury rate data:

one-year bills: HV = 8 per cent;
five-year notes: HV = 11 per cent;
20-year bonds: HV = 16 per cent.

Recalling equation (6.1) above we know that we have to adjust the HV to the appropriate confidence level by multiplying by 1.28 and we have to take into account the time factor element *via* the square root rule.

Based on the above, our calculations will yield the following risk factors:

One-year bills
one-month RF = 1.28 × 0.08 × square root of 0.08 = 2.89 per cent;
three-month RF = 1.28 × 0.08 × square root of 0.25 = 5.12 per cent;
six-month RF = 1.28 × 0.08 × square root of 0.50 = 7.24 per cent;
12-month RF = 1.28 × 0.08 × square root of 1.0 = 10.24 per cent.

Five-year notes
one-month RF = 1.28 × 0.11 × square root of 0.08 = 3.98 per cent;
three-month RF = 1.28 × 0.11 × square root of 0.25 = 7.04 per cent;
six-month RF = 1.28 × 0.11 × square root of 0.50 = 9.96 per cent;
12-month RF = 1.28 × 0.11 × square root of 1.0 = 14.08 per cent.

20-year bonds
one-month RF = 1.28 × 0.16 × square root of 0.08 = 5.79 per cent;
three-month RF = 1.28 × 0.16 × square root of 0.25 = 10.24 per cent;
six-month RF = 1.28 × 0.16 × square root of 0.50 = 14.48 per cent;
12-month RF = 1.28 × 0.16 × square root of 1.0 = 20.48 per cent.

Placing this into a grid we obtain Table 6.1.

If a credit officer gets an urgent call from a trading desk wanting to sell $50m of Treasury notes for delivery in six months to a given client, the officer will quickly be able to determine the risk attributable to the trade as just under $5m. This method of developing risk factor grids for all products is convenient and allows an officer to be responsive in 'short fuse' situations.

With this information in mind, we have effectively created a useful framework by means of which we can apply risk equivalency to an instrument or

Table 6.1. Risk Factors for Extended Settlement Treasuries (per cent)

	One-month	Three-month	Six-month	12-month
Bills	2.9	5.1	7.2	10.2
Notes	4.0	7.0	9.9	14.1
Bonds	5.8	10.2	14.5	20.5

product. Armed with this background (as well as our general knowledge of different types of risk), we are prepared to begin analysing the financial instruments commonly encountered in the financial markets; this discussion forms Part III of the text.

As a final note on risk factors it should be pointed out that in the individual product descriptions in Part III the derivation of specific factors for each market risk product follows the methodology detailed above. The exception is swaps and swap derivatives, where a slightly more complex approach is required.

Part III
Financial Instrument Risk Analysis

7: Repurchase/Reverse Repurchase Agreements

DEFINITION

The first product covered in this section is the repurchase agreement, one of the fundamental instruments in the money markets. A repurchase agreement (or repo, as it is commonly known) is essentially an agreement to sell and repurchase a security. The actual repurchase of the security may come as soon as the next day or as far away as one or two years in the future. Repos can also be booked on an 'open' basis; that is, the transaction can be 'rolled' (rebooked) daily until one of the two parties involved decides to close it out. In a standard repo transaction the bank will sell its securities (perhaps Treasury notes) to a third party, while at the same time entering into a contract to repurchase them at some point in the future. Both sale and repurchase prices are agreed prior to entering the deal. In return for the securities, the bank will receive cash from the third party; the inflow of cash can be used to fund the balance sheet and a repo transaction is thus often thought of as a financing or a short-term, collateralised borrowing.

The motivation for an institution to enter into a repo transaction is that it can finance the purchase of securities, or otherwise fund its balance sheet, at relatively competitive rates in a quick and informal manner and in a very liquid market (particularly in repos with shorter maturities where the underlying collateral is a US Treasury instrument). In addition to pure funding reasons, a bank may be holding securities it does not currently want but does not wish to liquidate. It can repo the securities and, with the proceeds, acquire other securities it may favour. At some point in the future it will liquidate these new securities, return the cash and receive its original securities without having liquidated its original position. Note that the repo counterparty, although not in physical possession of the securities during the transaction, is entitled to the interest which accrues on the underlying collateral.

On the opposite side of the repo transaction is the reverse repurchase agreement (also known as a reverse repo or simply a reverse). The counterparty who is entering into a reverse is, in essence, making a short-term, collateralised loan to the bank by providing funds in return for holding securities. When the reverse matures, the counterparty returns the securities to the bank and receives its cash (plus the profit spread). The motivation for an institution to enter into a reverse repo is that it earns some extra income on what might otherwise be 'idle' cash.

The major players in the repo and reverse market tend to be financial institutions with substantial portfolios of government securities. Primary dealers (a group of securities dealers which act as the US Government's main link in the distribution of Treasury securities to investors) often hold large inventories of government securities, which they repo out in exchange for cash. Another high volume business for the largest dealers on Wall Street is to fill customer orders. A customer will deposit securities in exchange for a loan at, say, 7.5 per cent; the dealer will then repo the securities out for cash at a rate of, say, 7.48 per cent, locking in a small spread for the duration of the repo/reverse. The dealer's large size and active market participation allow it to borrow at rates which are lower than those available to a smaller customer. This type of business is known as a 'matched book' (ie the dealer is reversing in securities and repoing out identical, or matched, securities); major Wall Street dealers run matched books of billions of dollars.

In order to execute a repo or a reverse, securities and cash must change hands. In the US this is usually, but not invariably, accomplished through the exchange of immediately available funds (*via* Federal Reserve Bank or commercial bank deposits, for example) for securities transferred through the CPD wire or Fed Wire (the Commissioner of Public Debt wire which is operated by the Federal Reserve). The rate charged by the lender, in this case the counterparty who is doing the reverse repo, is typically related to the Federal Funds rate (the rate at which banks can borrow from each other). Repo rates tend to be slightly lower than the associated Fed Funds rate, since a repo is a secured transaction and Fed Funds borrowing is not. As one might expect, the largest and most creditworthy borrowers get the lowest repo rates. Overnight repo rates tend to be the lowest rates in the market; open repo rates are slightly higher and term repo rates are higher still. This is in line with the standard, upward sloping yield curve.

The instruments most commonly repoed and reversed by banks and dealers are US Government securities, ranging from three-month Treasury bills to 30-year Treasury bonds. Given the underlying security, a US Government obligation, the risk of default on the collateral is virtually non-existent. However, agencies, CDs, mortgage-backed securities, whole loans and various other instruments can also be used. As the collateral becomes more speculative, so the chances for default on the underlying security become greater and the chances of the loan's becoming unsecured increase. These factors will change the risk profile of the deal significantly and an institution granting a reverse on the basis of such an underlying security may find itself in a difficult situation. The credit quality distinction on the collateral must be factored in when calculating the appropriate overcollateralisation level, as discussed below.

In a typical repo/reverse repo transaction, the counterparty which is borrowing (ie the repo counterparty) will put up more collateral than the amount being borrowed. The primary reason for this overcollateralisation (or 'haircut' in Wall Street parlance) is that the institution holding the reverse repo (ie holding the securities) is subject to market movements on the value of the collateral and, in a default, could lose money if it has to liquidate the collateral it is holding to make up for the money it has lent out.

In a period of rising interest rates the value of a bill, note or bond declines. If a bank enters into a 30-day reverse with a dealer and interest rates spike sharply up, the value of the securities it is holding may not be sufficient to cover the value of the loan being extended. The overcollateralisation alleviates this problem by adding a 'buffer', based on market practice or historical market movements. From a market practice standpoint, dealers generally take haircuts of 10 to 20 basis points on Treasury bill repos from one to four weeks; for notes and bonds, this increases to 15 to 25 basis points.

If all repos and reverses involved US Government securities, there would be no concern over the underlying collateral's going into default and the reverse counterparty's being left with an unsecured loan. However, other securities require different overcollateralisation factors. If the haircut on a six-month Treasury bill is 0.25 per cent, the haircut on a risky security might be 15 or 20 per cent. This extra overcollateralisation covers the volatilities inherent in more speculative securities. Examples of securities where additional overcollateralisation is warranted include AA-rated collateralised mortgage obligations (CMOs), asset-backed securities, senior/subordinated participation certificates, conforming whole loans, CMOs rated lower than AA, CMO residuals and interest-only and principal-only (IO and PO) strips.

While overcollateralisation exists at the start of a transaction, it should be noted that a bank with a reverse position can call for additional collateral should market movements warrant it, while a bank with a repo position can have collateral returned to it should market movements allow it. Most major dealers and banks mark their repo books to market on a daily basis and, where necessary, will call for additional collateral or will return collateral. In practice, many major dealers and banks will not call for additional collateral among themselves unless absolutely necessary. However, when dealing with smaller or less creditworthy counterparties, where risk of default on the repo is much greater, collateral calls are apt to be more frequent.

In addition to regular repos and reverses, defined as open (rebooked daily by mutual agreement), overnight and term (any repo not maturing the next day), there are several variations of the product of which analysts should be aware.

Due Bill Repo

Here, the counterparty borrowing the funds and giving collateral will keep the collateral in a segregated, 'in-house' account. Although the repo counterparty does not have legal claim over the securities while in possession of cash, it does have physical possession of them. This type of repo can be an attractive alternative for banks considering repo business with a counterparty which has a relatively low rating. All other terms and characteristics found in a regular repo would apply.

Tri-party Repo

Here, the securities from the repo party and/or the cash from the reverse party are routed through, or kept with, a third party custodian. The custodian will not release cash or securities until it has received both sides of the transaction. This type of arrangement ensures that there will be no customer fails on either side and can be utilised when dealing with clients with lower ratings. Again all other characteristics of a regular repo apply.

Liquid Repo

This is a repo where one party allows the other to terminate a term repo transaction at a point prior to maturity. As the name implies, this adds liquidity to the transaction and can be used when dealing with less liquid types of collateral or longer-term deals. All other characteristics of a regular repo apply once more.

Reverse to Maturity

This is a repo by a counterparty with securities which it is unwilling to sell (particularly if they are at a loss). Through a reverse to maturity it will repo the securities for cash and set the maturity of the transaction to match the maturity date of the underlying securities. On the maturity date it will then be able to liquidate its securities at par. This type of repo can be long-term in nature, so an analyst needs to be aware of the final maturity of the underlying security. All other characteristics of a regular repo apply.

Markets outside the US

While our descriptive section has focused on standard US Government repos and reverses, it should be mentioned that there are active, and growing, markets for similar financing arrangements in other countries. In Europe there are 'bond borrow/bond lend' and 'sale/buyback' markets involving the government securities of the UK, France, Germany and Italy and in Japan there is a 'gensaki repo' market involving Japanese Government Bonds (JGBs). While these markets have specific characteristics of liquidity, over-collateralisation levels, mark-to-market procedures and so on, they are similar in concept to the standard financing transactions we have just discussed.

GENERAL CREDIT CONSIDERATIONS

When considering repo and reverse transactions in the decision-making framework, there are several items to consider.

Risk

Risk is low, particularly when dealing with US Government securities. The risk weighting for repos is 100 per cent under the BIS, while for reverses it can be as low as 20 per cent (depending on the collateral taken).

Return

Return is low for medium quality counterparties utilising generic collateral; although the risk weighting for repos is 100 per cent, this is offset by low risk factors, so capital charge spreads for repos and reverses are very low.

Maturity

Maturities are typically short, particularly if an open position is marked to market on a daily basis.

Motivation

Motivations are either yield enhancing (reverse) or pure funding (repo).

Enhancement

Since repos and reverses represent collateralised borrowing and lending, risk enhancement is already present in the standard structure.

Creditworthiness

Repos and reverses, as secured, short-term transactions, can be viewed as appropriate for a broad range of credit qualities. Even counterparties with low ratings can be considered for these transactions so long as the analyst has confidence that the client is viable for the duration of the transaction (typically short-term in any case).

If it appears that the company is viable but additional protection is warranted, the analyst will then have to decide how to approach the collateralisation issue. If the bank is to enter into a reverse with a low rated company, it may decide that it wants extra collateral over and above normal requirements to protect it from market movements (ie it does not want any portion of its loan unsecured at any point). Alternatively, it may decide that it will limit the reverses to overnight maturities or will strictly enforce a daily mark to market and call for additional collateral as the market moves away from it.

Certain adjustments may also have to be made in the case of a repo. Instead of giving additional collateral in exchange for the institution's cash, the bank may want to put the repo on a 'flat' basis, ie $50m of securities are exchanged for $50m of cash and the company takes the market risk on the securities. Further, it may want the company to give up any future appreciation in the value of the securities over and above the amount of cash it has lent to the bank.

Beyond altering collateral levels, the variations discussed above can be used. Both due bill and tri-party repos are suitable for customers of lower credit quality, as both reduce some of the risk inherent in a standard transaction.

In either a repo or a reverse, however, the analyst should obviously not extend approval if there is a substantial chance that the counterparty will default. Although security exists, there is clearly no point in engaging in any transaction where the risk of default is high.

RISK QUANTIFICATION

Repos and reverses are affected by market rate movements which alter the value of the underlying collateral. They are thus considered market risk products and must be risk-adjusted.

In all instances market risk must be evaluated to see whether movement in the price of the underlying security being reversed in will leave the bank either partially or completely unsecured, thereby altering the appropriateness of the transaction for certain clients. In the case of a repo, it will also indicate whether excess collateral should be returned because of market movements.

From an intuitive standpoint, it is relatively simple to derive the appropriate risk equations for both repos (7.1) and reverses (7.2), if we refer back to our original equation (5.1) which says that

$$\text{REE} = \text{RF} \times \text{N}$$

In a repo securities (plus a haircut) are given in exchange for cash. Exposure is therefore twofold: first, the securities given as collateral, termed N in the equation below, might increase in value over the life of the trade. If the reverse party defaults when the market value of securities is higher than when the trade was booked, the repo party will lose this extra amount. As we have already discussed, use of the risk factor RF will give us an indication of possible future rate movements during the life of the transaction; this risk factor, applied to the notional amount N, will give us a maximum potential exposure with respect to future rate movements. This concept is captured in the first term of the equation, (RF × N). The second item at risk is simply the differential between the securities given as collateral and the cash received as a loan. This amount is the haircut, or overcollateralisation level. Since the institution has given more securities than cash, this amount is also at risk and is captured in the second term of the equation, (N − cash borrowed). Combining these two items yields

$$\text{REE} = (\text{RF} \times \text{N}) + (\text{N} - \text{cash borrowed}) \tag{7.1}$$

where RF is the appropriate risk factor,
N is the market value of securities lent (and would include the initial overcollateralisation level).

The equation for a reverse follows the same thinking, with one exception: while the reverse party is susceptible to future rate movements which could decrease the value of the collateral securing the cash lent out, it has taken a haircut which can be used partially to offset potential risk due to future market movements. As in the equation above, we still need to reflect the idea that future rate movements will alter the collateral levels; we do so using (RF × N). However, we are now in a position to reduce the potential exposure through overcollateralisation; this is done in the second portion of the equation, using (cash lent − N). The reverse equation is, therefore:

$$\text{REE} = (\text{RF} \times \text{N}) + (\text{cash lent} - \text{N}) \tag{7.2}$$

where RF is the appropriate risk factor,
N is the market value of securities borrowed (and would include the initial overcollateralisation level).

Recall from (5.1) that REE = RF × N, where N is the notional amount of the transaction. Formulae (7.1) and (7.2) capture a version of the original equation by allowing for the market value to be calculated at any point in time by substituting the new market value of the securities in place of N. Thus, (7.1) and (7.2) can be thought of as being both PREE (potential REE) and AREE (actual REE); PREE is calculated at inception, while AREE is calculated on an ongoing basis as the market value of the securities changes. Note that all collateral calls are made following a mark-to-market evaluation.

Depending on the type of security being repoed or reversed and the maturity of the underlying instrument, RF will yield the appropriate decimal percentage risk factor to apply to the notional amount. As always, the longer the maturity, the higher the RF. However, since repo and reverse positions are generally marked to market on a daily basis and collateral can be called for as required, the actual maturity of the repo becomes less of a concern unless the bank or dealer in question does not have the correct operational framework in place to make daily mark-to-market adjustments or there is an operational error in executing the mark-to-market and the call. For the purposes of our discussion, we can assume that all the major players in the market have strong back offices which allow for daily marking to market and collateral calls.

Applying a numerical example to the above equations, assume the following scenario. A dealer wants to borrow from a bank, which has an excess cash balance of $10m to invest for seven days. The dealer has a portfolio of six-month Treasury bills which it is able to use as collateral. Under the transaction the dealer will also be giving a 0.25 per cent, or $25,000, haircut. Based on (7.1) above and a risk factor of 0.9 per cent, the dealer's risk would be as follows:

$$
\begin{aligned}
\text{REE} &= (\text{RF} \times \text{N}) + (\text{N} - \text{cash borrowed}) \\
&= (0.009 \times \$10{,}025{,}000) + (\$10{,}025{,}000 - \$10{,}000{,}000) \\
&= \$90{,}225 + \$25{,}000 \\
&= \$115{,}225
\end{aligned}
$$

The $115,225 represents the exposure the dealer has to the bank because, even though the dealer has $10m in cash from the bank, the bank has an additional $25,000 of its securities. If the bank were to default or walk away from the trade today, the dealer would have to attempt to recover that differential. In addition, our risk factor RF covers the potential that interest rates will fall and the market value of the collateral given will rise. That adds $90,225 of potential risk to the transaction, based on a 0.9 per cent RF. If rates decline, the value of the securities rises and the bank defaults before returning the excess collateral, the dealer will face that additional loss. As always, we must remember that the RF captures the potential for interest rates (or any other relevant rates) to move and add exposure to the transaction.

It is worth highlighting that the actual market value of the securities is relevant to the ongoing risk-adjusted calculation; it is calculated by replacing our original N with the new market value of the securities. For example, if interest rates rose sharply and the value of the Treasury bill declined by, say, \$200,000, we would have the following:

$$\begin{aligned} \text{REE} &= (\text{RF} \times \text{N}) + (\text{N} - \text{cash borrowed}) \\ &= (0.009 \times \$9{,}825{,}000) + (\$9{,}825{,}000 - \$10{,}000{,}000) \\ &= \$88{,}425 + (-\$175{,}000) \\ &= -\$86{,}575 \end{aligned}$$

This negative figure implies that the bank now has exposure to the dealer and, accordingly, has the right to call for additional collateral to bring the market value up to its original level.

We can view the same transaction from the bank's point of view (as the reverse party) by incorporating the same details into formula (7.2):

$$\begin{aligned} \text{REE} &= (\text{RF} \times \text{N}) + (\text{cash lent} - \text{N}) \\ &= (0.009 \times \$10{,}025{,}000) + (\$10{,}000{,}000 - \$10{,}025{,}000) \\ &= \$90{,}225 + (-\$25{,}000) \\ &= \$65{,}225 \end{aligned}$$

This figure represents the bank's exposure to the dealer and is intended to capture potential market movements in the underlying value of the collateral which might leave the bank exposed at some point during the trade. If interest rates rise and the value of the collateral falls to an amount which is less than the cash lent, the bank will be forced to call for additional collateral. Until the additional collateral is received, the bank remains exposed to the dealer in the amount of the shortfall.

If, however, interest rates fall and the market value of the six-month bill increases by \$100,000, we can see that the bank will have more comfort than before:

$$\begin{aligned} \text{REE} &= (\text{RF} \times \text{N}) + (\text{cash lent} - \text{N}) \\ &= (0.009 \times \$10{,}125{,}000) + (\$10{,}000{,}000 - \$10{,}125{,}000) \\ &= \$91{,}125 + (-\$125{,}000) \\ &= -\$33{,}875 \end{aligned}$$

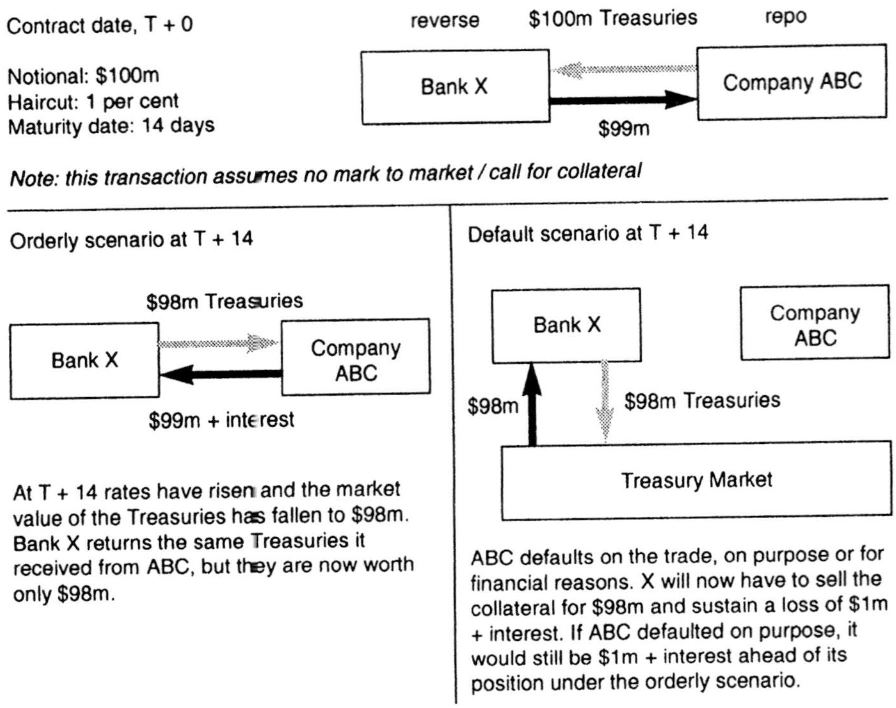

Figure 7.1. Repo/Reverse Repo: Orderly and Default Scenarios.

A negative REE figure in this instance implies that the trade is in the money for the dealer, which means that the dealer has exposure to the bank. Under this scenario the bank has eliminated its potential risk of $65,225 and should return to the dealer an amount which would bring the haircut back to its original level. Let us consider, as a final example, Figure 7.1.

Default in the Repo Markets

To place some of the issues discussed above in the context of actual credit losses, consider some notable failures of the 1980s which caused financial institutions and other customers to lose millions of dollars. In one of the most widely quoted cases, the default by Drysdale Government Securities in 1982 on its repo obligations left several financial institutions with losses of nearly $300m (including Chase Manhattan, which is believed to have lost $160m). The failure of Lombard-Wall in late 1982 caused losses of the order of $20m.

The 1985 failure of ESM Companies caused investors and other participants to lose approximately $300m. Other defaults in the past 15 years have involved Lion Capital Group, Comark, RTD Securities and Bevill, Bresler and Schulman. As a result of these cases, banks and securities firms running large repo operations tend to be attentive to credit risk issues and many employ some of the techniques discussed above.

The 1982 Lombard-Wall case was also important from a legal standpoint. Following the bankruptcy filing, Lombard-Wall asked for, and received, a stay in bankruptcy. This effectively meant that parties holding collateral securing transactions were unable to liquidate that collateral immediately to cover losses. In granting the stay, the courts ruled that repos were effectively secured borrowings and, as with other secured borrowings, the automatic stay was relevant. For dealers, however, that obviously had serious implications, as collateral could no longer be liquidated immediately in the event of default. For a bank holding especially volatile collateral, this could translate into additional risk exposure while waiting for permission to liquidate.

With the precedent set in the Lombard-Wall case, repo dealers, through the Public Securities Association (PSA), lobbied Congress for an amendment to the US Bankruptcy code. The amendment, which was ultimately approved in 1984, provides an exemption from the automatic stay in bankruptcy, effectively allowing dealers to liquidate collateral immediately upon default. As a further step, the PSA drew up a standard repo agreement which includes each party's rights and obligations under standard transactions; most (though not all) participants active in the market today use the PSA Agreement.

A second amendment to the US Bankruptcy Code, applicable in the case of repos as well as other instruments such as swaps and foreign exchange, protects financial institutions from 'cherry-picking' by bankruptcy receivers. If a dealer is active on both sides of the business with a counterparty which declares bankruptcy, it is likely that some transactions will have value to the dealer and some will have value to the bankrupt company. Receivers, acting in the best interests of the bankrupt company, had the power in the past to honour only those contracts with value to the bankrupt company, while disallowing those detrimental to it. With an amendment to the U.S. Bankruptcy Code now in place, all repo/reverse transactions under a single contract with a bankrupt counterparty are honoured, whether they have value to the bankrupt company or not; in practice, contracts are effectively netted down to a single payment in one direction or the other. Thus, dealers no longer run the risk of having transactions cherry-picked. These two amendments are now incorporated in the Financial Institutions Reform, Recovery and Enforcement Act, 1989 (FIRREA).

RISK FACTORS

In the previous examples we demonstrated the risk calculation utilising an RF of 0.9 per cent, the risk factor for a Treasury bill. Any number of factors are used for the calculation of REE, depending primarily on the type and maturity of the instrument being repoed. Given differences in the credit, trading and risk management areas between different institutions, many banks and dealers have their own methods for calculating risk factors for repos and reverses. Within a single institution these risk factors can even differ from the credit area to the trading desk, with the credit area focusing on historical volatilities and a general statistical model, as demonstrated in Part II, and the trading desk following common practice among players in the market. This is particularly true with repos involving government securities.

When more esoteric instruments are involved – whole loans, CMO residuals and IO/PO strips, for example – it is generally wise to be conservative. There is insufficient price history or liquidity to give an accurate picture of potential volatilities for many of these new instruments.

Despite the fact that there are various factors which can be used to value the exposure on repos and reverses, it is helpful to review the relative risk factors which can be used by a credit committee in evaluating a transaction request. The risk factors listed in Table 7.1 assume that the institution has the ability to mark the position to market and either call for additional collateral or ask for collateral to be returned, depending on the type of trade. The list provides factors for the most commonly used instruments in the repo markets; it is based on recent estimates of historical volatilities and is adjusted to a 90 per cent confidence level against a lognormal distribution.

Note that these risk factors may be considered too conservative if a position is being marked to market daily or weekly, with a call for collateral should the market movement exhaust the initial haircut. If a dealer has an active book which it marks to market daily and a dedicated operations unit which makes margin calls as required, a one-week or two-week risk factor may be sufficient. If no marking to market takes place, then the relevant risk factor would be one equal to the maturity of the trade. Term risk factors are included for illustrative purposes.

Table 7.1. Sample Risk Factors for Repos and Reverses (per cent)

	One week	Two weeks	One month	Two months	Three months	Six months	12 months	24 months
Treasury bills HV = 5.1%	0.9	1.3	1.9	2.7	3.3	4.6	6.6	9.3
Treasury notes, under five years HV = 13%	2.4	3.4	4.8	6.9	8.4	11.9	16.9	23.9
Treasury notes or bonds HV = 14.5%	2.7	3.8	5.4	7.7	9.4	13.3	18.9	26.7
FNMAs or GNMAs HV = 5.8%	1.1	1.5	2.1	3.1	3.7	5.2	7.4	10.5
CMOs AA, one to five years HV = 7.5%	1.4	2.0	2.8	3.9	4.8	6.8	9.6	13.6
CMOs AA, five to 10 years HV = 9.8%	1.8	2.6	3.6	5.2	6.3	8.9	12.6	17.8
CMOs AA, over 10 years HV = 22.8	4.2	6.1	8.4	12.1	14.6	20.7	29.2	41.3

8: Treasury Securities and Treasury Derivatives

DEFINITION

A Treasury security (or simply Treasury) is the name given to a debt obligation of the US Federal Government. Without spending any length of time detailing why and how the US Government funds itself, the vital component in this discussion is the end result of the funding process, the Treasury security itself. When the government decides it needs to raise a certain amount of dollars to finance its operations, one of its primary means is through the issuance of bills, notes or bonds. These three instruments make up Treasury securities. The distinction between the three is primarily a question of maturity, issuance frequency and coupon payment.

Treasury Bill

These are securities at the short end of the maturity spectrum. The minimum maturity for a Treasury bill is three months and other maturities include six months and one year. Both the three-month and the six-month bills are auctioned on a weekly basis (ie new issues are brought to market every week to replace maturing issues), while the one-year issues are auctioned on a monthly basis. The market, as one might expect, is extremely liquid. No periodic coupons are paid but the securities are sold on a discount basis and the investor will receive par at redemption.

Treasury Note

These securities occupy the middle of the maturity spectrum. Notes are available with two-, three-, five-, seven- and 10-year final maturities. The two-year is offered every month, the three- and 10-years every quarter (during the quarterly refunding) and the five- and seven-years once a quarter at different times during the first and the second month respectively. In contrast to Treasury bills, all Treasury notes bear interest, with investors receiving a coupon on a semi-annual basis.

Treasury Bond

These are long-term securities. Bonds are available with 20- and 30-year final maturities. The 30-year bond is offered every quarter during the quarterly refunding, while the 20-year is offered every quarter at the end of the third month. All Treasury bonds are interest-bearing securities and investors receive a coupon semi-annually.

Development of Treasury Securities

In the mid-1970s the Treasury created a schedule for the issuance of different maturities as a way of helping to manage its debt requirements and of organising maturities. Additional issues have been added to the cycle as required to assist in the general management of the many Treasury issues in the market. Note that refunding issues come about to replace maturing issues, while new issues provide additional cash to the government for the financing of its operations, over and above that provided by the replacement of maturing issues.

Regular settlement of Treasury securities among the major players is accomplished within two business days following sale or purchase *via* the Fed Wire (through accounts at the Federal Reserve, eliminating the need for the physical movement of paper between counterparties).

In a typical regular settlement transaction, Bank A may sell to Bank B $10m worth of Treasuries. In order to execute the transaction, Bank A sends a message *via* the Fed Wire instructing the Fed to debit its Treasury security account by $10m, while crediting Bank B's Treasury account in the same amount. At the same time the Fed debits Bank B's cash account in the amount of the purchase price and posts the corresponding credit to Bank A's account. At that point the transaction is complete and there will have been no physical movement of paper.

Given the scenario above, an analyst might think to ask what risk an institution is exposed to in trading Treasury securities with a counterparty, if the risk of the issuer's going bankrupt is virtually nil (ie US Government credit risk) and sales and purchases appear to settle in standard fashion *via* the Fed Wire. The answer to that question is 'none'. However, as with many other instruments in the securities business, certain derivatives exist which contain very real elements of risk. Specifically, any Treasury trade which is forward settling, any trade done on a 'when issued' basis or any trade involving options on Treasury securities will carry elements of risk which an analyst must consider. Before describing the risks associated with each, it is helpful to review the definitions of these Treasury derivatives.

Forward (Extended) Settlement Trades

Normal settlement for Treasury trades is within two business days and any settlement period beyond that is considered forward or extended. For practical purposes, however, many institutions also view 'skip day' trades (ie those falling within a three-day timeframe) as a regular settlement, while still others view a full five-day settlement period as regular (corporate settlement of securities is typically on a five-day basis). From a practical standpoint, many large institutions involved in securities purchases and sales will not monitor 'cash settlement' or 'corporate settlement' trades (five business days or fewer from trade date to settle date) because the volume is large and the risk of market movements during that time is relatively small.

'When Issued' Trades

Prior to the issuance of a new Treasury security (either a replacement of a maturing issue or an altogether new instrument), there is a period between the announcement and selling of the security and actual physical settlement, during which trading can take place. Trading of the new security during this period is done on a 'when, as and if issued' basis and is known as a 'when issued' or WI trade. All WI trades are executed on a yield basis (as derived from the Treasury auction process), since traders are dealing in securities on which the actual coupon is still unknown. Following the WI period and the settlement of the new instrument, all yield-based trades are calculated into a price format.

Given the nature of the trade and the fact that it will not physically settle until some point in the future, this type of transaction is an extended settlement deal and carries market risk; in fact a WI trade is simply a subset of the forward (or extended) settlement transaction described above. It is worth noting, however, that, while every WI trade is an extended settlement transaction, not every extended settlement transaction is a WI trade. The actual time between announcement and selling of a new security and settlement can range from a few days for bills to weeks for notes and bonds. There have been efforts recently by regulators to shorten the 'when issued' period for all instruments.

Treasury Options

Markets exist for the trading of both listed and over-the-counter (OTC) Treasury options. The focus of this discussion will be on the OTC market. As with other options, there are two parties to a given transaction: the writer (or seller) and the buyer A writer of Treasury calls provides the buyer with the right, but not the obligation, to buy the underlying Treasury securities at a specific strike price during a certain period of time, in exchange for a premium from the buyer. Conversely, the writer of a Treasury put gives the buyer the right to sell the underlying Treasury securities to the buyer at some point in the future. In either case, depending on whether the option is American-style or European-style, the exercise can take place at any time up to and including maturity (American) or only at maturity (European).

Should the buyer of a Treasury call desire to exercise the option (because it is 'in the money' and has value to him), the writer must honour the obligation either by delivering Treasury securities to the buyer in exchange for the cash equivalent based on the strike price and the dollar amount of the option or by cash-settling the option.

Consider the following example: Bank X sells Corporation Y 10 Treasury calls (with each call representing $100,000 of one-year Treasury bills), maturity April, strike price 99. Corporation Y pays Bank X a premium for the right to buy the Treasury bills should market movements allow. The option is 'out of the money', so the premium paid is relatively small.

Assume that, one month on, one-year Treasury rates fall and the value of the bills increases to 100. At this point the option is in the money. Corporation Y decides to exercise its option. It can pay Bank X $99mm (10 × $100,000 × 99) and receive the Treasury bills from Bank X, which it could then sell in the market for $101mm and earn a gross profit of $2mm (net profit would depend on the amount of premium initially paid). Alternatively it can cash-settle the option with Bank X, receiving $2mm (10 × $100,000 × (current market price–strike price)). For all practical purposes, Bank X will take its underlying securities (assuming it wrote covered, not naked, calls) worth $99mm, sell them in the market for $101mm and deliver the $2mm difference to Corporation Y.

Each of the above has the same end result, which is to deliver $2mm in profit to Corporation Y, although variations on the theme exist. Corporation Y might decide to hold the securities after receiving them from Bank X because it requires them for some other reason. Bank X might have written naked options, which substantially increases the risk to Bank X if the options are exercised but means that it does not need to have the securities on hand initially. The above example can be reversed into a 'sell' scenario for puts, with interest rates rising and bill prices falling.

GENERAL CREDIT CONSIDERATIONS

We can now consider the various aspects of the framework discussed in Part I of this book.

Risk

For forwards (including WIs) risk is low, for a bank's short options positions it is non-existent and for long options positions it is low to medium, depending on how far in or out of the money the option is and whether the counterparty's short position is naked or covered. The BIS risk weighting for both options and forwards is flexible among member countries and can range from 50 per cent to 100 per cent; the risk weighting for simply holding Treasuries is 0 per cent.

Return

On standard forwards, return is low for medium quality credits. For options, return for in-the-money transactions with medium quality counterparties can be high. Although risk weightings for options and forwards can be as high as 100 per cent, capital charge spreads are reasonably low due to low risk factors associated with short-term trades.

Maturity

Maturities for forwards are generally short. Option maturities are also usually short but can go beyond 12 months with no marking to market, effectively making them medium-term transactions.

Motivation

For forwards, motivations can range from hedging, arbitrage and yield enhancing to outright speculation. The same is true for options.

Enhancement

Credit enhancement of any type is unusual for standard forwards and options.

Creditworthiness

Forward trades, including WIs, are generally acceptable across the spectrum of credit qualities, although a credit analyst may want to limit the settlement period and/or the amount transacted with sub-investment grade counterparties. Obviously, as one gets to the lowest tier of sub-investment grade companies, trades settling two or three weeks forward become inadvisable. Unlike the repos and reverses discussed in Chapter 7, forward trades have no security or collateral attached to them, so care must be exercised with clients of lower credit quality.

Consideration of treasury options involves distinguishing short options from long options. If a bank is to sell Treasury options to a counterparty (a short position), it is expecting to receive premium income in exchange for the possibility of having to honour the option obligation at some future date should market movements warrant its exercise. Thus, a bank has no risk in a short position once premium is received, so sales of Treasury options can be appropriate for the entire range of credit qualities.

In a long position (i.e. where the bank is buying a Treasury option from a counterparty), it is the bank which is both paying premium and expecting future performance from the counterparty. In this scenario a credit analyst needs to be much more careful about approving a trade or facility. A lower quality counterparty may not have the financial wherewithal to support a large options line with extended maturities of three months or more.

Risk is increased if the counterparty is writing naked options, ie selling options to a bank without actually possessing the underlying Treasury securities. In this case the writer of the options is attempting to generate premium income by taking a view that the market will not move enough to push the option into the money. Should this happen, the writer may have to deliver either the securities or cash; this means that the company has to raise sufficient cash to buy the securities to deliver to the bank or to buy the securities from the bank. For a lower tier counterparty, either scenario might be financially constraining, particularly if the sums involved are large. In summary, it is vital for an analyst to focus on long options positions and to determine whether lower rated clients warrant a modified and conservative position involving a small amount and/or a limited maturity or, indeed, whether they are unsuitable for a facility at all.

Also worth considering is the motive for a potential Treasury transaction, particularly in the higher risk options market. While a counterparty's own long positions may well be acceptable because they may constitute legitimate hedges or yield enhancing strategies, short positions, particularly if they are naked, may be deemed speculative. Although writing naked options is a way to earn extra income, it is clear that a weak counterparty engaged in such a practice could find itself in substantial financial difficulties should the market move against it. It is therefore vital that any such strategies be examined closely by the analyst.

RISK QUANTIFICATION

Treasury forwards and options are affected by market movements in underlying Treasury rates and are thus considered market risk products. This means that they need to be risk-adjusted to provide the relevant dollar risk exposure.

As in all market risk situations, a credit analyst will have to deal with risk only when an actual default by the counterparty occurs. So long as a counterparty continues to perform on a forward settlement or options trade, the amount of ongoing market risk is transparent to the analyst. It is important, however, to know how much risk is being assumed at the inception of the trade; once this is quantified, the analyst will know whether the transaction or limit under consideration is advisable. Returning to equation (5.1), we know that

$$\text{REE} = \text{RF} \times \text{N}$$

Using this equation, we can determine the risk inherent in forward settlement and options trades of Treasury securities. In the case of forward settling transactions, it is clear that the movement of interest rates has a direct impact on the value (and risk) of the unsettled deal. If a bank sells a Treasury for settlement in four weeks, the value of that security in four weeks' time will be greater if interest rates have fallen and lower if interest rates have risen. From the bank's point of view, the risk on a sale occurs when interest rates rise and the value of the Treasury falls; it is at this point that a loss can occur if the counterparty fails. If the bank has an opposing transaction to cover from the sale of the Treasury, it will have to alter its strategy and sell at a lower price, thus sustaining a loss. The opposite scenario obviously holds true when a bank buys a Treasury for forward settlement. Thus, any risk equation must consider the impact of rate movements on the unsettled notional amount. The forward settlement risk equation takes the following form:

$$\text{REE} = \text{RF} \times \text{Greater of LV} \vee \text{SV} \tag{8.1}$$

where RF is the appropriate risk factor,
LV are long trades where the bank has bought Treasuries forward,
SV are short trades where the bank has sold Treasuries forward.

Note that we take only the long or the short value for a given client, since a movement of rates in one direction will help one position and hinder another but cannot hinder both. The selection of one of these two 'legs' gives us the dollar magnitude of the trade(s) in question (we term this N in equation (5.1)). The selection of the appropriate RF will give us a frame in which to capture both the maturity of the trade and the underlying Treasury being traded. The longer the maturity of the trade, the higher the possibility of market movements and, therefore, of market risk. The greater the maturity of the underlying Treasury, the greater the price volatility and, therefore, the greater the potential market exposure.

Consider the following example: Bank X sells \$10m worth of Treasury notes to Corporation ABC for settlement in one month. At the inception of the trade we know that rates will not yet have moved and so the risk on the deal is

$$\begin{aligned} \text{REE} &= \text{RF} \times \text{N} \\ &= 0.019 \times \$10\text{m} \\ &= \$190{,}000 \text{ (using a 1.9 per cent risk factor)} \end{aligned}$$

The \$190,000 is the risk the analyst must consider when approving the transaction. From a practical standpoint, assuming that the correct statistical analysis has been performed in the derivation of RF, the REE derived initially represents the maximum potential risk the bank will face during the next 30 days. WIs and forwards are not typically marked to market and, as a general rule, margin is not taken; most banks would not have a dedicated operational unit calculating mark-to-market values for Treasury forwards as they would with, say, repos and reverses. The equation above thus represents the simplest and most likely procedure for assigning risk to a forward.

If an analyst has concerns regarding the mark-to-market value of the trade, the equation above can be refined to include this component as well. The form would now be

$$\text{REE} = [\text{MTM} + (\text{RFc} \times \text{MV})] \tag{8.2}$$

where MV is the new market value of the Treasuries,
MTM is the difference between the original value of the Treasuries and the new market value (MV),
RFc is a constantly adjusted risk factor.

As time passes and rates begin to move, the MV of the Treasuries begins to move as well. Assume that rates increase by 5 basis points two weeks after the trade was booked, such that the MV moves down by \$5,000. The numerical example would yield

$$\text{REE} = [\$5000 + (0.013 \times \$9{,}995{,}000)] = \$134{,}935$$

Note that, although the MTM exposure has increased by \$5000, our new RFc is 1.3 per cent (down from 1.9 per cent). As a result, total risk on the

Buy/sell	*Put/call*	*Market risk*
Sell	Put	none
Buy	Put	↑ if the price of the underlying security falls
Sell	Call	none
Buy	Call	↑ if the price of the underlying security rises

from the perspective of a bank buying/selling

Figure 8.1. Options Exposure: Market Risk.

trade is now just under $135,000. Intuitively it makes sense that the RFc being used is lower than the original RF, since there is less time until maturity of the trade and, as a consequence, less time during which rates can move against the bank. Note also, however, that the MTM value is already positive at $5000. If ABC defaulted at this point, XYZ would face a certain loss of $5000.

Formula (8.2) is conservative in that it displays two distinct items: how much a bank will lose today if a counterparty defaults (the MTM or actual market risk component) and how much risk may yet occur given potential market movements and a default in the future (the RFc × MV component). This idea parallels very closely the concept of actual and fractional exposure discussed in detail in Chapter 13 on swaps. If a credit analyst were particularly concerned about a given client, he might institute a special operational arrangement such that margin would be posted once the MTM moved to a certain deficit level. Again, MTM and margining arrangements are not typical for this type of business, so that general equation (8.1) is usually a sufficient measure for the risk a bank might face during the life of a trade.

Prior to considering the risk inherent in options trades, it is helpful to recall when an institution dealing in options faces market risk and when it faces no risk at all. The different scenarios are captured in Figure 8.1.

The market risk inherent in options trades is somewhat different from the risk encountered in forward settlements. We know from basic options pricing theory that an option's value consists of both intrinsic value (how far in the money or out of the money the option is) and time value (how much time remains until expiry, whether the option is deeply in the money or out of the money, the volatility of the underlying security and the level of short-term interest rates). An option with high intrinsic value and high time value will be more valuable than an option with low intrinsic value and low time value.

It seems obvious that a buyer of an option will pay more premium for a more valuable option and, as a result, will face greater risk. The risk is greater not only because a higher option premium has been paid out but also because the chances of exercise are much higher, so reliance on the performance of the option writer is more critical. With these concepts in mind, it is relatively easy to develop a basic risk model for a long Treasury call or put option. As before, we can turn to our basic equation (5.1) and make some adjustments. N and RF are important in order to reflect both the dollar magnitude of the trade (N) and the particulars of the trade (RF reflects maturity and underlying Treasury type, as discussed above). These components will measure the maximum market risk an option buyer will encounter during the life of the trade.

We cannot, however, ignore the upfront payment of premium which is characteristic of long options. Since this is cash out at the inception of the trade by the buyer of the option, the buyer has additional exposure. He is not only expecting performance on the option, should exercise occur, but must also consider that, if the writer defaults on the transaction, the premium is lost. Thus, the appropriate risk model can be expanded as follows:

$$\text{REE} = \text{premium paid} + (\text{RF} \times \text{N}) \tag{8.3}$$

This can be thought of as a general, albeit static, equation that measures the risk of the trade by returning a figure which equates to the likely maximum risk faced during its life plus the premium paid out. We shall also see below that this equation represents the standard form for valuing the risk of at-the-money options.

Just as in equation (8.2) above, where we focused on the ongoing market value of a Treasury forward, a more conservative option equation might also look at initial and ongoing changes in market value. To assess the market value accurately, we need to compare the option's strike price SP with the current market price CMP; this will allow us to determine the option's intrinsic value.

As one might expect, the greater the intrinsic value, the higher the loss should the option seller default. If, however, an option is deeply out-of-the-money with a short time to expiry, the likelihood of exercise, and thus the reliance on performance by the seller, is almost non-existent. In our new equation, then, we take the greater of 0 or the term reflecting the current value of the option. If it is deeply out of the money, we ignore any chance of market risk exposure and simply value the premium. These changes can be captured by utilising the greater of 0 or ((CMP − SP)/CMP)) for calls and the greater of 0 or ((SP − CMP)/CMP)) for puts. These components effectively compare market prices with strike prices to quantify how far in-the-money or out-of-the-money a given contract is. We still need to apply our constantly adjusted risk factor RFc to the notional amount in order to determine which potential market movements may yet occur to alter the risk of the transaction. In order to reflect these concepts, we alter our equation to the following form for calls:

$$\text{REE} = \text{premium} + 0 \vee [(\text{RFc} \times \text{N}) + (\frac{(\text{CMP} - \text{SP})}{\text{CMP}} \times \text{N})] \quad (8.4)$$

where CMP is the current market price,
SP is the strike price of the option,
RFc is a constantly adjusted risk factor,
N is the notional amount of the trade.

For puts the equation is:

$$\text{REE} = \text{premium} + 0 \vee [(\text{RFc} \times \text{N}) + (\frac{(\text{SP} - \text{CMP})}{\text{CMP}} \times \text{N})] \quad (8.5)$$

where
CMP is the current market price,
SP is the strike price of the option,
RFc is a constantly adjusted risk factor,
N is the notional amount of the trade.

A deeply out-of-the-money option, particularly if it has a short time to expiry, clearly has little or no market risk. The bank will have no incentive to exercise the option and, as a result, will not expect performance from the counterparty. Once the value of the option begins to move into the money, the bank will expect performance if it decides to exercise and the calculated risk figure will reflect the value of the potential gain (ie the intrinsic value). Ongoing calculation of the RFc and in-the-money or out-of-the-money parameters will allow the analyst to focus on the continuous changes in potential market risk.

Consider the series of European-style Treasury bill put options below.

An Out-of-the-money Option

$$N = \$1m$$
$$SP = 100$$
$$CMP = 105$$

maturity is two weeks, RF is 1.2 per cent, premium paid is $10,000

For puts the equation is:

$$REE = \text{premium} + 0 \vee [(RFc \times N) + (\frac{(SP - CMP)}{CMP} \times N)] \quad (8.5)$$
$$= \$10{,}000 + 0$$
$$\text{or} \quad [(0.012 \times \$1m) + (((100 - 105)/100) \times \$1m)]$$
$$= \$10{,}000 + 0 \text{ or } [\$12{,}000 - \$50{,}000]$$
$$= \$10{,}000$$

Since the chances of exercise are extraordinarily small, given both the short time to expiry (two weeks) and the large price differential, the buyer of the call need not concern himself with the potential for market risk due to non-performance by the seller. The model presented above indicates that only the premium paid out is at risk since, if the counterparty defaults, the bank will have lost that amount of money even though it may not have exercised the option.

It is worth noting that, if the expiry date of the option were further away, the associated risk factor would be higher. If the risk factor is sufficiently high, it will convert the second portion of the equation into a positive value, indicating additional risk exposure. This makes sense, since an out-of-the-money option with a great deal of time to expiry still has a chance of ending at-the-money or in-the-money. Equations (8.4) and (8.5) take this into account.

An At-the-money Option

$$N = \$1m$$
$$SP = 100$$
$$CMP = 100$$

maturity is two weeks, RF is 1.2 per cent, premium paid is $50,000

$$REE = \text{premium} + 0 \vee [(RFc \times N) + (\frac{(SP - CMP)}{CMP} \times N)] \quad (8.5)$$

$$= \$50{,}000 + 0 \text{ or } [(0.012 \times \$1\text{m}) + (((100 - 100)/100) \times \$1\text{m})]$$

$$= \$50{,}000 + 0 \text{ or } [\$12{,}000 + 0]$$

$$= \$62{,}000$$

In this instance there could be value to the option. Depending on its delta (how much the option value moves for a given price movement in the underlying Treasury), it stands a chance of terminating either in the money or out-of-the-money. Options purchased at the money typically have a delta of 0.5 (ie they have a 50 per cent chance of ending with value). Given that there is at least some probability that the option will end up with value, the potential exposure which might be faced during the life of the trade cannot be ignored; this is added to the premium paid out to obtain a total REE figure. As one might expect, the premium paid for an at-the-money option is higher than that for one which is out of the money. Note here that no adjustment is actually made to the risk factor, as the second portion of the equation condenses to 0; this is precisely the result of equation (8.3), the standard form for valuing risk of at-the-money options.

An In-the-money Option

$$\begin{aligned} N &= \$1\text{m} \\ SP &= 105 \\ CMP &= 100 \end{aligned}$$

maturity is two weeks, RF is 1.2 per cent, premium paid is \$100,000

$$REE = \text{premium} + 0 \vee [(RFc \times N) + (\frac{(SP - CMP)}{CMP} \times N)] \qquad (8.5)$$

$$= \$100{,}000 + 0 \text{ or } [(0.012 \times \$1\text{m}) + (((105 - 100)/100) \times \$1\text{m})]$$

$$= \$100{,}000 + 0 \text{ or } [\$12{,}000 + (0.05 \times \$1\text{m})]$$

$$= \$162{,}000$$

It is easy to see that this option has value, as the buyer could exercise today and obtain a profit of \$50,000. The chances of exercise are much higher than if the option were at the money or out of the money, so our associated REE is higher. Note that, in addition to the option's being nearly 5 per cent above market, we still include our original risk factor of 1.2 per cent in the calculation. The reason for this is that we need to account for the fact that the default might occur not today but at some point during the next two weeks. During that time the option may move even further in the money, making the potential loss higher than it is today.

Table 8.1. Risk Models for a Put Option

Time to maturity	CMP	RF	REE of static model	REE of dynamic model
Four weeks	100	1.9 per cent	\$69,000	\$69,000
Two weeks	99	1.3 per cent	\$69,000	\$73,101
One week	100	0.9 per cent	\$69,000	\$59,000

It becomes obvious in examining the two risk models presented above that they will always yield slightly different figures. This occurs because equation (8.3) is static and equations (8.4/8.5) are dynamic. Depending upon the system used to track the trading exposure, one model may be more feasible or desirable than the other. Although differences exist, it is also clear that both provide some reasonable estimate of the risk likely to be incurred during the trade. If we were to track the risk of the put at various points during the trade detailed below, we would obtain the following:

$$N = \$1m$$
$$SP = 100$$
$$CMP = 100$$

maturity is four weeks, RF at inception is 1.9 per cent, premium paid is \$50,000

where our static model equation is

$$REE = \text{premium paid} + (RF \times N) \tag{8.3}$$

and our dynamic model equation is

$$REE = \text{premium} + 0 \vee [(RFc \times N) + (\frac{(SP - CMP)}{CMP} \times N)] \tag{8.5}$$

The results are reflected in Table 8.1 above. The dynamic model is more helpful in that it will constantly adjust for changes in price and risk factor, yielding a more accurate assessment of the risk being faced; it will not overestimate or underestimate risk, as the static model will. However, the trade-off is that it is somewhat more complex to calculate and, operationally, more difficult to update constantly.

As a final example of the risks faced in dealing with the Treasury option product, we can consider Figure 8.2. This presents both orderly and default scenarios on a Treasury option transaction to demonstrate how a given deal can go against normal settlement practices. It is important to recall that a

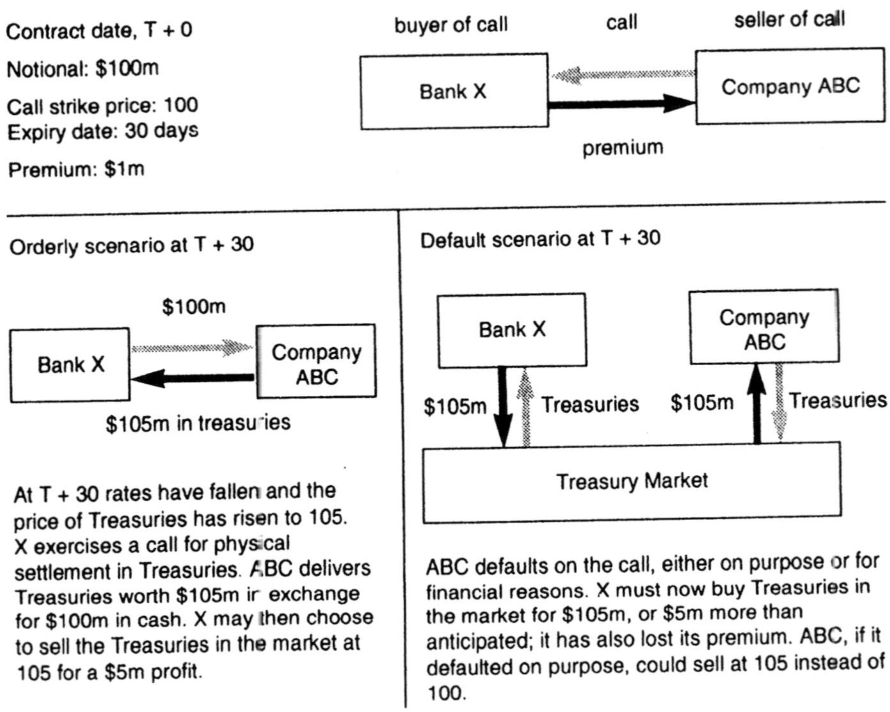

Figure 8.2. Treasury Option: Orderly and Default Scenarios

default can occur because of financial difficulties of the counterparty or because default is particularly attractive economically (ie the default will allow the counterparty either to gain more or to lose less).

The above discussion has focused on instances of risk where a bank buys Treasury options from another counterparty (paying the premium upfront and expecting performance in the event of exercise). It has not touched on instances where a bank sells Treasury options. Where the bank is short an option, it incurs no risk as it will have received the premium from the client (in a normal cash settlement timeframe) and will then have to perform should the client decide to exercise. Although the bank's dealing team might have certain risk management considerations (ie hedging its short options position), the credit team will not have to deal with the credit risk issues discussed above.

RISK FACTORS

As with repos, every bank and investment bank (if it uses a risk model similar to the one discussed above) will have slightly different risk factors to apply to

Treasury forwards and options. However, a sample listing of risk factors appears for information in Table 8.2; this is derived from historical volatility studies with a 90 per cent confidence level on a lognormal distribution. Note that Table 8.2 provides the appropriate RF (or RFc) for forwards, WIs and options. As one might expect, notes and bonds have higher historical volatilities than bills, so the associated RFs are higher. Likewise, the longer the maturity of the underlying trade (within a given category), the greater the chance for rate movements and the higher the associated RF.

Table 8.2. Sample Risk Factors for Treasury Forwards and Options (per cent)

	One week	Two weeks	One month	Two months	Three months	Six months	12 months	24 months
Treasury bills HV = 5.1%	0.9	1.3	1.9	2.7	3.3	4.6	6.6	9.3
Treasury notes, under five years HV = 13%	2.4	3.4	4.8	6.9	8.4	11.9	16.9	23.9
Treasury notes or bonds HV = 14.5%	2.7	3.8	5.4	7.7	9.4	13.3	18.9	26.7

9: Mortgage-backed Securities and Associated Derivatives

DEFINITION

Mortgage-backed securities (MBSs), or pass-through securities, are instruments backed by 'pools' of mortgages, which pay a periodic (generally monthly) coupon of interest and principal. In essence, MBSs represent the securitised and tradeable form of residential and commercial mortgages. The most commonly traded MBSs are based on mortgages packaged by loan originators and guaranteed by one of three US Government agencies: the Government National Mortgage Association (GNMA or Ginnie Mae), the Federal National Mortgage Association (FNMA or Fannie Mae) and the Federal Home Loan Mortgage Corporation (FHLMC or Freddie Mac).

The process involved in creating a tradeable instrument from a mortgage is comparatively simple. A residential mortgage is extended to a borrower, either conventionally or through a government-guaranteed or insured programme (eg the Federal Housing Administration (FHA) or Veterans Administration (VA)). If it originates under an FHA/VA programme, the mortgage itself will meet certain criteria, including maximum size, loan to value ratio, maturity and so on; such loans are said to be 'conforming mortgages' and are eligible for inclusion under certain agency programmes.

The actual process of originating mortgages is typically undertaken by a mortgage banker, a thrift or a commercial bank. In most instances a mortgage originator will originate and close a loan and then market the loan (along with others which have been closed) to secondary market participants (one of the three agencies mentioned above, private investors, primary dealers, other financial institutions and so on). This is called the 'warehousing' period and generally covers one to two months. Once a mortgage loan is sold to a secondary market participant, the originator may still be involved by retaining servicing rights. Servicing is the process of collecting principal and interest payments from the underlying borrower and passing the flows on to the appropriate secondary market participant (who in turn will pass them on to investors). Since the servicing function generates a fee for the servicer, rights have value and can be bought or sold in the secondary market. When an originator relinquishes rights to servicing, the loan (or group of loans) is said to be 'servicing released'.

After a group of loans has been sold to a secondary market participant, the participant can pool them into a tradeable form and issue a security (a private label pass-through, FHLMC MBS, FNMA MBS, etc). Note that GNMA does not purchase loans directly; it simply guarantees conforming pools upon receipt of documentation from the originator, who retains the pools. Each pool will have certain characteristics (dependent upon the underlying mortgages), including initial coupon, weighted average maturity, weighted average coupon, prepayment speed and so on.

Once packaged into securities, MBSs are sold to the market, where they are actively traded, primarily by institutional investors. Each investor holding an MBS will receive a monthly interest and principal repayment associated with the underlying pool of mortgages. A bank issuing a private label security will 'pass through' all flows it receives from borrowers to investors. Should a borrower default on a mortgage payment, there may be a delay of interest and principal repayment. Securities of the three agencies also 'pass through' all flows to the investor but also guarantee timely repayment of interest and timely or ultimate repayment of principal in the event of default by the borrower.

One of the difficulties surrounding MBSs is the question of prepayment. While an investor holding a non-callable, fixed income security (such as a non-call Treasury) will always be aware of the final (and average) maturity of the investment, the same cannot be said about MBSs. A mortgage may cease to exist for at least three different reasons: refinancing, sale of the home or default. Cessation of a mortgage within a pool will have an impact on the average life of the underlying MBS.

In a period of falling interest rates, holders of the underlying mortgages are apt to refinance their mortgages at lower rates. If refinancing takes place, a significant number of prepayments will occur within the mortgage pools, the end result being a decline in the average life of the security. Likewise, a sale of the underlying property or an actual default on the mortgage will cause the mortgage to 'disappear' from the pool, reducing the principal and interest balances and lowering the average life of the security.

Alternatively, a borrower may choose to repay a larger portion of his mortgage every month (although without full prepayment), which again will affect the outstanding principal and interest balances and, in turn, the average life of the security. Most mortgage prepayment models begin with an assumption of 'level pay' mortgages but must factor in the notion that not all mortgages will be repaid according to schedule.

For those investors with sophisticated portfolios incorporating concepts of bond immunisation and duration (which rely heavily on average life calculations), the inclusion of MBSs can be challenging. A great deal of research goes into analysing prepayments and the factors which most affect prepayments (interest rates and interest rate forecasts, inflation expectations, the state of the economy, etc), so that when an investor buys a given MBS, it will have an estimated prepayment level associated with it. This assists in determining the average life and yield of the security, although there can still be discrepancies based on the factors mentioned above. There are various models available to help calculate the prepayment rates of MBSs, including the Conditional Prepayment Rate (CPR) model and the Public Securities Association's Standard Prepayment Model.

The term MBS is applied generically to GNMA, FNMA and FHLMC securities; each has its own procedures and parameters but the end product is much the same (indeed, the three are often referred to as 'generics'). Liquidity for generics is very high, since the market is large and US Government ownership and/or implicit support translates into top credit ratings for the three main agencies. The bulk of our discussion will centre on the description and risks of generics.

Commercial mortgages and non-conforming residential mortgages (also known as 'whole loans') represent a much smaller, but still important, market. They are often packaged in pools and traded in the same fashion as the generics above, although the lack of a large market and the absence of AAA/Aaa ratings mean that liquidity is much lower. Many whole loans are privately placed.

GNMA

This agency is owned by the US Government *via* the Department of Housing and Urban Development (HUD) and is the primary guarantor of MBSs (accounting for roughly 80 per cent of the market). Pools guaranteed by GNMA comprise FHA-insured and VA-guaranteed mortgages and conform to a variety of other standards (pool size, minimum purchase price, minimum maturity, etc). The securities themselves are expressly guaranteed by the government. GNMA offers a number of pool programmes reflecting different underlying characteristics. These include Program I (single issuer pools), Program II (multiple issuer pools), Midgets (shorter maturity pools) and Mobile Homes (mobile home loan pools). Repayment of both interest and principal is guaranteed on a timely basis.

FHLMC

Currently the second largest guarantor of MBSs, this agency, owned by the US Government *via* the Federal Home Loan Banks (FHLBs), guarantees pools comprising solely conventional, single family, residential mortgages. FHLMC securities guarantee the timely repayment of interest but only the ultimate repayment of principal (ie the investor will get his/her money back but perhaps not immediately). Although the government owns Freddie Mac *via* the FHLBs, the absence of the FHA/VA component in its pools, the lack of an explicit government guarantee and the restricted guarantee of repayment of principal, mean that FHLMC MBSs trade at a small premium to GNMA MBSs.

FNMA

FNMA is the newest and smallest of the three agencies involved in MBSs. Although the government owns a portion of FNMA *via* the HUD, FNMA is essentially a private corporation. It is involved in both the conventional and the FHA/VA sectors of the mortgage market and has various programme pools to accommodate the differences. The agency guarantees the timely repayment of principal and interest and, since the issues are not specifically backed by the government, they again trade at a small premium to GNMA MBSs.

Private Label Pass-throughs

These securities, typically originated and pooled by a financial institution, are not guaranteed by any of the agencies detailed above. If an originator chooses not to seek an agency guarantee, it will require other forms of credit enhancement (such as third party insurance, senior/subordinated structure, overcollateralisation or letter of credit) to obtain a credit rating which investors will find attractive. If sufficient credit enhancement is obtained, rating agencies will typically grant private labels a AA/Aa or AAA/Aaa rating. Mortgages included in these pools can vary depending on institution but may be conventional or FHA/VA-backed. There is typically no explicit guarantee as to the timely repayment of principal and interest, as the institution issuing the security will only pass through the flow it receives from the underlying mortgages. Private pass-throughs account for only a small portion of the total MBS market. Note that commercial banks and investment banks account for nearly two-thirds of this market, followed by thrifts and other conduits.

Other MBS Products

While the securities discussed above represent the fundamental building blocks of the MBS market, certain financial institutions have created other MBS derivatives. These securities generally consist of the same instruments as discussed above but are repackaged in different fashions to yield different results.

Among the most widely traded of the mortgage derivatives is the collateralised mortgage obligation or CMO. A CMO is essentially nothing more than a pool of mortgage-backed securities (or packaged whole loans) and represents the next step after a pool of mortgages has been packaged to create an MBS. In a typical CMO structure (which is established as a trust), the investor can elect to buy one of several tranches of the CMO, with each tranche representing a different maturity (most CMOs have four tranches). Investors in all tranches (except the Z tranche) will receive interest payments from the underlying mortgages throughout the maturity of each underlying tranche. However, investors in the first tranche (or A tranche) will receive all their principal repayment first. Once they have been paid out, the principal flows are directed to the second tranche (the B tranche) and so on until all investors have been repaid; this is called a sequential pay CMO and is the standard structure in the CMO market.

The creation of the CMO allows investors greater flexibility in choosing the appropriate maturity of a mortgage-related investment. Although investors are still subject to prepayment risk, the ability to select shorter-term tranches represents a clear advantage over traditional MBSs (which limit investors to a few, long-term maturity options, eg 15 years or 20 years).

At the end of the CMO payout comes the accrual bond or Z tranche. This portion is structured like a zero coupon bond in that it receives no interest until all other tranches are paid out. If the tranche immediately ahead of it has a 10-year final maturity, the Z tranche holder can expect no income until that time. To compensate the Z tranche investor for the longer waiting period and the greater volatility, the coupon is significantly higher than coupons on other tranches. As an example, a GNMA 9.5 per cent CMO with 4 tranches might pay coupons of 7.9 per cent (A tranche), 8.6 per cent (B tranche), 9.1 per cent (C tranche) and 9.25 per cent (Z tranche).

A final item included in a traditional CMO is the residual. The residual is the riskiest portion of a CMO structure, as payout is dependent on there being a residual cash flow associated with the CMO. In formal terms, the investor in a residual will receive cash flow generated by the collateral in excess of that required to service the investors in other tranches. The residual cash flow is simply equal to premium interest (the differential between the coupon on the underlying collateral and the highest paying coupon in the CMO, ie 25 basis points in the example above) plus the bond interest differential (the differential between the highest coupon and the remaining coupon on all tranches; in the example above the differential would vary between 135 basis points for Tranche A and 15 basis points for Tranche C) plus reinvestment income (interest generated by investing the income between the monthly receipt of interest from the MBS collateral and the quarterly CMO interest payment) less any expenses incurred in operating the CMO structure.

The above describes a typical CMO structure. As with other instruments, there is any number of alternative CMO structures, each with its own characteristics. Some CMOs pay no interest to the second and third tranches until all interest and principal is paid to the first tranche investor; others have more than one accrual (or Z) tranche; still others have a floating rate component instead of a fixed coupon structure (a CMO floater). In a novel derivative, some CMOs are split between fixed rate coupon tranches and a floating rate coupon tranche, with every dollar of principal repayment split on a *pro rata* basis between the fixed tranches and the floating tranche (this is known as a split principal floater). In addition, there are reverse floaters, CMOs with ascending rate tranches, CMOs with sinking fund tranches and so on.

Although there are various mechanisms for the timing and distribution of cash flows, the most important aspect from a credit standpoint is the underlying security being used to structure the CMO. If government agencies are being utilised, we know that risk of default on the underlying security is minuscule. However, if whole loans are used, we no longer have explicit or implicit government support; it is important to determine the actual composition of the collateral.

There might be instances where the collateral is unacceptably risky (eg commercial whole loans extended to businesses in a weak economic area). In such cases a bank being asked to finance the paper (*via* a reverse repo, for example) may not want to be involved or may only be involved with a substantial 'haircut' (as discussed in Chapter 7). In other instances CMOs with more questionable collateral underlying the structure may have to obtain a third party guarantee or insurance in order to make the deal attractive to investors.

Aside from CMOs, there are other derivatives and packaged combinations of MBSs which have been created over the past few years. Among the most interesting (and volatile) are interest-only (IO) and principal-only (PO) strips. At least two major institutions have suffered losses in these securities; Merrill Lynch lost over $377m in 1987 (although a portion of the loss was attributable to unauthorized trading activity) and JP Morgan is believed to have lost over $50m in late 1991 and early 1992. IOs and POs are MBSs which are 'stripped' into two separate components, one paying interest (based on a fixed rate pool), the other paying principal; FNMA strips its own securities directly, while strips involving GNMA/FHLMC instruments are created through trusts designed expressly for that purpose.

An investor buying an IO would receive only the interest flows from the underlying MBS, while the PO investor would receive only principal amortisations. As one might expect, these securities act and react very differently in rising and falling rate environments. In general, in a typical MBS the prepayments on the underlying mortgages tend to increase as interest rates fall (as mortgage holders look to refinance in the lower rate environment); as with other fixed income instruments, the price of the security increases in a falling rate (and yield) environment.

However, the price of an IO strip falls with interest rates, since prepayments will increase and refinancings will follow. In a high (and rising) interest rate environment, prepayments slow down, interest income remains high and the value of the IO increases. IOs are one of the few fixed income securities to react in this fashion. POs, in contrast, do well when interest rates are low and falling; prepayments increase, principal is returned to the investor more quickly and the yield to maturity on the security is logically much higher. It should be noted that MBS strips are highly volatile and care must be exercised when considering them in an extended settlement or financing transaction; we demonstrate at the end of this chapter the very high risk factors associated with these instruments.

Most MBSs trade on a book entry cash basis once they are in the secondary market; that is, settlement is typically within five days (and is generally completed within two business days). Payment is generally on a delivery *versus* payment (DVP) basis: the seller of the MBS will deliver (*via* book entry) the security to the buyer; when the buyer accepts the security, his cash account is automatically debited and the seller's cash account is automatically credited.

Returning to the discussion covered in Chapter 8, an analyst might again pose the following question: since the risk of the issuer's going bankrupt is virtually nil with agency securities as they are US Government-guaranteed or implicitly supported and since securities sales and purchases appear to settle on standard five-day corporate terms, what risk is an institution exposed to in trading MBSs with a counterparty? Again, the answer to the above questions is 'none'. However, as with Treasuries, there exist certain MBS derivatives which contain very real elements of credit risk.

Any MBS trade which is forward settling, any trade done on a 'TBA' basis or any trade involving options on MBSs will carry elements of risk which must be considered. Before describing the risks associated with each, it is useful again to review the definitions of these derivatives:

Forward (Extended) Settlement Trades

If normal settlement for MBS trades is within two business days, any settlement period beyond that would be considered forward or extended. As in the case of Treasuries, many institutions opt to view a full five-day settlement period for MBSs as regular (recalling that corporate settlement of securities is typically on a five-day basis).

TBA Trades

In MBS parlance, 'when issued' trades are referred to as TBAs (short for 'to be announced'). When the GNMA, the FNMA or the FHLMC are in the process of putting together a new pool of securities, there is a period during which trading takes place. If a mortgage originator has approved loans from the FHA/VA, for example, it can take them to one of the agencies, which will authorise a TBA contract. While waiting for the entire pool to be formed (which can take several weeks or months), the mortgage banker will contact MBS dealers and sell them the issue on a TBA basis; since the mortgage banker has a TBA contract from one of the agencies, most dealers are likely to be interested in trading the new pool. As with WITs, given the fact that TBAs will not physically settle until some point in the future, this type of transaction is considered an extended settlement deal and carries with it market risk exposure. Recall that a TBA trade is always a forward settlement transaction but not every forward settling transaction is a TBA.

MBS Options

There is an active, and growing, market for the trading of OTC MBS options. Options on MBSs are no different from other OTC options. There are two parties to the transaction, the writer (or seller) of the option and the buyer. A writer of MBS calls is offering the buyer the right, but not the obligation, to buy the underlying MBS, say FNMA 9s of 2001 (ie 9 percent coupon, maturing in the year 2001), at a specific strike price during a certain time-frame, in exchange for a premium from the buyer. Conversely, the writer of an MBS put is giving the buyer the option to sell the underlying FNMA to the buyer at some point in the future. In either case, depending on whether the option is American-style or European-style, the exercise can take place at any time prior to, and including, maturity (American) or only at maturity (European).

If the buyer of an FNMA call wishes to exercise the option because it is in the money (ie has value), the writer must honour the obligation either by delivering FNMA securities to the buyer in exchange for the cash equivalent based on the strike price and the amount of the option or by cash-settling the option.

Consider the following example: Bank X sells Corporation Y 10 FNMA calls (with each call representing $100,000 of FNMA 9s of 2001), maturity 30 April, strike price 99. Corporation Y pays Bank X a premium for the right to buy the FNMA should market movements allow. The option is out of the money and, as such, the premium paid is relatively small, say $100,000.

Assume that, one month on, rates fall and the value of the FNMA 9s increases to 101. At this point, the option is in-the-money. Corporation Y decides to exercise its option. It can pay Bank X $99m (10 × $100,000 × 99) and receive the FNMA MBSs from Bank X, which it can then sell in the market for $101m and earn a gross profit of $2mm (net profit of $1.9m after subtracting premium paid). Alternatively, it can cash-settle the option with Bank X, receiving $2m (10 calls × $100,000/call × (current market price − strike price)). For all practical purposes, Bank X will take its underlying securities (assuming it wrote covered, not naked, calls) worth $99m, sell them in the market for $101m, and deliver the $2m difference to Corporation Y. Each of the above transactions has the same end result, which is to deliver $2m to Corporation Y.

GENERAL CREDIT CONSIDERATIONS

We now return briefly to the discussion of elements in the decision-making process.

Risk

For forwards (including TBAs), the risk is generally low unless dealing with an exceptionally long forward settlement period and/or an esoteric MBS derivative. For a bank's short option position the risk is non-existent. For a long position it is typically low, unless the option is struck well in the money and the counterparty's short option position is naked. In addition, long options on certain MBS derivatives can be medium risk as they may be especially volatile, illiquid and difficult to price. The BIS risk weighting for forwards and options involving MBSs varies from 50 per cent to 100 per cent, depending on individual countries and individual government agencies. In the US, for example, a 0 per cent weight is assigned to GNMA MBSs, 20 per cent to FNMA and FHLMC MBSs, agency CMOs and private label CMOs utilising agencies and 100 per cent to IO/PO strips.

Return

Return on generic TBAs and forwards for medium quality counterparties is low. For at- or in-the-money options the return increases and for options or forwards involving esoteric MBS derivatives return tends to be high. Although risk weightings for MBS forwards and options can be as high as 100 per cent, capital charge spreads are typically small given the low risk factors associated with the transactions.

Maturity

For forwards the maturities are typically short-term. For most options the same is true, although certain transactions may be executed over 12 months with no mark-to-market provisions.

Motivation

For both forwards and options the motivations can include hedging, speculation, arbitrage and yield enhancing.

Enhancement

Standard MBS forwards and options (and MBS derivatives) carry no credit enhancement.

Creditworthiness

Generally speaking, forward trades can be acceptable across the spectrum of credit qualities, although a credit analyst may wish to limit the settlement period and amount transacted with sub-investment grade counterparties. For the lowest tier of sub-investment grade companies forward settling MBS trades of several weeks become inadvisable, particularly if dealing with volatile derivatives such as IOs and POs. It must be recalled that there is no security or collateral in dealing with forward settling MBSs, so a bank will be exposed to market risk. Care must therefore be taken when dealing with lower credit quality clients.

If a bank is selling MBS options to a counterparty (a short position) it is expecting to receive premium income in exchange for honouring the option obligation at some future date (should market movements warrant exercise of the option). Thus a bank has no risk in a short position once the premium is received (which is generally within two days), so sales of MBS options can be appropriate for the entire range of credit qualities.

In a long position (when the bank is buying an MBS option from a counterparty), it is the bank which is both paying premium and expecting future performance from the counterparty. In this scenario a credit analyst needs to be much more careful about approving a trade or facility. A lower quality counterparty may not have the financial backup to support a large options line with extended maturities of six months or more.

The motivation for transacting MBS options, particularly for sub-investment grade clients, must be analysed with care. These transactions can represent outright speculation and may involve risks which are unacceptable in dealing with the lower tier of clients. While a counterparty's long positions may well be acceptable because they may constitute legitimate hedging or yield enhancing, short positions, particularly if they are naked, can be deemed speculative in some situations.

Although the strategy of writing naked options in certain market conditions is a way to earn extra premium income, it is clear that a weak counterparty engaged in such a practice can get into substantial financial difficulties should the market move against it. It is therefore vital that any such strategies be examined closely by the analyst, as they are generally inappropriate for weak clients.

RISK QUANTIFICATION

MBS forwards and options involving generics or derivatives are affected by rate movements. As such, we view them as market risk products and adjust risk exposure *via* the risk equivalency process. As in all market risk situations, a bank will have to deal with its market risk exposure only when an actual default by the counterparty occurs. If a client continues to perform on an extended settlement or options trade, the amount of market risk present is less vital to the bank. It is important, however, to know how much risk is being assumed at the inception of the trade; once this is quantified, the analyst will know whether the transaction or limit under consideration is advisable. Recalling equation (5.1) we know that

$$\text{REE} = \text{RF} \times \text{N}$$

We can use this equation to determine the risk inherent in forward settlement and options trades of MBS securities.

In the case of forward settling transactions (including TBAs) it is clear that the movement of interest rates has a direct impact on the value (and therefore the risk) of the unsettled deal. As with other fixed income securities, the bank faces risk on a sale when interest rates rise and the value of the MBS falls. It is at this point that a default could occur, since the counterparty could renege on the transaction and buy the MBS in today's market at a price lower than that contracted several weeks ago; an outright default for financial reasons would have the same effect. If the bank had an opposite transaction to cover from the sale of the above MBS, it would have to alter its strategy and sell the MBS at today's lower price; thus it would sustain a loss. In the same fashion, a bank will sustain a loss on a forward purchase if rates fall, the value of the MBS rises and the counterparty defaults. This will force the bank to cover its position in the more expensive cash MBS market.

Based on the above, any risk equation must consider the value of the trade as it is affected by future movements in interest rates. The new equation takes the following form, which is identical to the equation used for forward settling Treasuries:

$$\text{REE} = \text{RF} \times \text{Greater of LV} \vee \text{SV} \tag{9.1}$$

where RF is the appropriate risk factor,
LV are trades where the bank has bought MBSs forward,
SV are trades where the bank has sold MBSs forward.

As with Treasuries, we need take only the long or short value for a given client, since a movement in rates in one direction will help one position and hinder another but cannot hinder both (the only exception being a situation which involved forward sales or purchases of IOs which, as we have seen, move in the opposite direction to traditional fixed income securities). The selection of one of these two positions gives us the dollar magnitude of the trade(s) in question.

As always, use of the appropriate RF will give us a measure by which to capture both the maturity of the trade and the underlying MBS being traded. The longer the maturity of the trade, the higher the possibility of market movements and therefore of market risk. The greater the maturity of the underlying MBS (eg a 20-year FNMA against a 30-year FNMA), the greater the price volatility and therefore the greater the potential market exposure.

Consider the following example: Bank A sells \$100m worth of FHLMC 8s of 96 to Bank B for settlement in two months. At the inception of the trade rates will not yet have moved, so the risk on the deal is

$$\begin{aligned} \text{REE} &= (0.018 \times \$100{,}000{,}000) \\ &= \$1{,}800{,}000 \end{aligned}$$

Note that the RF being used is 1.8 per cent. The \$1,800,000 represents the risk the analyst must consider when approving the transaction today. Since TBAs and MBS forwards are not typically marked to market and no margin is taken, the equation above represents the most straightforward procedure for assigning risk to these forwards.

If an analyst needs to focus on the mark-to-market value of the trade, the equation above can be refined to include a MTM component as well. The form would now be

$$\text{REE} = [\text{MTM} + (\text{RFc} \times \text{MV})] \tag{9.2}$$

where MV is the new market value of the MBS,
MTM is the difference between the original value of the MBS and the new market value (MV),
RFc is a constantly adjusted risk factor.

For example, as time passes and rates begin to move, the MV of the MBS begins to move as well. Assume that rates increase 30 days after the trade was booked (with 30 days left to settlement) such that the MV moves down by \$500,000. The numerical example would yield

$$\text{REE} = [\$500{,}000 + (0.01 \times \$99{,}500{,}000)] = \$1{,}495{,}000$$

Note that the RFc has changed to 1 per cent from 1.8 per cent. As settlement draws nearer, the potential movement in rates is much smaller, so a lower RFc is used. In the example above, even though there has been a market movement of \$500,000, the remaining potential movement (according to the statistical model) is less than \$1m. The total risk is \$1.495m because it takes into account the MTM value; if Bank B defaulted on the trade today, Bank A would face a certain loss of \$500,000. The remaining \$995,000 captures potential movements which might yet occur before the trade settles (if the counterparty does not default today).

To put the issues raised above in a scenario reflecting both orderly and default settlements, we can consider figure 9.1.

The market risk inherent in an MBS option trade is different from the risk encountered in a forward settlement. Recalling the discussion in Chapter 8, we

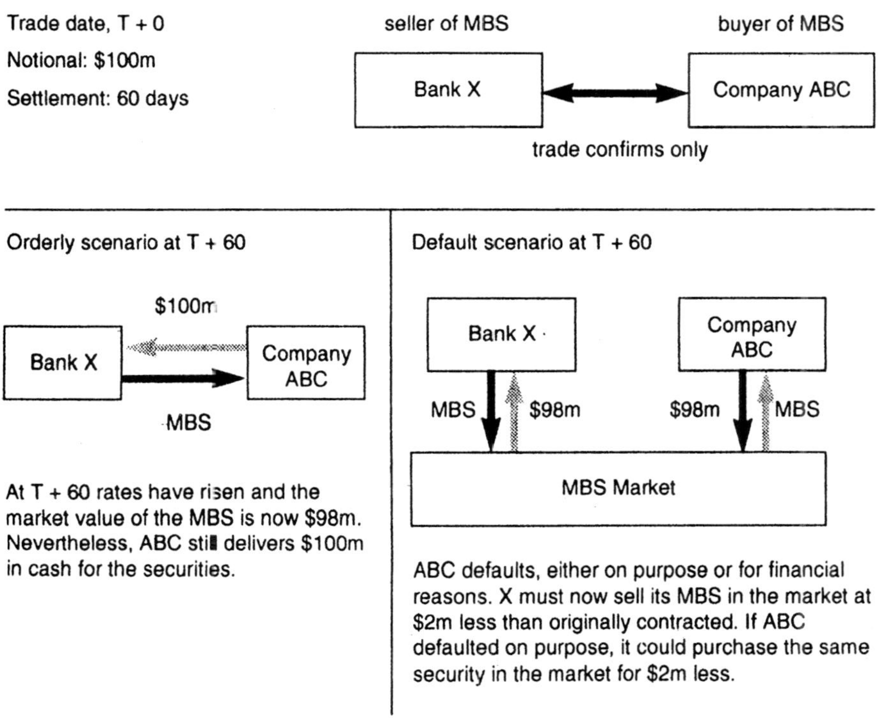

Figure 9.1. MBS Extended Settlement, Orderly and Default Scenarios.

know that an option's value comprises both intrinsic value (how far in the money or out of the money the option is) and time value (how much time remains until expiry, whether the option is deeply in the money or out of the money, the volatility of the underlying security and the level of short-term interest rates). An option with high intrinsic value and a high time value will be more valuable than an option with low intrinsic value and a low time value.

As before, it seems obvious that a buyer of an option will pay a larger premium for a more valuable option and, as a result, will face greater risk. The risk is greater not only because a higher option premium has been paid out but also because the chances of exercise are much higher and reliance on the performance of the option writer is thus more critical. With these concepts in mind, it is easy to apply the framework from Chapter 8 to our discussion of MBS options. We can return to our basic equation (5.1) and make some adjustments. The notional amount of the trade (N) and the appropriate risk factor (RF) remain unchanged and are important in order to reflect both the dollar magnitude of the trade and its particulars (maturity and underlying MBS type). This will yield a potential market risk figure. As with Treasury options, however, we must also factor in the upfront payment of premium. Since this is cash out at the inception of the trade by the buyer of the option, the buyer has additional exposure. The buyer is not only expecting performance on the option, should exercise occur, but must also consider that, if the writer defaults on the transaction, the premium is lost. Thus, the appropriate risk model can be expanded as follows:

$$\text{REE} = \text{premium paid} + (\text{RF} \times \text{N}) \tag{9.3}$$

This represents the same basic risk model as was developed in the previous chapter and measures the risk equivalent exposure of the MBS options trade by providing a figure which equates to the likely maximum risk to be faced during the life of the transaction, plus premium paid out. As we shall see below, this equation is actually a standard risk valuation form for at-the-money options.

A second model examines changes in the option value as market prices move. From a buyer's perspective, a given option may or may not have value over and above the premium already paid out, depending on where the market price stands in relation to the strike price. It would not make sense to allocate risk to an option which is not likely to be exercised (ie one which is deeply out-of-the-money with a very short time to expiry); in such situations the only amount at risk is the premium. Conversely, an option which is very likely to be exercised (ie one which is heavily in-the-money) exposes the buyer to a greater amount of risk.

In order for us to assess the extent to which an option is in the money or out-of-the-money, we focus on the difference between the current market price CMP and the strike price SP; this is simply a market value comparison. As before, for calls this will take the form of the greater of 0 or ((CMP − SP)/CMP), while for puts it will be the greater of 0 or ((SP − CMP)/CMP). If an option is out-of-the-money (and the time to expiry is reasonably short), the only portion of the trade which is at risk will be the premium, hence the use of 0. As an option moves into-the-money (or its expiry date is extended), the market risk exposure increases. We still need to include a risk factor component RFc in order to capture potential market movements which may yet occur; we do so with (RFc × N), by now familiar to the reader. The more detailed model for call options is now:

$$\text{REE} = \text{premium} + 0 \vee [(\text{RFc} \times \text{N}) + \left(\frac{(\text{CMP} - \text{SP})}{\text{CMP}}\right) \times \text{N})] \quad (9.4)$$

where CMP is the current market price,
SP is the strike price of the option,
RFc is a constantly adjusted risk factor,
N is the notional amount of the trade.

For puts the equation is:

$$\text{REE} = \text{premium} + 0 \vee [(\text{RFc} \times \text{N}) + \left(\frac{(\text{SP} - \text{CMP})}{\text{CMP}}\right) \times \text{N})] \quad (9.5)$$

where CMP is the current market price,
SP is the strike price of the option,
RFc is a constantly adjusted risk factor,
N is the notional amount of the trade.

To help illustrate how this formula can be used, consider the following series of European-style FNMA call options:

An Out-of-the-money Option

N = \$10m
SP = 110
CMP = 100

maturity is four weeks, RF is 1.8 per cent, premium paid is \$100,000

$$\text{REE} = \text{premium} + 0 \vee [(\text{RFc} \times \text{N}) + \left(\frac{(\text{CMP} - \text{SP})}{\text{CMP}}\right) \times \text{N})] \quad (9.4)$$

$$= \$100{,}000 + 0 \text{ or } [(0.018 \times \$10\text{m}) + (((100 - 110)/100) \times \$10\text{m})]$$
$$= \$100{,}000 + 0 \text{ or } [\$180{,}000 + (-0.1 \times \$10\text{m})]$$
$$= \$100{,}000 + 0 \text{ or } [-\$820{,}000]$$
$$= \$100{,}000$$

Since the chances of exercise are virtually non-existent given both the short time to expiry (four weeks) and the large price differential (10 points out of the money), the buyer of the call need not concern itself with the potential for market risk due to non-performance by the seller. As before, in such situations the risk equation chooses to focus strictly on the risk of the premium paid out. Note that if the time to expiry were greater, the associated risk factor would be greater. As maturity increases the RF, the chance that the second portion of the equation will be positive (implying additional exposure) increases. Intuitively this makes sense, as an option that is deeply out-of-the-money still has an opportunity of moving into the money when the time to maturity is long. In the example above, once the RF is greater than 10 per cent the risk on the entire equation will be positive. For a FNMA option any maturity in excess of 18 to 24 months will generally yield a risk factor of over 10 per cent.

An At-the-money Option

$$N = \$10\text{m}$$
$$SP = 100$$
$$CMP = 100$$

maturity is four weeks, RF is 1.8 per cent, premium paid is $250,000

$$REE = \text{premium} + 0 \vee [(RFc \times N) + \left(\frac{(CMP - SP)}{CMP)}\right) \times N)] \qquad (9.4)$$

$$= \$250{,}000 + 0 \text{ or } [(0.018 \times \$10\text{m}) + (((100 - 100)/100) \times \$10\text{m})]$$
$$= \$250{,}000 + 0 \text{ or } [\$180{,}000 + 0]$$
$$= \$430{,}000$$

In this instance there is clearly value to the option. Depending on its delta (how much the option value moves for a given price movement in the underlying MBS), it stands a chance of terminating either in-the-money or out-of-the-money; as previously mentioned, options purchased at-the-money typically have a delta of 0.5 (that is a 50 per cent chance of ending with value). Given a 50 per cent probability of exercise, we would need to incorporate possible market risk into our REE calculation (together with premium paid). With an at-the-money call no adjustment is actually required to the risk factor (it will remain at 1.8 per cent in this example). We note that the market value portion of the equation actually condenses to 0, so the entire result is equal to the general form reflected in equation (9.3).

An In-the-money Option

N = \$10m
SP = 100
CMP = 110

maturity is four weeks, RF is 1.8 per cent, premium paid is \$700,000

$$\text{REE} = \text{premium} + 0 \vee \left[(\text{RFc} \times \text{N}) + \left(\frac{(\text{CMP} - \text{SP})}{\text{CMP}}\right) \times \text{N})\right] \qquad (9.4)$$

$$\begin{aligned} &= \$700{,}000 + 0 \text{ or } [(0.018 \times \$10\text{m}) + (((110 - 100)/110) \times \$10\text{m})] \\ &= \$700{,}000 + 0 \text{ or } [\$180{,}000 + (0.091 \times \$10\text{m})] \\ &= \$700{,}000 + 0 \text{ or } [\$180{,}000 + \$910{,}000] \\ &= \$1{,}790{,}000 \end{aligned}$$

In the final instance it is relatively easy to see that the option has more risk, as the buyer could exercise in four weeks' time and achieve a 10-point profit. Since the intrinsic value is so high and exercise is virtually certain, the buyer has more at stake and will be looking to the seller for performance. The associated REE must therefore be higher. Note that, in addition to the fact that the option is already above the market, the 1.8 per cent risk factor is also included in the calculation to reflect the possibility that default might occur at some point in the next four weeks (when the option might be even further in the money).

Comparing the two risk equations (9.3) and (9.4) in a simple example yields Table 9.1.

GNMA call N = \$10m
SP = 100
CMP = 100

maturity is three weeks, RF at inception is 1.8 per cent, premium paid is \$500,000

where our static model equation is

$$\text{REE} = \text{premium paid} + (\text{RF} \times \text{N}) \qquad (9.3)$$

and our dynamic model equation is

$$\text{REE} = \text{premium} + 0 \vee \left[(\text{RFc} \times \text{N}) + \left(\frac{(\text{CMP} - \text{SP})}{\text{CMP}}\right) \times \text{N})\right] \qquad (9.4)$$

Table 9.1. Comparison of Static and Dynamic Models

Time to maturity	CMP	RFc	REE of static model	REE of dynamic model
Three weeks	100	1.8%	$680,000	$680,000
Two weeks	101	1.5%	$680,000	$780,000
One Week	100	1.1%	$680,000	$610,000

It will be clear to the reader that there will always be slight differences in the calculation of REE in the static, as against the dynamic, model. While the dynamic model is more accurate because it tracks ongoing movements in market prices and relates such movements to the strike price, it is also operationally and technically more complex to monitor. Thus, any institution involved in this type of business would face trade-offs in using one equation or the other.

This discussion has focused solely on risks inherent in transactions where a bank is long MBS options (and the counterparty is short options). In transactions where the bank is short an option it incurs no risk, as it will have received the premium from the client (in a normal cash-settlement time-frame) and will then have to perform if the client decides to exercise. Although certain risk management considerations (such as hedging requirements) may exist when a bank is short options, there are no credit considerations.

Table 9.2. Sample Risk Factors for MBS Forwards and Options (per cent)

	One week	Two weeks	One month	Two months	Three months	Six months	12 months	24 months
GNMA/FNMA HV = 5.8 per cent	1.1	1.5	2.1	3.1	3.7	5.2	7.4	10.5
CMO AA one to five years, HV = 7.5 per cent	1.4	2.0	2.8	3.9	4.8	6.8	9.6	13.6
CMO AA five to 10 years, HV = 9.8 per cent	1.8	2.6	3.6	5.2	6.3	8.9	12.6	17.8
CMO AA over 10 years, HV = 22.8 per cent	4.2	6.1	8.4	12.1	14.6	20.7	29.2	41.3
IO/PO strip HV = 24.8 per cent	4.6	6.6	9.1	13.1	15.9	22.5	31.8	45.0

RISK FACTORS

A sample listing of risk factors is given in Table 9.2 for information purposes. These are derived from historical volatilities and 90 per cent confidence levels against a lognormal distribution. Note that Table 9.2 provides the appropriate RF (or RFc) for forwards, TBAs and options. As one might expect, GNMA, FNMA and FHLMC MBSs tend to have lower volatilities than CMOs, AA-rated pass-throughs and other MBS derivatives, so the associated RFs are lower. As always, the longer the maturity of the underlying trade (within a given category), the greater the chance of rate movements and the higher the associated RF.

10: Money Market Instruments

DESCRIPTION

In general terms, money market instruments are defined as short- to medium-term, senior, unsecured debt obligations of the company or bank issuing the notes. In most instances the notes are issued in shelf or programme form and are utilised, or drawn down, as required. Use of the notes is typically for general financing purposes (in lieu of, or in addition to, bank financing, equity financing or long-term bond financing). Money market instruments are often used to meet a short-term or seasonal need for funds (while equity financing and long-term bond issuance might be regarded as more 'permanent' forms of funding).

The purpose of this chapter is to cover several of the major categories of money market instrument commonly dealt in by banks. These include commercial paper (CP), Eurocommercial paper (ECP), medium-term notes (MTNs) and certificates of deposit (CDs). There are, of course, other money market instruments in the marketplace, including retail CDs, bankers' acceptances (BAs), deposit notes and so on, but they either represent 'derivatives' of the major categories above or account for only a small fraction of money market instruments currently issued. From a risk point of view, it will become clear that most money market instruments have very similar risk profiles.

Commercial Paper

Overview

CP notes are short-term, unsecured, unsubordinated promissory obligations issued by industrial, utility, financial and governmental institutions, generally for short-term financing purposes. The notes are typically marketed to institutional investors on a discount basis. CP can also be issued on an interest-bearing basis, though this is less common. Notes are issued in bearer form and are not subject to US Securities registration, provided one of the exemptions from the Securities Act of 1933 (the 1933 Act) is utilised; this concept is covered in depth below.

Notes can be issued for up to 270 days without the need for registration; actual maturities typically range from seven to 45 days, although this depends on both the current state of the yield curve and the actual borrowing needs of the issuer. While there is no provision for automatic maturity extension, issuers typically replace or 'rollover' maturing notes with new notes as long as funding is required and investor demand for the paper is present. Dealer paper (ie paper issued by one of the major CP dealers on behalf of an issuer for a 'spread' or commission of several basis points) is normally sold in lots of $250,000. Given a fairly high minimum denomination (generally not lower than $100,000), CP is not typically considered a common investment for the retail market.

Once a CP programme is established, the entire process of issuing the paper takes place in one day. The issuer decides how much paper to issue, the dealer or issuer markets it to investors and the CP is delivered to, and paid for by, the investor. At the same time investors may be presenting maturing paper for redemption. The issuance of CP involves the physical delivery of a note, although attempts are currently underway to change this practice into a book entry format. The entire process is routed through an independent third party (called the issuing and paying agent or depository), who is charged with the safekeeping of the notes prior to issuance, their delivery to the dealer after the sale and paying for them at maturity. Investors and issuers (often *via* the dealer) generally have their own independent agents (safekeeping and clearing agents) acting to verify that funds and notes have been received as required.

Approximately half of all CP outstanding is placed directly by the issuer with investors (direct paper); the other half is issued through dealers (dealer paper). Within the CP market as a whole approximately one-third is issued by the industrial sector (public utilities, manufacturers and retailers) and a further half by finance companies, banks and bank holding companies. Bank holding companies very often issue CP to finance non-bank activities such as leasing and real estate. Funds can also be channelled into the bank for various uses. The balance of the market consists of other issuers, including municipalities and sovereigns. The most active CP dealers are currently Merrill Lynch, Goldman, Sachs, Lehman Brothers, Morgan Stanley and First Boston; Salomon Brothers, which was active for a time, withdrew from the market in the mid-1980s.

Bank Lines

Nearly all paper sold today carries ratings from one or more recognised rating agencies (Standard & Poor's, Moody's Investor Service, Fitch Investors' Services, Duff & Phelps). Paper is often priced by dealers based on these ratings, while investors will look to the ratings to determine, or to assist in determining, the credit quality of the issuer.

In addition to ensuring that the credit fundamentals of the CP issuer (or the support provider in the case of guaranteed or letter of credit-backed programmes) are sufficiently strong, the agencies will generally require corporate CP programmes to be backed by a line of credit from a bank; such bank lines serve as secondary liquidity support for the paper in case issuers are unable to sell new notes to replace maturing ones. From a rating agency's point of view it is normally sufficient to have the full amount of any single day's maturities covered by a line of credit, although exceptions to this obviously exist. Paper issued by medium or lower quality corporations (ie those in the A-2/P-2 or A-3/P-3 range) generally have committed backup facilities equal to 100 per cent of the programme size.

Some backup lines carry no legal commitment, in other words they can be withdrawn at will with no liability to the bank. These are often referred to as 'standby' or 'advised' lines. With a standby or advised facility, a borrower will not have paid the bank any fee for the facility, so the bank is under no legal obligation to maintain the lines (or to allow them to be drawn). Their use in acting as a backstop to a commercial paper programme is questionable and analysts and rating agencies would not view them as part of the company's backup liquidity.

'Committed' lines, in contrast, carry the strongest assurance because the borrower typically pays the bank a fee to have such lines in place (whether or not they are used). While committed lines are typically a sound source of support, some caution must be used, since even these facilities can include strict financial covenants or 'material adverse change' clauses to protect the bank. Such covenants or clauses allow the bank to withdraw its commitment or to keep from funding if it is believed that there has been a breach. In the case of financial covenants this is typically not subject to interpretation, as issuer and bank will have agreed beforehand on the appropriate formula to use in the calculation of covenant ratios (leverage, interest coverage and so on). However, the nature and interpretation of a 'material adverse change' clause (which allows the bank to cancel its facility if it believes a 'material adverse change' to have occurred) has been the subject of discussion in the recent past, as there is some debate as to events which constitute a 'material adverse change'. In the case of Mortgage and Realty Trust (MRT), which defaulted on $167m of CP in early 1990, the lead bank providing the credit facility was unwilling to fund MRT prior to the paper's maturing. The bank used a 'material adverse change' clause in the documentation to allow it to keep from funding. As a result, the company's supposed 'committed' lines were not in place and the lack of financing forced MRT to default on its paper and declare bankruptcy.

Registration Exemptions

Under the 1933 Act all securities sold in the US are required to be registered with the Securities and Exchange Commission (SEC). The process of registering an issue of securities can be a lengthy and expensive one, given the amount of detailed information which must be filed with the SEC (see the end of this chapter for additional details). For companies in need of a short-term financing facility and those not wanting to go through the registration process, an alternative is available through the use of one of several registration 'exemptions'. By using one of the exemptions described below (and adhering to the various constraints each carries) an issuer can enter the market without having to go through the registration process.

There are four types of commercial paper which are exempt from registration under the 1933 Act: open market, privately placed, letter of credit and tax-exempt. Tax-exempt commercial paper, which has certain specific characteristics, is not discussed in this text as it is more narrowly focused on US municipalities.

Open Market Paper (Section 3(a)(3))

Open market paper is prime quality commercial paper typically purchased by a broad range of institutional investors (and only rarely by the general public). It is exempt from registration under Section 3(a)(3) of the 1933 Act.

This section provides an exemption for CP which arises out of a current transaction or in which the proceeds are to be used for a current transaction. Proceeds from the sale of open market paper are not to be used for permanent or fixed investment, for speculative transactions or for transactions involving the purchase of securities, except for direct obligations of the US Government. Proceeds generally cannot be used for the discharge of existing indebtedness unless the indebtedness itself is exempt. Proceeds may be used for the funding of assets easily convertible into cash (eg liquid inventories of an industrial or mercantile company, short-term receivables, etc).

Maturity of 3(a)(3) notes is not to exceed nine months, exclusive of any days of grace. Any renewal of the security is subject to the same maturity limits. Any security with a provision for automatic rollover is not exempt from registration under Section 3(a)(3).

In practice a great deal of paper is reissued as existing notes mature, in effect creating an ongoing source of financing for the issuer of the paper. This process is, of course, dependent upon both pricing considerations and continued investor demand for the paper and is certainly not automatic.

The large number of issuers in the 3(a)(3) market and the considerable dollar amounts of paper issued have enabled a secondary market to develop. Liquidity for prime names is considered to be excellent.

Privately Placed Paper (Section 4(2))

Privately placed paper is paper which is exempt from registration under Section 4(2) of the 1933 Act. The purpose of this provision is to permit an issuer to make a specific or isolated sale of its securities to particular persons without incurring the expense of registration.

Securities issued under this section must meet all conditions relating to the limitations on the manner of offering, the nature of the offerees (potential purchasers), access to information about the issuer, the number of purchasers and subsequent disposition of securities.

Normally the number of offerees is limited to 100. They must be sophisticated investors with knowledge of the issuer, although they need not be 'insiders'. The issuer must still provide the information contained in any proxy statement as well as the information contained in an annual report (or in a registration statement on Form S-1 under the 1933 Act or on Form 10 under the Exchange Act).

The offeree must have knowledge and experience in financial and business matters such that he or she is capable of evaluating the investment and can bear the economic risk of the investment. The issuer must inform the offeree in writing of the need to bear the economic risk of the investment because of the stringent restrictions on resale. This is typically covered in the information prospectus. Since resale of private placement paper is severely restricted (unlike open market paper), the potential investor must be prepared to hold paper until maturity.

Rule 146(c) under the 1933 Act prohibits the issuer or any person acting on its behalf from offering or selling the securities through any form of advertising or solicitation.

As mentioned above, resale is permitted only under limited conditions; if resale occurs, it must be proven that such was not the original intent of the investor. The longer the period of retention, the more persuasive the argument that the purchase was made as an investment strategy, not a trading strategy. 4(2) paper must be resold to the dealer or, in the case of direct issue, back to the issuer; it cannot be resold to third parties.

If a dealer repurchases a block of 4(2) securities from the original investor and discovers the investor's original intention was not to hold them, the dealer's own resale of the securities at a subsequent date may not be exempt from registration. Dealers may typically resell the securities provided the conditions meeting exemption requirements are maintained.

Based on all the above, it is clear that the issuance of 4(2) paper represents a more involved process than the issuance of 3(a)(3) paper. Despite the various rules which must be followed, however, there is still an active group of 4(2) issuers.

Letter of Credit Paper (Section 3(a)(2))

Letter of credit (LOC) commercial paper is paper that is supported or guaranteed by any bank and is therefore exempt from registration under Section 3(a)(2) of the 1933 Act. Paper issued by a branch or agency of a foreign bank located in the US is also covered by this exemption; such foreign bank issues currently dominate the market, as these institutions are in general more highly rated than US banks. LOC-backed commercial paper notes are also occasionally referred to as 'documented discount notes'.

Issuing LOC paper has several advantages: it enables the issuer to obtain a better rating than might otherwise be possible because of credit considerations. If the underlying issuer is a weaker credit, it will be forced to pay a premium to investors in order to obtain financing. Rather than constantly pay this risk premium, it can elect to pay, on a yearly basis, a more highly rated bank for the use of its rating and can enter the market in this fashion. From an investor's point of view, the paper is being purchased on the basis of the support provider's name and rating, not the issuer's. Most such programmes are supported by direct pay letters of credit, so that the investor is at no time exposed to the credit or performance of the underlying issuer (this is discussed in greater detail at the end of the chapter).

Companies which are not large enough to obtain a rating can also use this method, as can companies which do not want to disclose financial information to the general public but do not mind disclosure to the rating agencies. US subsidiaries of Japanese companies often issue LOC paper rather than having their parent companies guarantee the securities.

Other characteristics found under Section 3(a)(3) also apply in the case of 3(a)(2) paper: nine-month maximum maturity, no provision for automatic rollover and so on.

Eurocommercial Paper

In some respects ECP is similar to CP: the notes represent short-term, unsecured, unsubordinated obligations of the issuer of the paper and are typically sold by dealers to investors on a discount basis (with two-day settlement, in physical or book entry form). Unlike CP, the ECP market and product exist only offshore (ie no ECP may be sold in the US or to US investors) and the maximum maturity of the paper can be beyond 12 months if using a Euronote facility. Participants in the market are similar to those in the USCP market: industrial, financial and sovereign issuers. Recent entrants include sovereign and blue chip industrial companies based in Latin America (these issuers are either unrated or carry sub-investment grade ratings, so have not used the USCP market, which is more restrictive in both ratings and regulations).

ECP can (but does not have to) be issued under a note issuance facility (NIF) or a revolving underwriting facility (RUF). Under a NIF or RUF a borrower issues notes through an agent or dealer; notes which are not taken up by investors are purchased by a syndicate of banks, all committed to providing the borrower with funds as required. Some NIFs are structured so that the syndicate places notes on a *pro rata* basis (instead of assigning a single dealer to the task); notes which cannot be placed are retained by the bank, which provides the borrower with funds.

Other facilities are structured with a 'tender panel', where each of the placement agents submits a bid for the notes a week prior to issuance; the winning bid (ie the one providing the lowest cost to the borrower) will receive the greatest allocation of notes and will then attempt to place them with investors. Other issuance mechanisms include transferable RUFs (TRUFs), where a bank's funding commitment can be transferred to another bank, standby NIFs (SNIFs), generally a backstop, rather than a main borrowing facility, and multiple option facilities (MOFs), where the borrower can access funds through the issuance of notes or can elect other borrowing facilities, currencies, and so on.

Generally speaking, documentation for ECP tends to be similar to that required in the US market (ie each programme requires a dealer agreement, an issuing and paying agency agreement, a prospectus or selling document, legal opinions, a note, board resolutions and a certificate of incumbency). Since the paper is issued offshore, there are no registration requirements (or exemptions from registration) as in the US market. In addition, there is no formal regulatory body with complete jurisdiction over the ECP market (as the SEC has in the USCP market).

The market developed in the 1970s, grew in earnest during the early and mid-1980s and underwent fundamental changes in the later 1980s and early 1990s. During the boom years many unrated and low quality issuers tapped the ECP market for funds and competition among dealers for business was substantial (to the point where paper was issued at negligible or negative spreads to the dealer).

ECP defaults in the late 1980s by Integrated Resources, with \$63m outstanding, Lomas Financial, with \$17m outstanding, Development Finance Corporation of New Zealand (DFC), with \$270m outstanding, and Wang Laboratories, with \$96m outstanding, appear to have signalled a turning point for the market. Following the defaults, many dealers re-evaluated the business, the profitability and the risks and at least three top tier dealers (Merrill Lynch, CSFB and SG Warburg) decided to withdraw from what was then a high risk/no return market. Today the focus by those still active in the market is on creditworthy issuers (most, though not all, rated) and on profitable transactions and the market appears to have recovered from some of the excesses of the late 1980s.

Medium-term Notes

Medium-term notes (MTNs) can be thought of as commercial paper notes with a longer maturity. In standard form, MTNs are again unsecured, unsubordinated promissory notes issued by industrial companies, financial institutions (issuance is in the form of 'deposit notes') and sovereigns. The notes are not underwritten but are sold by dealers or agents on a continuously offered basis. Standard maturities start at nine months (where commercial paper maturities end) and go out as far as 30 or 40 years (though most issuance does not occur in those maturities).

As with CP, MTNs are set up as programmes, allowing issuers to use them as required. Depending on rates and funding needs, the company can simply instruct its dealer or agent to issue a tranche of notes when needed (in a similar manner to issuing a tranche of bonds from a 415 shelf registration, as discussed in Chapter 11). Once they mature, the company can elect to issue more paper. Alternatively, it may want to issue two-year and five-year notes at the same time to coincide with specific funding requirements. Within the MTN product in general an issuer is free to select any number of different types of note structure: fixed rate notes, floating rate notes (based on LIBOR, CP, Federal Funds, etc), amortising notes, multicurrency notes and so on.

The MTN market originated in the early 1980s and grew steadily through much of the decade in terms both of new programmes and of total paper outstanding. Documentation for MTN programmes (and EuroMTN programmes, representing paper issued offshore) has evolved from a complex, negotiated (and generally onerous) process to a simple, standard and relatively quick one. As a result, the number of issuers which can come to the market in a short time to take advantage of particular interest or currency rate situations has increased dramatically and even complex structures such as multicurrency issues can be effected with ease. In this respect MTNs have a distinct advantage over traditional non-shelf registered fixed or floating rate bonds.

The primary institutions involved in the selling and trading of MTNs include Merrill Lynch, Goldman, Sachs, Lehman Brothers, Morgan Stanley, Salomon Brothers and First Boston.

Certificates of Deposit

Certificates of deposit (CDs) are a traditional bank funding instrument. Banks have been actively issuing CDs since they were developed as negotiable instruments in 1961. CDs represent unsecured, unsubordinated obligations of the bank and can be issued with maturities ranging from one week to several years. CDs are interest- bearing obligations and are generally issued at par. Certain instruments can be sold on a discount basis; these are known as 'discount CDs' (and are very often issued through a bank's Cayman Islands branch or *via* a subsidiary in Canada, known as a Schedule II Bank).

Most banks issue their own CDs and sell them to institutional clients in either fixed or floating rate form, onshore or offshore, in denominations generally starting at $100,000. Certain investment banks are involved with another sector of the market, which involves the issuance of bank CDs sold directly to the retail client base (these are sometimes known as retail CDs). As one might expect, these instruments have a much smaller minimum denomination (generally $5000 or $10,000) and are insured by the FDIC up to a maximum of $100,000.

Banks can also issue EuroCDs (typically out of a London branch) and deposit notes (fixed or floating rate, characterised by longer maturities out to five years).

GENERAL CREDIT CONSIDERATIONS

We return once more to our credit decision-making framework.

Risk

The risk on all money market instruments is high. For CP specifically the risk is greater given the potential for underwriter's liability. The BIS risk weighting on money market inventories of private sector issuers is 100 per cent and for sovereign issuers in OECD countries it is 0 per cent. For banks providing standby letters of credit in support of 3(a)(2) programmes risk weighting is 50 per cent; for direct letters of credit or guarantees it is 100 per cent. Underwriting commitments under NIFs and RUFs are weighted at 50 per cent.

Return

The return on money market instruments for medium quality counterparties is low for instruments with shorter maturities but increases as maturities are extended. Theoretical capital charge spreads tend to be reasonably high, given both high risk weighting and high risk factors associated with inventories and underwriting commitments; the exception is for inventories involving sovereign issuers in OECD countries.

Maturity

Maturities cover a wide range. For MTNs, EuroMTNs and certain CDs final maturity may be many years away. For CP (and certain CDs) it will always fall within nine months.

Motivation

Issuance of a money market instrument represents a pure funding transaction. It cannot have any other use.

Enhancement

Standard money market programmes carry no enhancement but, as discussed above, the 3(a)(2) market is specifically for programmes enhanced by letters of credit. In addition, a growing sector of the CP market, the asset-backed CP product, may be enhanced by receivables or other assets. Although bank lines are a part of most programmes, these are typically viewed as necessary backup, not as enhancement.

Creditworthiness

In previous chapters we have indicated that certain financing and trading instruments (such as repos, forward Treasuries, MBS options, etc) are acceptable across a range of credit qualities. The same is not true for money market paper; such instruments are generally acceptable only for high and medium quality companies. This is clearly evidenced when looking at the characteristics of the markets today (whether CP, ECP, MTN/EuroMTN or CD). Virtually all issuers are rated and most are investment grade.

The market for sub-investment grade and unrated money market issuers has all but vanished with recent, highly publicised defaults. The unrated paper market was active for a time but a combination of defaults and low profitability has confined almost all activity to the investment grade sector. The only exceptions to the rule which exist today are in the ECP and EuroMTN markets, which have seen activity from various Latin American issuers (a good deal of them sovereign issuers, although large, blue chip private sector issuers are increasingly penetrating the market). It should be noted, however, that these issuers have not up to now tapped the USCP market, where regulations and requirements are far stricter (and potential liabilities for dealers far greater, as will be discussed below). Many low quality banks and Savings & Loan institutions issued CDs in the late 1980s as well and the subsequent failure of many of these also reflects the inappropriateness of the CD product for low quality issuers.

RISK QUANTIFICATION

Inventories may be temporarily or permanently impaired in value either by the actions of the issuer or, to a lesser degree, by movements in market rates.

Since the former tend to be more detrimental to a bank in a worst case scenario, we focus our discussion of risk quantification on counterparty difficulties or default. As mentioned in Part II, there is no adjustment for inventory risks. In addition to inventory risk, dealers may also face a series of provisional risks, as detailed below.

Note that in a given money market programme there is risk not only to the dealer holding inventory in the issuer's paper but also to the investor, who is a third party participating in the transaction. While all our other discussions have centred on two-party transactions, ie the bank and its counterparty, we must now also consider that paper being issued is held by investors outside the bank.

Position (Inventory) Risk

With regard to rate movements, we know that a rise in interest rates after paper has been issued will cause a decline in the market value of the paper. If an investor or dealer needs to sell the paper prior to maturity, after such a movement has taken place, there will be a capital loss. Obviously, for dealers and investors able to hold paper to maturity, no loss will occur, as notes will be redeemed at par or face value.

Although market risk can affect the value of paper on a dealer's books, a far more serious impairment or loss can occur as a result of the financial actions and performance of the issuer itself. Such risks will far outweigh any loss attributable to market movements.

To illustrate, assume that XYZ issues $100m of MTNs through its dealer, with $20m held by the dealer and $80m by third party investors. While the notes are outstanding, XYZ has a bad year; financial performance is off sharply, the company is being sued by dissatisfied customers, etc. The market, upon hearing the news, may assign a lower value to the obligations of XYZ. We may further assume that third party investors panic at the news and liquidate their positions by selling either to the original dealer or to other 'bargain hunters' in the financial community. The large amount of sales will drive the value of the paper down further, either temporarily or permanently. The $100m of notes may now be worth only $90m. The dealer, holding $20m, will now find its position worth only $18m and will have to mark it down accordingly. Third party investors who sold out as the market was falling will have sustained a loss of $8m. This reflects the effect of an issuer's financial difficulties on an inventory position.

An actual default on money market paper is the most extreme example of position risk and will expose paper holders to the largest amount of market loss. If we suppose XYZ's problems to be so critical that it files for bankruptcy while its $100m of MTNs is still outstanding, the market will assign to the paper a value of less than 100 per cent; it will not necessarily be worth nothing, since the company may have some residual value and creditors (including MTN holders, who are senior and unsecured) may receive some value in a bankruptcy court. Certain financial institutions actively take positions in 'distressed' securities, analysing the fundamentals, assigning a value to the paper and buying it from those investors who feel that they may receive nothing from bankruptcy proceedings. No one can say for certain what the securities will be worth until all proceedings have been completed. In the interim the dealer and investors with inventory may find their holdings worth only 10 per cent of their face value. Thus the $100m of MTNs will be valued at $10m and losses on inventory positions will have to be recorded.

There is a fundamental difference between the risk on a money market instrument and the other instruments we have dealt with so far: if a counterparty defaults on a money market instrument, the investment bank or investor holding paper will always face a certain loss. Whereas with an option or an extended settlement, for example, a bank would have to experience a counterparty default while the value of the trade was in its favour to lose money (which we have already seen is dependent upon the difference between original and current level of rates), with a money market default this is not the case.

A counterparty default will always result in a fall in the value of money market paper, regardless of the level of interest rates. It is for that reason that money market inventory is close to a loan equivalent, with a 100 per cent risk factor. The actual market loss a dealer or investor may sustain cannot be calculated or estimated ahead of time because it is dependent largely upon the value of the company defaulting on the paper after bankruptcy proceedings (we emphasise once more that dealers and investors are unsecured). The most prudent approach is to assume that the entire amount of paper being held is at risk (ie there is no value in bankruptcy), although some fractional amount may actually be recovered.

From a credit officer's point of view there is a clear need to control the amount of a given issuer's securities held by the bank. This is accomplished through the establishment of an inventory limit. The typical uses of an inventory limit by a bank are twofold: to provide secondary market support for the securities (ie to facilitate trading between those investors wanting to sell and those wanting to buy; the bank will generally position the paper for a period of time until a new buyer is found, enabling the market to flow smoothly); and to allow own account or proprietary trading (ie if the bank feels that the paper is particularly attractive from an interest rate point of view, it may elect to hold the securities itself).

However, for an analyst the relevant question is not the use of the inventory but how large the limit should be. A general guide followed by most dealers is that an ongoing inventory limit should range from 20 to 30 per cent of the total programme where there is only one dealer, or $20m to $30m in the case of XYZ's programme above. Since a programme of this size is unlikely to be drawn down at once for final maturity on the same day and sold to a single investor, the percentage range indicated above can generally accommodate very comfortably both secondary and proprietary trading. Most maturities are staggered and paper is sold to a number of investors, so that a limit equal to the amount of the programme is unnecessary. Exceptions to the rule can, and do, exist and depend on the specific financing requirements of the issuer in question.

An inventory limit of 100 per cent of a programme would be unwise in credit terms, as the bank would then be at risk to a decline in market value for the full programme if it found itself holding all outstanding paper. In addition, if the bank found itself with an inventory position of 100 per cent of the programme (fully utilised), it would be assuming the role of a major unsecured lender; that is not the function of the money market dealer. Where there is more than one dealer, the size of the inventory limit can be reduced to 10 to 20 per cent of the programme because there will be other dealers performing the same functions in the secondary market.

Beyond setting an individual inventory limit for each programme, the credit officer may also want to limit inventory risk in total for a given issuer. In other words, if an issuer has a $100m CP programme, a $100m ECP programme and a $100m MTN programme (all sole dealerships), which would normally equate to up to $90m in inventory limits, the officer may choose to cap the total limits at some fraction of that, say $50m. Since it is unlikely the issuer would be tapping all three programmes simultaneously, it would not make sense to provide full limits for each one at the same time.

The credit officer must be also be vigilant towards actual usage of inventory limits over time. If an officer notes that the CP limits are almost constantly utilised (and determines from the trading desk that the positions are not for proprietary reasons), then he must examine why such a large amount is consistently being held by the bank instead of by investors. An inventory limit for secondary market support is intended to be a temporary bridge until new investors are found; it is not a permanent source of finance for the company. If new investors are not being found, it may be that the investor base has fears about the issuer or that the paper is being mispriced. In either event it should serve as a warning signal to the credit officer, who should establish the reasons and take appropriate action. In no circumstances does a bank want to be the sole financier under an unsecured money market programme inventory limit; that is the function and purpose of traditional bank lending.

The details regarding inventory risk as outlined above can be applied equally to CDs, CP, ECP, MTNs, EuroMTNs, BAs and other money market instruments. From an inventory risk standpoint, all money market products have the same risk characteristics. As an example, if an issuer is active with a

EuroMTN programme and a CP programme and bad news affects the value of the company's paper, it is very likely that the dealer and investor will sustain losses on both inventory positions. Although the relative amounts may be different (depending on coupons, amounts of paper outstanding, maturity considerations and other variables), the central point is that dealers and investors will have an inventory loss on both products.

Provisional Risk

NIF/RUF Underwriting Commitments
A bank providing an ECP underwriting commitment through a RUF or NIF, perhaps as a tender panel member (although tender panel members may sometimes be only placing agents and need not commit to any underwriting), could well find itself in a traditional lending position if the placement agents fail to allocate the borrower's notes to investors. Once a bank has funded the borrower through its underwriting commitment, it faces a set of risks equal to those found in traditional unsecured bank lending (ie a full 100 per cent exposure on the amount funded). The risks associated with an ECP programme supported by a bank syndicate generally apply only to the commercial banks participating as agents or tender panel members with underwriting commitments. Investment banks, who might be active as dealers, do not generally provide any direct funding commitments and would therefore not find themselves as direct lenders. Recall from Part I that a potential funding commitment under a RUF or NIF can be counted as a provisional risk, ie a risk which may increase exposure (and ultimately, perhaps, losses) should a future event occur.

Underwriter's Liability
Our discussion of risk in money market products is not complete until we turn to the question of underwriter's liability. This concept is most clearly and readily applied to USCP issuers, rather than to ECP, MTNs or EuroMTNs, so we limit our discussion to CP. As a note, it should be pointed out that in the defaults of Wang, Lomas, DFC and Integrated Resources in the ECP market dealers involved in the programmes were not found to have underwriter's liability; in other words, they were not required to reimburse investors in the paper for losses sustained.

Commercial paper is a unique security in that an investment bank involved in dealing in it is generally exposed to risks beyond the inventory exposure discussed above. According to the 1933 Act (which regulates public offerings), dealers of commercial paper are required to inform prospective investors about financial and other relevant details regarding an issuer and to ensure that no false statements or omissions occur in conveying this information. Much of the information disclosed to investors is gathered through due diligence.

Due diligence can best be described as the process of evaluating the financial performance and outlook of a given company by examining financial statements and associated documents (bank lines, forecasts and so on). Part of the process also involves interviewing officials from the company and having them personally review material issues relating to the company. Items which are considered material include merger, divestiture and acquisition plans, new products, new contracts, changes in the valuation of assets, changes in management, financial condition, pending litigation and so on. Information gathered from the due diligence process is generally compared with the disclosure or information statement distributed to investors to ensure that there are no omissions or false statements.

The need for due diligence and accurate communication of information has its foundation in Section 12 of the 1933 Act (paragraphs 681 and 683).

> Section 12. Any person who (1) offers or sells a security in violation of Section 5, or (2) offers or sells a security (whether or not exempted by the provisions of Section 3, other than paragraph (2) of Subsection (a) thereof), by the use of any means or instruments of transportation or communication in interstate commerce or of the mails, by means of a prospectus or oral communication, which includes an untrue statement of a material fact or omits to state a material fact necessary in order to make the statements in the light of the circumstances under which they were made, not misleading (the purchaser not knowing of the such untruth or omission), and who shall not sustain the burden of proof that he did not know, and in the exercises of reasonable care could not have known, of such untruth or omission, shall be liable to the person purchasing such security from him, who may sue either at law or in equity in any court of competent jurisdiction, to recover the consideration paid for such security, interest thereon, less the amount of any income received thereon, upon the tender of such security, or for damages if he no longer owns the security.

Several key phrases above reveal that if a person (ie a CP dealer) sells a security and, in doing so, either makes a false statement or neglects to inform the investor of some material fact, the investor purchasing the paper has recourse to the dealer, which will be required to reimburse the investor for funds lost in the transaction.

The particulars of a CP programme are generally communicated in an information memorandum or a disclosure statement, which contains facts on the programme structure as well as details on the issuer itself. It is by this disclosure that accurate information must be conveyed to the investors. There is no statutory requirement as to the form of such information or disclosure; it can range from being relatively simple to very detailed. The courts have established that, in order to sue successfully, the plaintiff must establish that there was a false statement or omission in the disclosure, not necessarily that the plaintiff relied on the disclosure to reach a decision to buy the notes.

Note that Section 12 of the 1933 Act is more general in nature than Section 11. Section 12 is concerned with miscommunication of facts by any form (prospectus, disclosure statement, information memorandum and so on, provided there is use of mail or facilities of interstate commerce). Section 11, in contrast, is primarily concerned with miscommunication as it relates to the registration statement. Since CP is exempt from registration under the exemptions detailed above, the filing of a registration statement is not required. Thus, liability under Section 12 is applicable to our discussion of CP, while liability under Section 11 is applicable to our discussion of bonds (which are registered securities), covered in the next chapter.

It should be pointed out that an issuer and/or dealer may also be liable for the same omissions and false statements under Rule 10b-5 of Section 10(b) of the Securities Exchange Act of 1934 (the 1934 Act) which regulates public companies. Although 10b-5 liability is applicable primarily in instances involving the sale or purchase of a security (where security is defined in the 1934 Act as having a maturity of more than nine months), courts have found commercial paper within the scope of the 1934 Act (*Zeller* v *Bogue Electric Manufacturing Corp, (476 F 2d 795, 800 (2nd Cir), cert denied, 414 US 908 (1973))*), despite a maturity of less than nine months. A key difference with 10b-5 liability, however, is that the plaintiff must demonstrate '*scienter*' (a state embracing intent to deceive, manipulate or defraud) as an element in the action; no such requirement is necessary under Section 12 liability. As such, it is generally believed that legal action against a commercial paper dealer is easier under the 1933 Act than the 1934 Act. A full quotation of Rule 10b-5 is included in the next chapter for reference.

From a practical standpoint we can consider the following scenario. Assume that Company Y is a commercial paper issuer with middle tier credit ratings. The paper of Company Y is placed by Investment Bank X on a regular basis. As part of the annual credit due diligence process a credit officer at X goes to visit Y to review past and expected financial results, as well as any other topics which might affect the quality of the credit in the future. During one of these sessions the credit officer learns that within 30 days Y will probably lose five of its largest sales accounts, which together account for more than 60 per cent of the company's gross sales. Upon his return to the bank, the credit officer documents the results of his visit with the company for the bank's credit files but omits to include any reference to the potential loss of its major accounts (this may be because he did not want to, he forgot to, he was being negligent, etc). The bank's dealers continue to issue the paper and continue to represent to investors that the paper is a good middle quality investment (because they are unaware of any problems).

Thirty days later the news of the account losses becomes public and the company decides that it will have to seek bankruptcy court protection because loss of the sales revenue will leave it unable to service its interest obligations. Investors holding Y's now defaulted paper demand that the investment bank repurchase the notes at a price which will reimburse them for losses sustained.

After an internal review by the bank reveals that the credit officer omitted to inform the dealers and the investors of a very material fact it becomes apparent that the bank will have no option but to repurchase the paper at 100 per cent of its value on the date it was sold. The market value of the paper following the announcement may have fallen to 30 (its perceived or estimated value in bankruptcy) and the bank must bear this loss. In addition to reimbursing investors for their losses, the bank would also suffer a loss on any inventory holdings it had.

The bank was clearly negligent in performing its duties and it withheld material information which affected the value of the paper being sold. From an investor's point of view it does not matter where the 'weak link' in the due diligence chain occurs; if the credit officer neglects to inform the bankers and traders of the problem, or if the officer informs the bankers and traders who elect to issue more paper in any event, the result is the same: the bank acting as dealer has been negligent in its duties and the investor has lost money and will have to be reimbursed. Underwriter's liability is, then, the means by which an investor can protect itself from the negligent actions of the commercial paper dealer.

Consider for a moment the opposite scenario, where a dealer fulfils the role outlined in the 1933 Act. Investment Bank Y performs its due diligence and, learning of the potential loss of accounts, urges the company not to reissue new commercial paper when existing notes mature until disclosure of these facts can be made public (care must be taken not to follow any steps which would result in the bank's profiting from what is very obviously 'inside information'; a defensive posture, such as not reissuing new paper and urging the company to make an immediate and full public disclosure of the problems, could be one solution. That, however, may have ramifications of its own if CP is the sole or primary source of funding for the issuer. In any event it is vital that a bank's legal counsel be involved throughout the process).

If paper is already outstanding when the negative information comes to light, it is quite clear that the bank should not be held liable. Investors should have no recourse to the bank as it was not in possession of material information nor did it omit any facts at the time of the original sale of paper. It was only upon learning of the new information through the due diligence process that the investment bank took action designed to avoid possible losses for all those involved, dealer and investor alike.

There is, of course, precedent in determining and assigning underwriter's liability and it has commanded increased attention in recent years. The watershed case occurred in March 1970 when the Penn Central

Transportation Company defaulted on its CP; at the time of default the company had $82m in notes outstanding, sold through its dealer, Goldman, Sachs. Following the court cases (including *Franklin Savings Bank of NY* v *Levy (F 2d 521, 527 (2nd Cir 1977))*, *University Hill* v *Goldman, Sachs (422 F Supp 879 (SDNY 1976))*, *Alton Box* v *Goldman, Sachs (418 F Supp 1149 (EDMo 1976))*, *Welch Foods* v *Goldman, Sachs (398 F Supp 1393 (SDNY 1974))*, etc) it was determined that Goldman was at fault for not taking proper care in determining the deteriorating financial condition of Penn Central and advising investors of such deterioration. As a result, Goldman was forced to reimburse investors for losses sustained through reliance on its declaration that the Penn Central CP they were purchasing was prime quality.

Other similar precedent exists in *Sanders v John Nuveen & Co (463 F 2d 1075 (7th Cir) cert denied, 409 US 1009 (1972) and 619 F 2d 1222 (7th Cir 1980))*. In this case Nuveen sold Winter & Hirsch's CP with disclosure indicating that there would be no question of the company's being able to repay its obligations at maturity. When Winter filed for bankruptcy there was $1.6m in paper outstanding and investors sued to recover. Nuveen had relied on fraudulent financial statements prepared by the company and its auditors in its assessment of Winter's ability to repay. The courts ruled that Nuveen should have been in a position to know that the financials were fraudulent and, knowing that, no CP should have been sold. Nuveen was found liable and was forced to repay investors.

Recent defaults involving Lomas Financial, Colorado Ute, Mortgage and Realty Trust and Columbia Gas have also served to focus attention on the due diligence process and the potential liability of dealers; those cases are currently being resolved.

The implications of the above are far-reaching. Since the USCP market is now in excess of $550b, the volume of potential liability is substantial. While virtually all unrated issuers are out of the market (and low rated issuers make up only a small fraction of it), banks active as dealers must still account for the fact that good credits can become bad credits very rapidly (particularly in trying economic times). As a result, dealers need to be vigilant across the entire range of issuers, performing due diligence on a regular basis, updating disclosure statements to reflect changing conditions at a particular issuer and limiting, in some instances, the total amount of paper issued for a given company. Many dealers have dedicated credit units whose sole function is to monitor the CP process and to perform due diligence.

As indicated above, a credit officer will very often want to 'cap' the amount of CP sold by the trading desk (generally after discussion with the banking and trading teams), in accordance with both the creditworthiness of the issuer and the number of other dealers active on the programme. Where a particular issuer has selected only one dealer to sell its commercial paper, a maximum issuance limit may not be an option but several dealers are generally assigned to most large programmes, so that a limit on paper sold is a reasonable idea.

From a credit officer's point of view the risk faced in dealing CP is not so easily quantified as the risk on some of the products dealt with so far. We have already seen that, with an inventory position, the investment bank will have dollar-for-dollar exposure; if the issuer defaults on its paper and the investment bank has a position, it will sustain some loss (whether 100 per cent or a smaller proportion cannot be determined beforehand).

The proportion of risk on CP accounted for by underwriter's liability is not, however, so easily assessed. If an investment bank has performed its due diligence function properly (has put forth material facts in its disclosure and has not omitted any material information or made any false statements) and the issuer defaults, investors will have no recourse to the bank. The bank's exposure will then be limited to any inventory position it might be carrying on its own books. However, if due diligence was not properly conducted and the courts rule the bank to be liable under Section 12 (or under 10b-5), then it will clearly be forced to reimburse investors up to the amount of paper sold.

Thus, an investment bank's exposure can be thought of as provisional, as discussed in Part I. Ignoring inventory positions, it will have no direct exposure to the issuer in performing the dealer function so long as the issuer does not default and it has performed its due diligence requirement properly.

Letter of Credit Support

The same line of thinking can be applied to LOC-backed CP programmes (Section 3(a)(2) paper). Under a typical arrangement an issuer (perhaps sub-investment grade or a private concern unwilling to disclose detailed financial information publicly) will essentially 'rent' the rating of a given bank for a fee. If Bank XYZ is rated A−1+/P−1 by Standard & Poor's and Moody's, the issuer will pay XYZ a fee so that those ratings are transferred to its paper. Now the issuer has an A−1+/P−1 programme, while Bank XYZ has an off-balance sheet exposure to the issuer (plus a fee of several basis points).

For an investor, the credit risk being faced is that of XYZ, not the issuer. Most common among such programmes is the direct pay letter of credit. This forces the bank to pay the investor at maturity and the bank then seeks reimbursement from the issuer. This is the safest mechanism for an investor because at no time will he or she be exposed to the credit of the issuer. Under a standby letter of credit the investor will seek its funds directly from the issuer at maturity. Should the issuer be unable (or unwilling) to pay, the support bank will reimburse the investor and then attempt to get its own funds back from the issuer; in essence, the bank 'stands by' until its services are required.

For a dealer involved in selling LOC-backed paper, the due diligence concepts discussed above are applicable. Nevertheless, the focus of the due diligence will be on the bank providing the letter of credit (as the true provider of the credit rating), rather than on the issuer. If a dealer sells paper (and positions some for its own account), the credit exposure taken on the books must be attributed to the LOC bank. Thus, in our discussion of provisional exposure arising from the sale of CP (and in any direct inventory position taken), the credit officer must allocate these limits from its total exposure to the bank. This is always true when dealing with direct pay LOCs, since at no time is the dealer facing the issuer.

In a standby LOC the dealer technically has exposure to the issuer until a default occurs; for all practical purposes, however, it may make sense to attribute the exposure to the LOC provider immediately. In a worst case scenario (admittedly difficult to picture) we can imagine a situation where the issuer defaults on its CP and, shortly thereafter, the LOC bank goes under as well. The credit officer needs to know its total exposure to the LOC bank at all times, including third party CP exposures carried through the LOC support mechanism; this can effectively be captured as a provisional risk.

RISK FACTORS

While in other chapters we have used the concept of the risk factor (RF) for risk equivalency calculations, money market instruments require no such adjustment. Inventories carry dollar-for-dollar risk weighting (implying an RF of 100 per cent), while underwriter's liability carries some risk weighting which could potentially be 100 per cent, should an issuer default and the dealer be held liable. Thus, no sample RFs are required for this chapter.

A FINAL NOTE ON REGISTRATION REQUIREMENTS

Schedule A of the 1933 Act (paragraphs 901–933) states the requirements for registration of securities (for non-foreign government issuers). These requirements indicate that any institutions wishing to issue securities (and not using one of the exemptions) must provide the following information:

1. The business name of the issuer.
2. The name of the state or other sovereign power under which the issuer is organised.
3. The business address of the issuer.
4. The names and addresses of the executive personnel and promoters.
5. The names and addresses of the underwriters.
6. The names and addresses of all persons owning 10 per cent of any class of stock of the issuer within 20 days prior to the filing of the registration statement.
7. The amount of securities of the issuer held by any person named under 4, 5 or 6.

8. The general character of the business.
9. A statement of capitalisation of the issuer.
10. A statement of the securities covered by options outstanding or to be created, together with the names and addresses of all persons to be allotted more than 10 per cent of such options.
11. The amount of capital stock of each class.
12. The amount and description of the funded debt outstanding.
13. The purpose and amount devoted to such purpose of the funds.
14. The remuneration paid by the issuer to the directors and officers wherever such remuneration exceeds $25,000 during any year.
15. The estimated net proceeds derived from the security.
16. The price at with the security shall be offered.
17. All commissions or discounts paid or to be paid by the issuer or the underwriters.
18. The amount, itemised in reasonable detail, of expenses, other than commissions, in connection with the sale of the security.
19. The net proceeds derived from any security sold by the issuer during the two years preceding the filing of the registration statement, the price of the security and the names of the underwriters.
20. Any payment to any promoter within two years preceding the filing of the registration.
21. The names and addresses of vendors and purchase price of any property acquired in part or whole from the proceeds of the security to be offered.
22. The full particulars of the nature and extent of the interest of every director, principal executive officer and every stockholder holding more than 10 per cent of any class of stock in any property acquired, not in the ordinary course of business of the issuer.
23. The dates and parties to any contract made, not in the ordinary course of business in excess of $2,500 per year.
24. A balance sheet of the issuer.
25. A profit and loss statement of the issuer.
26. A profit and loss statement for the acquired business.
27. A copy of any agreement made with any underwriter.
28. A copy of the opinion of counsel in respect of the legality of the issue.
29. A copy of all material contracts.
30. A copy of all organisation papers.
31. A copy of the underlying securities agreements or indentures.
32. Miscellaneous items as required.

Note: foreign government issuers must adhere to a lesser list of requirements contained in Schedule B of the 1933 Act, paragraphs 941–954.

11: Bonds

DESCRIPTION

Any discussion of bonds and the bond markets will be lengthy and detailed because the market is large and the variations on the standard bond concept are substantial and growing. In the very simplest form a bond is an interest-bearing debt obligation or corporate IOU. It is a security which represents a company's promise to repay at some time in the future (and to make periodic interest payments to) an investor who has lent it money. The 'promise' also includes details of when and how the investor will be fully repaid. When a company needs to raise funds and elects to do so using debt (as opposed to equity) one of the main vehicles available to fulfil the requirement is a bond.

In a typical bond arrangement Company A contacts its investment bankers, who structure a deal with certain characteristics (interest rate, frequency of interest payments, final maturity, call provisions, sinking fund and other important details) described in a document called a bond indenture. Once the particulars have been agreed and finalised, the investment bank sells the bonds to investors, who provide the cash to Company A (and in the process become creditors of the company). Over a period of time Company A pays all investors (also known as bondholders) a certain amount of interest on an agreed, periodic basis. The original investors may hold the securities to maturity or sell them to a bond dealer or another investor. Depending on such factors as the credit quality of the issuer, the interest rate on the paper in comparison with current market rates and so on, there will be varying degrees of liquidity in the secondary market for that paper. At maturity Company A will repay investors the initial principal lent to the firm and the bond will have been 'retired'.

In a market that must respond to the individual financing requirements of diverse issuers there are many variations on the theme. The first part of this chapter will explore some of the most common forms of bond but does not attempt to deal with all of them. There are many excellent works devoted solely to the study of bonds to which the reader may (and should) refer.

Eurobonds

Bonds can be issued in any of several different markets. The offshore market, or Euromarket, is a primary source of financing for many companies. Bonds issued in the Euromarket are known as Eurobonds and carry with them certain unique characteristics. First, they may not be sold in the US or to US investors. US companies may, of course, issue Eurobonds and do so through offshore subsidiaries to offshore investors. Secondly, Eurobonds can generally be brought to market very quickly with documentation and due diligence to be formalised and finalised after the security has been issued. In addition, there are no formal registration requirements such as those in the US markets. These last two points enable an issuer to enter the market quickly to benefit from a favourable move in rates. The bulk of Eurobond trading takes place in London, with issues generated in a variety of offshore currencies: Eurodollars, Euroyen, Eurodeutschmarks and so on. Eurobonds may be publicly or privately placed.

US Domestic Bonds

The domestic US market is home to both US public bonds and private placement bonds. As with CP, bonds issued in the public market can be bought and sold without restriction, whereas private placement bonds are traded only between a small group of parties (the original investor, the dealer and perhaps a second investor). Recent changes to the Securities Act allow the use of Rule 144A language in private placement deals; such language allows 144A bonds to be traded among a certain amount of qualified institutional buyers (or QIBs) and not simply among original investors and the dealer. The hope is that 144A language will help develop liquidity in the private placement market for bonds (and certain money market instruments such as MTNs and EuroMTNs). Bonds issued in the US market must adhere to SEC registration requirements, which will be discussed in greater detail in this chapter.

Foreign Bonds

Foreign companies issuing dollar-denominated bonds in the US markets are said to be issuing yankee bonds. Non-resident companies issuing in local currencies in other local markets are said to be issuing matilda bonds (A$ bonds in Australia), matador bonds (peseta bonds in Spain), samurai bonds (yen bonds in Japan), bulldog bonds (sterling bonds in the UK) and so on.

Junk Bonds

Certain corporate, financial and sovereign issuers have been active over the past few years in the issuance of high yield (or junk) bonds. Junk bonds are bonds issued by sub-investment grade companies and are priced accordingly. Since the risk of default is thought to be greater, the coupons on the bonds are much higher. Where an investment grade company might issue at 1 or 2 per cent above a Treasury benchmark of 6 per cent, a sub-investment grade company might be forced to pay 15 per cent or more (ie a 9 per cent premium) on its paper. There has been substantial press reporting in the past two years on the junk bond market (which was brought into the limelight by Drexel Burnham Lambert in the mid-1980s), junk bond defaults and the abuses of the market during the 1980s. While the market for junk bonds slumped after the collapse of Drexel in 1990, activity in late 1991 and early 1992 appears to reflect some renewed interest among investors. Entities tapping the high yield market now (albeit in the Euromarkets) include some Latin American sovereign and corporate issuers.

Zero Coupon Bonds

Another type of security which has been popular for several years is the zero coupon bond. Where a typical bond will pay interest on a periodic basis and principal at maturity, a zero coupon will pay the investor no interest. In exchange for not receiving the periodic coupon the investor will purchase the zero coupon at a deep discount to face value; at maturity the zero coupon will be redeemed at par. For example, rather than paying $100m to receive 8 per cent semi-annually on a 10-year $100m bond (and the $100m back in 10 years' time), an investor might pay only $30m for a $100m zero coupon bond. Instead of collecting interest every six months, however, the investor would receive nothing until maturity, when he would receive the full $100m. At inception and at maturity the investor will be indifferent between the two schemes, as they are financially identical. However, the characteristics of the zero coupon mean that its volatility (ie the movement of the bond's price relative to the movement in interest rates) is much greater than that of a normal bond. An investor not holding the bond to maturity could face a larger capital gain or loss as a result. Zero coupons are available on certain US Government and corporate securities.

Convertible bonds

Convertible bonds are a hybrid, in that they are issued as regular bonds but may end up being converted into equity. As the name suggests, a convertible gives the investor the right to change a debt obligation into an equity participation should a specified conversion level be reached (conversion levels, known as premia, are typically 15 to 20 per cent above the issuer's equity price at the time the convertible is issued). If conversion takes place, the investor no longer has an interest-bearing debt obligation but an equity holding. As an equity holder, the investor now receives a dividend payment (if the company pays dividends) and ranks below subordinated debt holders and preferred stock holders in bankruptcy. However, the investor also stands to gain in the event of any capital appreciation in the underlying value of the stock. It is worth noting that not all convertible bonds will be changed into equity; if the conversion premium is not reached, they will continue to function as normal bonds until they are retired.

Bond Characteristics

Coupons on bonds may be either fixed or floating. Fixed rate bonds (also known as straight bonds) pay a fixed coupon throughout their lives, while floating rate bonds or floating rate notes (FRNs) adjust on a periodic basis to a new level dictated by the underlying benchmark rate (LIBOR-based, CD-based, CP-based or whatever). In addition to straight and floating bonds, there are various derivative structures, including step-up floaters (notes with spreads which increase on a certain schedule), step-down floaters (notes with spreads which decrease on a certain schedule), rating sensitive floaters (notes with rates which change depending upon credit quality) and so on.

Bonds can be issued in either bearer or registered form. As with other bearer securities, flows on bearer bonds are payable to the person in physical possession of the bond at the time of coupon or interest payment. The flows on registered bonds, in contrast, are payable only to the person registered with the bond trustee as the owner. When ownership changes the bond is re-registered with the trustee in the name of the new owner.

In addition to maintaining records of owners, trustees play other important roles in the bond issuance process. Chief among these is to monitor the issuer's compliance with terms stated in the bond indenture and to receive payments from the issuer ('sinking fund' payments) to be applied to repayment of principal at maturity. When a bond issuer pays a periodic coupon to investors it may also make a payment equal to some fractional portion of the total principal of the bond to the trustee. This payment will grow to an amount equal to the initial principal, which is returned to investors at maturity. The principal of bonds which have no sinking fund provision is repaid in full at maturity in a single payment to investors. These bonds are known as 'bullet bonds'. There is perhaps more comfort for an investor in the knowledge that a regular payment is being paid to the trustee than in relying on the issuer's ability to come up with sufficient funds to redeem the bond at maturity. New bonds will often be issued to replace maturing bonds.

The level of security or collateral associated with a bond is one of the main characteristics of which bond investors must always be aware. If a bond is issued with some express security or collateral attached to it (eg a commercial property, an aircraft lease, a cash deposit, etc), the bond is said to be secured. Investors in secured bonds rank at the top of the list of bond holders in the event of a bankruptcy, since they have first right to certain assets pledged in support of the bond. The assets securing bonds are real and should have some economic value, even in bankruptcy. Secured bonds can take a variety of forms (depending on the assets providing the security); escrow bonds, mortgage bonds, equipment trust certificates and collateral trust certificates are all examples of secured bonds.

Bonds which are not secured by any real assets are known as unsecured bonds or debentures. Within this category there are various levels to consider: at the top of the list are senior unsecured bonds, followed by subordinated bonds (or subordinated debentures) and junior subordinated bonds. The ranking within this category once again pertains to claims in bankruptcy. The senior unsecured bondholders will be repaid before subordinated bondholders (but after secured bondholders). Likewise, subordinated bondholders will receive proceeds before junior subordinated bondholders. Naturally, those investors willing to acquire the 'lower ranking' bonds will receive a higher coupon as a trade-off for the higher risk. Convertible bonds (discussed below) rank after subordinated bonds but ahead of preferred and common stockholders.

Many bonds have call provisions giving the issuer the right to redeem the bonds at some future date, prior to maturity. Since the call provision is potentially beneficial to the issuer (and potentially detrimental to the investor), the investor will typically be compensated *via* a slightly higher rate on the coupon. Since most bonds are not callable for an initial period of several years, the investor receives the additional spread during that time. Naturally, if rates fall dramatically during the life of the bond, an issuer will call and redeem the existing issue and reissue another bond at a lower coupon rate. In this case the bondholders will have to reinvest their principal at lower rates and are said to be facing 'reinvestment risk'.

Many bond issues are publicly rated by one or more of the rating agencies and, as with CP and other money market instruments, pricing of bonds in the secondary market will often depend on these ratings. As one would expect, issuers with the highest ratings (ie investment grade) will trade at narrower spreads to a Treasury or LIBOR benchmark than issuers with lower ratings.

Issuers of bonds cover a broad spectrum. Corporations, utilities, financial institutions, sovereign governments and municipalities are all active. The bulk of bond trading actually occurs in the over-the-counter markets, although certain bonds are also exchange-traded (though they account for a much smaller proportion of total outstanding paper). Settlement of most bonds generally occurs within five business days, although some foreign bond markets have somewhat different conventions. Eurobonds generally clear through Euroclear or Cedel, major bond clearing houses located in Brussels.

Bonds are brought to market through a bond underwriter (known as a lead manager) and, very often, a syndicate of co-underwriters. Although the precise mechanics of the process are dependent upon both market practice and any special circumstances surrounding a particular issue, in most cases it works as follows: a bank or investment bank contracts with an issuer to underwrite a bond In receiving the mandate to issue the bonds, the bank will have committed itself either to an underwritten offer (or 'bought' deal) or to a 'best efforts deal; in the former the bank commits to selling a certain amount of bonds, whether or not it actually can. If it cannot, it will take the bonds on its own books and attempt to sell them at a later date (or simply hold them to maturity, although that is not something it is likely to wish to do). From an issuer's point of view an underwritten bond is preferable because it allows the issuer to know exactly how much will be raised through the financing. In a 'best efforts' deal, however, the bank agrees only to sell as many bonds as the market will bear. If there is interest in only $50m of a planned $100m issue, the bank is under no obligation to sell more than $50m and will not have to take any bonds on its own books unless it chooses to do so. From a credit officer's perspective a 'best efforts' deal is generally preferable, since it does not commit the bank to a set amount of paper. As one might expect, fully underwritten deals typically carry a higher set of fees for the bank, since a greater amount of risk is being assumed in the transaction.

Once the mandate has been awarded, a syndicate of co-underwriters (the co-managers) is formed; they will assist in distributing the bonds (note that in certain issues an underwriting group and a selling group may also be formed to assist in the distribution process). The lead manager is the 'book runner' and decides the ultimate allocation of bonds among the underwriting syndicate. This is naturally the most coveted spot in any underwriting, since it gives the bank a great deal of power in allocating the bonds and dictating the progress of the deal.

Just prior to market entry the deal is priced and is then sold into the primary market by the syndicate. In the Euromarket it was formerly common practice for syndicate members to cut pricing during the primary offer in order to sell the bonds out (a good example of 'predatory pricing'). In recent years there has been a change to the 'fixed price re-offer' system more common in the US public markets: this involves a firm commission schedule for all syndicate members during the initial distribution phase. In exchange for this fee schedule, the syndicate members agree not to cut prices or to sell to the semi-professional market during syndication. Once the deal is fully sold out, the syndicate 'breaks' and the price is free to move as dictated by the market. This has added a certain amount of profitability back to the

Eurobond market, which went through a period of very tight margins (particularly on highly competitive, high profile deals).

It should be noted that, although the fixed price re-offer system has added profitability to the Euromarkets and has generally worked well, a number of deals in 1991 and 1992 have drifted away from the concept and are once again threatening the profitability of the sector. The eventual fate of the system in the Eurobond market remains to be seen.

Prior to the early 1980s, if a company wanted to enter the US bond market it would have to go through a lengthy registration process (see the end of Chapter 10 for a list of registration requirements). The time and detail required to complete the process did not permit a company to take advantage of rapidly changing interest rates or exchange rates. In 1982 the SEC passed a temporary rule allowing a company to register a specified or unspecified issue of securities to be underwritten at some point in the future. This temporary rule was extended in 1983 and became permanent in 1984. It is now Rule 415 of the Securities Act of 1933 (the 1933 Act) and is referred to in the financial industry as a '415 shelf registration' or simply a 'shelf registration' because it allows a company to take securities 'off the shelf' and sell them as required. Rule 415 specifically allows a company to issue a maximum amount of securities (debt or equity), on a continuous or delayed basis, over a two-year period, without the need for new registration. Naturally, an initial registration statement must still be filed prior to initial issuance.

The advantages of a shelf registration are clear. If Company Y establishes a shelf registration for $500m of senior debt securities in an environment where rates are relatively high, it can issue some small portion of the $500m in bonds right away. Should rates drop further during the two-year period, Company Y can quickly take advantage of the situation by issuing more securities without spending any additional time on the registration process. The advent of Rule 415 has meant that both issuers and underwriters can quickly get bonds (or equities) into the market in an efficient fashion.

GENERAL CREDIT CONSIDERATIONS

We return once more to our credit decision-making framework.

Risk

The risk on bond underwritings and subsequent market making can be high. The potential for underwriter's liability may also exist. The BIS risk weighting for private sector bond inventories is 100 per cent, while for OECD sovereign inventories it is 0 per cent. Guarantees in support of bond issues are weighted at 100 per cent.

Return

Return on a standard bond transaction with a medium quality counterparty is low to medium. With more esoteric or complex deals, such as convertibles or bought deals, the return is high. Capital charge spreads for private sector inventories are high, given both the substantial BIS risk weightings and the high risk associated with bond inventories. Charges are lower for sovereign issuer inventories.

Maturity

Maturities for bonds range from medium- to long-term.

Motivation

As with money market instruments, bond transactions are funding vehicles and cannot be characterised as hedging, speculation, arbitrage or yield enhancing.

Enhancement

Secured bonds are by definition enhanced by the assets on the issuer's balance sheet; debentures and convertibles have no enhancement. In certain instances weaker issuers may opt for third party support to enhance a particular transaction.

Creditworthiness

In the recent past the view of many professionals indicated that bonds were appropriate for virtually any company, regardless of credit quality. The late 1980s epitomised this phase of thinking and this was one of the primary reasons for the tremendous growth of the high yield market. Since historical data at one point suggested that default rates on high yield bonds were no greater than default rates on investment grade bonds, a rapid and widespread growth in sub-investment grade bond issuance ensued. While some of the debt issued on behalf of sub-investment grade companies was legitimate and perhaps ultimately useful, a threshold was crossed at which point any company, no matter how financially weak, could find a willing underwriter (who could find willing investors) to raise funds in the bond market.

Some of the high profile bond defaults of the recent past (eg Campeau Corp, Federated Department Stores, Memorex Telex, EII Holdings, TWA, Maxwell Communications and PanAm, to name but a few) have caused a change in thinking about the appropriateness of issuing bonds for the most uncreditworthy companies (see Chapter 2 for additional details). While there is certainly a role for high yield financing in the bond markets, it is also clear that more and better discrimination needs to be factored into the underwriting process. Some companies at the very bottom of the credit quality scale are not appropriate issuers of bonds and care must be taken to exclude them. While there are strong profit motivations for underwriting such deals, it is the job of the credit officer to examine, and reject, deals for those issuers which have no real chance of financial survival.

The maturity of the bond issue is something which the credit officer must also consider, particularly with sub-investment grade issuers. Where a two-year bond deal may be appropriate for a particular company, a five-, seven- or 10-year deal may not. Financial projections beyond a few years are a difficult task to perform with accuracy.

When a medium- or long-term underwriting is being considered for a weak counterparty, the credit officer will, of necessity, have to be as conservative as possible in making assumptions, projections and recommendations. Fully underwritten deals and ongoing inventory limits for sub-investment grade issuers are inadvisable.

As one might expect, the concerns about issuing bonds for the lowest quality clients disappear as one moves up the credit quality spectrum. Bond deals (including fully underwritten transactions) are quite appropriate for medium and high quality clients and ongoing inventory limits for these credits are usually in order.

RISK QUANTIFICATION

Dealing in bonds leaves a bank exposed primarily to counterparty performance and how it affects inventory positions; also, as with money market instruments, there is a degree of market risk present. As before, we take counterparty risk to be the greater of the two, so will focus this discussion on the losses a bank may face as a result of financial difficulties with the issuer. In this light, no risk adjustment is necessary. Note that a bond underwriter may also face provisional risk through underwriter's liability, as discussed below.

Position (Inventory) Risk

With regard to market risk, a temporary or permanent loss of value in inventories may occur because of adverse interest rate movements. Any

Table 11.1. Company X's Bonds: Values after Bankruptcy

Security	Original value	Value after Bankruptcy	Net loss
Bond 1	$10m	$7m	$3m
Bond 2, Tranche A	$5m	$2m	$3m
Bond 2, Tranche B	$5m	0	$5m
Total	$20m	$9m	$11m

investor or dealer holding bonds in position and needing to liquidate prior to maturity for any reason will sustain a market loss if rates increase. However, the loss sustained by a movement in rates will be insignificant compared with the loss sustained by counterparty default.

With any inventory position, a dealer or investor is also exposed to risk of loss stemming from the financial condition and performance of the issuer. Bad or unexpected news about the bond issuer (regarding earnings, sales, litigation, a takeover, etc) can temporarily or permanently impair the value of the bond position, resulting in a loss which must be recognised.

Permanent loss of value to the investor and dealer comes with an actual default on the bond by the issuer (this assumes that the dealer is holding a position in the bonds at the time of default, which is possible but not always true). If an issuer's problems are so severe that it can no longer service its interest payments (let alone repay principal in either amortised or bullet form), bankruptcy may be the only alternative. Once a company files for bankruptcy, there will be a lower value to any outstanding security, including bonds. From the point of view of the bond dealer and the investor bankruptcy is the critical point: those bondholders which are secured or senior will stand a better chance of recovering a portion of their original investment than will subordinated bondholders.

Consider the following scenario: Bond Dealer A, a major investment bank, underwrites two separate bond issues for Company X. Bond 1 is a $100m senior secured bond with five-year maturity and a 6 per cent fixed coupon. Bond 2 is in two tranches: Tranche A is a $50m senior unsecured bond with five-year maturity and an 8 per cent fixed coupon and Tranche B is a $50m subordinated bond with five-year maturity and an 11 per cent fixed coupon. One year into the deal Company X files for bankruptcy under the weight of customer litigation (which occurred after the underwriting). Bond Dealer A, as an active market player, had $10m bond inventory limits for each of the bonds (including $5m each of Tranches A and B). At the end of bankruptcy proceedings it finds its positions are worth the values set out in Table 11.1.

In bankruptcy proceedings (and subsequent asset liquidations) Bond Dealer A's secured position lost only 30 per cent of its value (because the office building securing the bond was acquired by another company at a reasonable price). The unsecured position held value reasonably well considering there was no security but the subordinated piece was worth nothing since, by the time the general creditors and senior secured and unsecured bondholders were paid out, there were no more assets to be distributed. Following logically from this point, preferred and common equity holders received no payout either. The above example does not suggest that a bond dealer should position only secured bonds; it simply means that the credit officer, in establishing limits to deal with position risk, must be aware of the fact that the subordinated and senior unsecured positions have less protection and are susceptible to more risk than secured positions.

As we have discussed before, an issuer defaulting on a bond or money market instrument will always cause a bank with inventory to face a loss, whereas a default on a swap or extended settlement, for example, may not necessarily result in a loss, depending upon the level and direction of rates since the beginning of a given trade. For that reason bond inventories are risk adjusted at a 100 per cent factor; in fact, as we have seen in Chapters 5 and 10, inventories are classified as a separate risk category. No one can be certain about the value of a company after bankruptcy; it may depend upon variables which come into play after the bond has been underwritten. Prudence dictates valuing an inventory position at zero when there is great uncertainty as to the true value (if any) after bankruptcy.

As with all inventories, there is a clear need to limit the total holdings of a given issuer's bonds; failure to do so could leave the bank exposed to unacceptably large risks. The typical uses of a bond inventory limit by a bank are to provide secondary market support and for own account or proprietary trading. From an analyst's point of view, however, the question is how large the limit should actually be (and whether secured, senior or subordinated tranches feature). It is unlikely that a bank will want to be a large, permanent source of finance for a given issuer, so total inventories may be limited to 10 or 20 per cent of a given bond issue, depending upon the size of the dealer syndicate, the quality of the issuer, the level of security (if any) and so on. Subordinated and junior subordinated inventories should be minimal (perhaps just enough to allow for market making), because it is these positions which stand a chance of being worth nothing in the event of a default.

Underwriter's Liability

The concept of underwriter's liability as discussed in Chapter 10 remains applicable to a certain extent in the discussion on bonds issued in the US markets (where US laws and regulations apply). It is difficult, however, to imagine the same concepts applying in the offshore markets, unless there are specific regulations to the same effect. To the best of the author's knowledge, there has never been a lawsuit in the Euromarkets involving underwriter's liability.

Section 11 of the 1933 Act calls for 'reasonable investigation' to be conducted prior to the issuance of debt or equity securities. False statements or omissions by the issuer in the registration statement or the disclosure document will leave the issuer liable for losses incurred by investors as a result of those statements or omissions. The underwriter will also be conditionally liable for the same damages, unless it has performed due diligence, disclosed all material facts and made no false or misleading statements.

Paragraphs 651–6, Section 11(a) of the 1933 Act state that,

> In case any part of the registration statement, when such part became effective, contained an untrue statement of a material fact or omitted to state a material fact required to be stated therein or necessary to make the statements therein not misleading, any person acquiring such security (unless it is proved that at the time of such acquisition he know of such untruth or omission) may, either at law or in equity, in any court of competent jurisdiction, sue –
> Signers of the Registration Statement
> Directors and Partners
> Persons Named as being, or about to become, Directors or Partners
> Accountants, Engineers, Appraisers or Other Professional Persons
> Underwriters

Paragraphs 658–661 state that no 'no person, other than the issuer shall be liable . . . provided that . . . before the effective date of the part of the registration statement with respect to which his liability is asserted . . . he had, after reasonable investigation, reasonable ground to believe and did believe . . . that the statements therein were true and that there was no omission to state a material fact required to be stated therein or necessary to make the statements therein not misleading'.

Recall from the previous chapter that dealer liability in the CP market is governed by Section 12 of the Act. As we indicate above, the potential liability facing a bond underwriter is captured in Section 11, which relates specifically to issuers filing a registration statement. Since all bond offerings in the US must be registered either prior to issuance or every two years in shelf format, a registration statement is the central document which must be focused on and, thus, Section 11 provides the primary legal base. Part of the task of the bond underwriter is to ensure that the results of the due diligence investigation correspond with the details contained in the registration statement.

It is also possible, as in the case of CP, for a bond issuer and/or underwriter to be found liable under Rule 10b-5 of the Securities Exchange Act of 1934. Under Rule 10b-5,

> It shall be unlawful for any person, directly or indirectly, by the use of any means or instrumentality of interstate commerce, or of the mails, or of any facility of any national securities exchange,
>
> (1) to employ any device, scheme, or artifice to defraud.
> (2) to make any untrue statement of a material fact or to omit to state a material fact in order to make the statements made, in the light of circumstances under which they were made, not misleading, or
> (3) to engage in any act, practice or course of business which operates or would operate as a fraud or deceit upon any person, in connection with the purchase or sale of any security.

As indicated in the previous chapter, 10b-5 liability is generally more difficult to establish, since the plaintiff must demonstrate *scienter*. Although there appears to be some overlap between liability under Section 11 and Rule 10b-5, courts have ruled that suit can be brought under 10b-5 for false statements or omissions in a registration statement under the 1933 Act (*Herman & MacLean* v *Huddleston, 459 US 375 (1983)*), which is normally the 'domain' of Section 11 liability. A bond underwriter, therefore, must be aware of possible liability under both Acts.

If the bond underwriter has performed adequate due diligence and the registration statement is shown to be complete and accurate, underwriter's liability is generally thought to be minimal. In addition, although a bond generally has a maturity of several years, the due diligence function is performed once and the disclosure is prepared once (although the registration statement is updated periodically by the issuer). After the initial due diligence and disclosure the investor cannot rely on the underwriter for updated information relating to the issuer. Thus, should an issuer default five years into a 10-year bond because of information or facts which were not in existence at the time of the initial due diligence, it is extremely unlikely that the underwriter could be held liable for losses sustained by investors.

In the commercial paper market, in contrast, the average maturity of notes is one to three months (with the maximum being nine months). Following the retirement of old notes and the issuance of new ones, the dealer may potentially face new liabilities. Since the instrument being issued is technically new and since information may have arisen since the issuance and maturity of the previous notes, a dealer may be held liable if it has not dealt with due diligence and disclosure requirements. As a result, the due diligence and disclosure processes are constant with the CP product.

To summarise, the bond underwriter is required to perform its due diligence function, to advise investors of all material facts and to make no untrue statements. Following the satisfactory performance of the initial function, however, the concept of underwriter's liability begins to subside; this is particularly true once the bond is well into its life. It is incumbent on the underwriter, therefore, to perform its due diligence function in a proper fashion at the outset.

There is, of course, precedent in the courts which demonstrates the liability an underwriter might face in not adequately performing the due diligence function (or not disclosing correct or sufficient information to investors). For example, in *Escott* v *BarChris Construction Corp (283 F Supp 643 (SDNY 1968))*, investors who lost money on an underwriting of convertible debentures after the issuer (BarChris) went bankrupt sued successfully in the courts.

In the BarChris case the courts ruled that all signers of the disclosure statement (including the company directors, the underwriting group led by Drexel Burnham Lambert and the audit firm, Peat Marwick) were liable to investors for not having completed adequate due diligence on BarChris prior to issuance of the notes, for not having adequately put forth all facts resulting from the investigation (some of which may have deterred investors from buying notes) and for including false statements in the disclosure document. The failure of BarChris 17 months after the issuance of the debentures demonstrated that the company was in poor financial condition prior to issuance. Had investors known this, from the prospectus or disclosure document, it is unlikely that they would have chosen to buy notes issued by the company.

RISK FACTORS

As discussed in Part II of this book, instruments involving inventory positions carry 100 per cent risk weighting. In the case of bonds a dealer holding inventory faces dollar-for-dollar risk. Thus, no risk adjustment is required and no sample risk factors are necessary.

12: Foreign Exchange and Currency Derivatives

DEFINITION

Although the trading of foreign exchange (FX) can be enormously complicated, in its simplest form an underlying transaction involves the exchange of one currency for a second currency, with settlement at some point in the near or medium-term future.

Virtually all currencies in the world can be traded. Foreign exchange traders make a 'price' for them by quoting a value at which they will buy (bid) or sell (offer). As one might expect, the more widely traded a currency, the narrower the bid/offer spread. Actively traded currencies are quoted to three or four decimal places, so the spread on a DM/$ trade might be 1.6511/1.6521, effectively 0.001DM per $ traded. The most actively traded currencies include the major European currencies (Deutschmark, Swiss franc, French franc, pound sterling, Italian lira, Dutch guilder and ECU), the Japanese yen, the Australian dollar and the Canadian dollar. The 'second tier' of currencies, those which are traded but do not have the liquidity of the 'majors', include other European currencies and certain Asian currencies. Illiquid, or thinly traded, currencies have wide spreads between the bid and the offer.

Most currencies are quoted and traded in terms of US dollars, although there is an increasing number of important 'cross rates' which are actively quoted and traded, including DM/yen, sterling/DM and so on. If an active cross rate does not exist, two or more FX transactions may be required to arrive at the desired currency position. For example, if a customer wants to execute a spot trade of Australian dollars against Finnish markkas, it will most likely transact an A$/$ trade followed by a FIM/$ trade. In the process it will pay the bid/offer spread on two trades instead of one, resulting in a more expensive deal.

Major participants in the market tend to be large, international commercial banks who deal for their own accounts and for customer accounts. Investment banks are beginning to get involved in the business as well, although they have a great deal of ground to cover to establish the volumes dealt in by commercial banks. Indeed, most investment banks have FX operations only to service customer orders; they tend not to be very involved in the interbank foreign exchange market, the professional market where large volumes are traded and where commercial banks dominate. On the customer side, many corporations are involved as active users of FX, particularly to hedge currency exposures resulting from overseas operations.

In a typical interbank FX transaction a bank will quote a price for, say, Deutschmarks against dollars. When the other bank agrees to the rate, the trade ticket is passed and confirmations are sent out by the operational units. FX transactions can be for spot or forward delivery. Spot delivery means that the two currency positions will be exchanged within the next two business days; this can be thought of as the FX equivalent of the 'cash' settlement found in the fixed income securities business. Forward delivery means that the two currencies will be exchanged at some point in the future; this can be one week or several months and in some instances it may be as far away as two or three years (these trades are known as 'long dates'). However, the most liquid portion of the forward market is for trades settling in less than a year. At some institutions FX forwards settling within the year are handled by the FX desk, while forwards more than one year out are handled by the swap desk, which has experience in dealing with instruments and cash flows in that time horizon.

A slight detour is required at this point to cover some fundamentals of spot and forward rates. Foreign exchange theory (and practice) states that the spot rate plus the interest rate differential between two currencies will equal the forward rate. This equation must hold true or else riskless arbitrage opportunities would exist. In point of fact, some covered interest arbitrage does occur, taking advantage of small price discrepancies existing for a short time; as more people attempt to arbitrage these small opportunities, the discrepancy quickly vanishes and the equation above once again holds true. Consider an extreme example, illustrating why the equation must hold true. If spot yen/$ is 120, 12-month forward yen/$ is 115, US 12-month interest rates are 7 per cent and yen interest rates are 6 per cent, the following could occur:

1. Bank A buys $10m worth of yen at the spot price of 120, receiving ¥1.2b. At the same time it contracts to sell forward yen for $ in 12 months at a rate of ¥115/$.
2. Bank A takes its ¥1.2b and invests in a 12-month yen CD yielding 6 per cent (assume simple interest). At the end of the year the ¥1.2b will be worth ¥1.272b (¥1.2b × 1.06).
3. Based on its initial forward trade of ¥115/$, Bank A converts its ¥1.272b to $11,060,869.
4. Had Bank A simply deposited its original $10m in a 12-month US dollar CD yielding 7 per cent (simple interest), it would have earned only $10,700,000. This implies a profit difference of $360,869 by engaging in the yen FX/deposit strategy.

With an arbitrage opportunity as wide as that, it is clear that a great many would be eager to exploit it. In fact, by investing not just \$10m, but \$10b, one's riskless profits would rise to over \$1b (or \$360m more than the dollar deposit strategy); there are not many places one can get a risk-free return of 10 per cent on as much money as one has available to invest (or can borrow and invest). Obviously, the economics of the situation would break down very quickly; thus, an arbitrage opportunity of that magnitude will not exist, particularly in an age of instantaneous information and sophisticated trading technologies.

In practice, the pressure of investors interested in buying yen spot and selling yen forward in order to implement the yen deposit strategy would be such that the two rates would reach an equilibrium point where there was no difference between engaging in the two strategies. Heavy demand to buy spot yen would drive the rate from ¥120/\$ to, say, ¥118/\$, making it more expensive to buy yen. At the same time the forward rate would begin to weaken as more yen were sold for dollars (implying that the dollar would strengthen from ¥115/\$ to, say, ¥117/\$).

We can again consider our transaction: \$10m would now be sold spot to yield ¥1.18b. The proceeds, invested at 6 per cent, would yield ¥1.25b at the end of 12 months. The forward sale at ¥117/\$ would convert the yen principal and interest to a total of just under \$10,700,000. The arbitrage opportunity has disappeared and the investor will be indifferent to selecting one strategy over another.

At this juncture it should be clear that the interest rate differential between yen and dollars determines the relationship between spot and forward rates. As the differential moves, so the spot and forward rates will move as well, adjusting to the new rate levels (and constantly kept in check by watchful arbitrageurs). As the world moved away from fixed exchange rates during the early 1970s, a by-product was increased volatility in both currencies and interest rates.

Foreign Exchange Options

In addition to spot and forward FX, there is also an active market in both listed and OTC FX options. As before, this chapter discusses only OTC products; in point of fact, more activity now takes place in the OTC market than on the exchanges, although some exchanges are very active in certain contracts; the Philadelphia Stock Exchange (sterling, Canadian dollars and Deutschmarks), LIFFE in London (sterling) and the Chicago Board Options Exchange (sterling, Swiss francs and Deutschmarks) are examples.

As one might assume, an FX option gives the buyer the right, but not the obligation, to buy (call) or sell (put) one currency for another at some point in the future. For example, a company may need to be in a position to buy

Deutschmarks against dollars in 90 days, if a particular sales contract is won. It is very concerned that Deutschmarks will rise in the next 30 days, before the contract is signed, making its purchase of the currency more expensive. A Deutschmark call at a particular strike price and maturity date will enable it to 'lock in' its desired rate today. Should the contract be signed, it will be able to exercise its call in 90 days and receive Deutschmarks in exchange for dollars. As with all other options, in exchange for this right the company pays a premium to the bank selling the call; should the contract not be signed, the company is effectively out of pocket by the premium paid for the option. While this is a cost, it is clearly preferable to entering into a forward contract which will lock the company into a particular transaction which it may or may not want.

FX options are available in a range of currencies, strike rates and maturity dates; the more actively traded the underlying currency in the spot and forward markets, the more actively traded the options on the same currency. As with other options, FX options can be for exercise in either European fashion (only at maturity) or American fashion (any time until, and including, maturity). It should also be remembered that options may not always be the most inexpensive way of accomplishing a given objective; depending on one's view of the currency markets, it may be preferable to leave a position uncovered or to use the forward market.

As in all options trading, there are motivations other than hedging which drive companies to execute FX options transactions. The counterparty may wish to earn extra income by engaging in call or put writing (naked or covered). Alternatively, it may wish to employ more complex strategies either to enhance yield on present currency exposures or to take an outright view on the direction of a particular currency. Many different strategies are available, such as calendar spreads (buying and selling options with different expiry dates), strangles (buying puts and calls with different strike rates but the same expiry date), straddles (buying puts and calls with the same strike rate and expiry date) and so on. For credit assessment the strategies must always be broken down into their component parts (buys/sells, puts/calls, delivery/no delivery, etc), so that the source and nature of the credit risk can be determined.

As an example, if a bank is buying a DM/$ strangle with an expiry date of 90 days, it is buying two different options, a DM/$ call (eg struck at DM1.65/$) and a DM/$ put (eg struck at DM1.63/$). If, 90 days from now, the market is DM1.66/$, only the call portion of the strangle will have value (because the bank can exercise at DM1.65/$ and sell at DM1.66/$). The put portion will have no value because the bank would gain nothing by selling at DM1.63/$, so the option will expire unexercised. The reverse can also be true; if the dollar weakens to DM1.62/$, the put will be exercised and the call will not. The credit officer needs to be watchful of the strategy employed, understanding that, since only one side of the deal will be exercised, the risk on only one portion of the trade need be counted.

FRAs

A third type of instrument encountered in the currency market is the forward rate agreement (FRA). This particular instrument has been likened to a type of single currency swap (with which it shares some similarities). However, an FRA can also be compared with a forward foreign exchange contract, except that both currencies in the transaction are the same. Many institutions elect to have FRA exposures carried under a counterparty's FX limits; however, they are often executed by a bank's swap desk. Given the mix of characteristics, the product may be described as an FX 'hybrid' or a swap 'hybrid'; for the purposes of this book, FRAs are dealt with as currency derivatives.

An FRA is an agreement where the amount paid (or received) is dependent upon the movement of certain underlying interest rates. It is a single currency contract, most often transacted in dollars, Deutschmarks, sterling or yen. In a typical deal Bank A would contract with Bank B as follows: A and B agree to a future interest rate (or forward rate), say DM LIBOR at 6 per cent, a settlement date, say 90 days from now, a maturity date, say 180 days from now, and a notional of DM10m. The deal is calculated on the basis of a notional amount, although there is no exchange of principal (as there would be in a currency swap). In market terminology the above would be described as a three/six DM FRA: the time between trade date and settlement date is three months and the time between trade date and maturity date is six months. On the settlement date A and B will compare the prevailing market rate for three-month DM LIBOR with the agreed forward rate (established at the trade date). Depending upon the level of LIBOR, A will make a payment to B or *vice versa*.

We can imagine the following example: a three/six DM FRA, where the forward rate, based on DM LIBOR, is 6 per cent and the notional amount is DM10m. If LIBOR for settlement three months after settlement date (ie at maturity date) is greater than 6 per cent, A will pay B the difference. If, 90 days on, DM LIBOR for settlement in 90 days is 5.5 per cent, B will pay A DM50,000 (DM10m × 6 per cent − 5.5 per cent). If the prevailing rate for 90-day DM LIBOR is 7 per cent, then A will pay B DM100,000 (DM10m × 7 per cent − 6 per cent).

In a typical FRA there is no exchange of principal, no upfront fee and no upfront premium. The only exchange of cash is a one-way payment at settlement date, based on the differential between the forward rate and the prevailing market rate.

FX Settlement

When settlement day arrives, whether we are referring to FX, FX options which have been exercised or an FRA, each bank will send payments to the location specified on trade date by its counterparty (recalling that in an FRA the payment is one-way, while in all other products it is two-way). Most banks keep local currency accounts at a local bank or one of their own local branches in order to receive payments in that currency. The process of settling FX positions is known as FX delivery.

As an example, if a US bank has sold dollars against Deutschmarks to a German bank and is expecting delivery of Deutschmarks on settlement day, its payment instructions to the German bank would include the appropriate local bank and account in Frankfurt at which DM funds can be credited. Conversely, the German bank, which is expecting receipt of dollars, will provide the US bank with its dollar account at a bank in New York. Because of timing differences between the debiting and crediting of accounts in different time zones there exists a phenomenon known as delivery risk (see Chapter 4); it is also referred to as free delivery, clean risk or split settlement risk. Delivery risk is the risk that a bank encounters when it temporarily loses control of its funds prior to receiving funds from its counterparty and is characteristic of FX trades. This concept is discussed more fully in the risk section below.

GENERAL CREDIT CONSIDERATIONS

We return once more to our credit decision-making framework.

Risk

Risk can be high for spot, forwards and options with delivery. For non-deliverable transactions risk is low to medium and for FRAs it is typically low. The risk weightings under the BIS for FX transactions (including spot, forwards and options) and FRAs vary from 50 per cent to 100 per cent, depending on individual regulators' preferences.

Return

Return on spot and forward FX trades and FRAs with a medium quality counterparty is low. At- or in-the-money options carry higher returns.

Although risk weightings are high, capital charge spreads for FX and FRA transactions are reasonably small, given the low risk factors associated with shorter-term deals.

Maturity

For FX forwards and options maturities can range from short to medium (spot trades are by definition short-term). FRAs are also short-term transactions.

Motivation

Motivations for FX spot and forwards, options and FRAs can range from hedging to speculation.

Enhancement

Taking collateral or other third party enhancement in the FX market is extremely unusual. However, certain product alterations can be considered in order to reduce risk; these are discussed later in the chapter.

Creditworthiness

An FX/FRA line is generally appropriate for high or medium quality credits. While a lower rated institution may have the need for such a facility, it may not always qualify on grounds of risk. In order for a credit analyst to be comfortable granting an FX line to a sub-investment grade counterparty, he or she may have to alter the nature of the facility by granting a non-delivery line or requesting some margin to cover market risk. On an unsecured or unaltered basis an FX line is probably not an appropriate product to grant to sub-investment grade clients.

FX options (both long and short positions) are certainly suitable for good quality counterparties. When considering FX options with lower rated counterparties, however, suitability may well be an issue. Unlike options we have considered in the past (on MBSs, Treasuries and so on), selling an FX option to a sub-investment grade counterparty will involve the bank in incurring risk, even after the premium is received.

Whereas with a Treasury option, for example, a bank selling the option is expected to perform on the underlying deal and thus has no risk to the counterparty, the same is not true with a short FX option. Although the bank selling the FX option will not sustain any market risk, because again it is the counterparty which is expecting performance from the bank, if the counterparty decides to exercise the option, the bank will have to deliver currency. At this point there is an exposure to delivery risk, something a bank does not face with other OTC options. Thus, if an analyst is uncomfortable granting a delivery limit on a normal foreign exchange line, he or she should also be uncomfortable engaging in short options. We know that long FX options (ie where the bank buys an option) are unlikely to be suitable with a weak counterparty, because the bank faces three different potential risks: loss of premium, market risk and delivery risk. Therefore, great care must be taken when considering an FX options facility of any kind for a weak counterparty. Very often it is not an appropriate product for the lower part of the credit spectrum.

It is again important to address the motives for engaging in foreign exchange, FX options and FRAs. All FX products, by their very nature, lend themselves well to hedging and obviously there is no difficulty in considering a hedging facility for top and medium grade companies. In addition, should a good, or even average, quality company desire to use FX to speculate, arbitrage or enhance yield, an analyst should not typically be concerned, as the counterparty should have the financial backing to absorb the risk of loss.

If the analyst is able to structure some level of security into an FX or options facility for a sub-investment grade counterparty to use for hedging purposes, the facility may also ultimately be beneficial. However, if a weak counterparty's desire to enter into foreign exchange deals is solely speculative, the motivation may be seen as unacceptable by the credit officer. An obvious key to determining whether a weak counterparty intends to speculate is to find out if it has any foreign currency assets, liabilities or receipts which need to be hedged. Without any, one may safely assume that the primary motive is speculation.

RISK QUANTIFICATION

FX and FX options are unique in that they carry two distinct types of risk: delivery risk and market risk. As we shall demonstrate, the quantification of delivery (or settlement) risk is relatively straightforward, as a bank sustains 100 per cent exposure for a short time. In addition, since FX transactions and FRAs are affected by underlying rate movements, they are considered market risk products; accordingly, they are adjusted through the risk equivalency process.

Delivery Risk

Delivery risk represents the risk that a counterparty will default after it has received a foreign currency flow from the bank but before it has effected payment on its portion of the deal. This risk exists because of the time differences involved in debiting and crediting local currency accounts where currencies are to be sent and received.

Consider the following example: Bank A, located in Frankfurt, is selling dollars for Deutschmarks to Bank B, located in New York. On settlement (or value) date Bank B will deliver Deutschmarks to Bank A in the Frankfurt time zone and will do so by crediting A's DM account. Recalling that Frankfurt is six hours ahead of New York, by the time A confirms receipt of DM in Frankfurt it will be too late in the day in Germany to send a payment of dollars to New York (although the FX market is a 24 hour market, the staff, systems and regulations governing payments are constrained to normal bank operating hours). What actually occurs, in practice, is that Bank B will send out its DM payment to Bank A 1 day in advance, so that it may receive its dollars as scheduled on settlement date.

It is during this time period that Bank B is left with no funds: it has lost control of the Deutschmarks, which are safely in A's account, and has not yet received the dollars. This is the nature of delivery risk and, although it generally lasts only 24 hours, it is true 100 per cent exposure. In risk equivalency an analyst is forced to assign a 100 per cent risk factor, as DM10m delivered out, with the equivalent $6m not yet received, means DM10m at risk. For those active in the FX market delivery risk will always be present. Banks operating in the US can confirm receipt of all currencies on value date, but have to pay away European and Asian currencies one day in advance. European banks can confirm same day receipt of Asian and European currencies, but not dollars; in addition, they need to issue early payment instructions for Asian currencies. Asian banks have no need to issue any early payment instructions, but cannot confirm same day receipt of European currencies or dollars. Thus, regardless of location, active FX banks will always be exposed to delivery risk via early payments or delayed confirmations, for up to 24 hours.

Since the risk is only 24 hours in length, some FX participants have questioned the advisability of establishing, or strictly adhering to, a delivery limit. In fact, instances of default on delivery have been comparatively few. The most memorable (and the one to focus attention on this category of risk) occurred in June 1974 when the Herstatt Bank in Germany failed after receiving, but before delivering, on currency transactions. The German authorities closed Herstatt down in the afternoon, after payments had been received, but not yet made, by the bank. Those institutions which had sold European currencies to Herstatt against US dollars were the primary losers in the bank's failure.

For many years there were no real instances of failure to deliver but the issue has been revived in the past few years: in 1989 Development Finance Corporation of New Zealand (DFC) failed with deliveries pending and in 1990 Drexel Burnham Lambert also failed with deliveries pending. In the most recent case, in 1991, the Bank of Credit and Commerce International also failed prior to completing delivery to certain counterparties.

Although actual cases of delivery failure have been few, it is not difficult to imagine that a bank, with several hundred million (or perhaps several billion) dollars in deliveries for a single day, could face severe trouble should a failure, no matter how remote, actually occur. The most prudent course of action is for a credit officer to establish, monitor and enforce a delivery limit.

An analyst establishing a delivery limit is in essence dictating the maximum amount of currency which can be deliverable on any single day. It does not dictate the number of trades which can be booked with a counterparty (which is the purpose of a gross limit, as described below) but the maximum that can be pending delivery for any business day.

Market Risk

As in other products we have dealt with, market risk is the risk a bank will face when the market begins to move in favour of or against FX positions on its books. We must remember that market risk will be transparent to the analyst so long as the counterparty continues to perform on its side of the trade. Should a default occur, however, the bank may suffer a loss created by market movements, if positions are in its favour. For FX spot and forward transactions a bank will very often establish a gross FX limit to control the amount of spot and forward trading risk being faced with a given counterparty. This limit controls the total notional amount of trades that a bank can book with a given counterparty at any point in time. It is distinguished from the delivery limit discussed above because the latter focuses solely on the amount of trades deliverable on a single business day, while the gross limit focuses on the total trades with an individual counterparty.

Consider Table 12.1, which shows Bank A's trades with Company Q.

Table 12.1. Bank A's Trades with Company Q

Value Date	Amount ($m)
March 15	100
March 16	50
March 17	50
March 17	100
March 25	100

Based on the above, Bank A is said to have \$400m in gross trades (ie the sum of all trades outstanding) and \$150m in delivery (ie the maximum of trades deliverable on a single day, March 17). If an analyst had established a gross limit of \$500m and a delivery limit of \$200m, traders would still be able to book another \$100m in trades, with no more than \$50m deliverable on March 17.

Use of the gross limit is helpful in establishing the maximum market risk a bank will face. Returning to our basic risk equation (5.1), we know that

$$\text{REE} = \text{RF} \times \text{N}$$

We can assume that N is equal to the total amount of possible FX trades outstanding with a given counterparty (in other words, the gross limit). In order to obtain our risk equivalent, we simply apply the appropriate risk factor to the notional or gross amount. For example, if we set a gross limit of \$100m and the appropriate RF is 6 per cent, then our risk equivalent exposure will equal \$6m. This tells us that the maximum market risk we will face for the sum of all trades will be less than or equal to \$6m. If we are dealing strictly with spot FX transactions, which settle in two business days or, at worst, carry over a weekend and/or bank holiday for a total of four or five days, the above equation should be satisfactory. The chances of a market movement of substance in several business days are small enough that we need not worry about an ongoing market value component in the risk calculation.

If we are considering forward FX transactions, however, we need to refine the equation somewhat so that there is more accuracy to our ongoing market risk calculation. To do so, we incorporate a mark-to-market element, which gives an indication of the value of the trade(s) at a particular point in time. We now obtain the following equation:

$$\text{REE} = [\text{MTM} + (\text{RFc} \times \text{MV})] \tag{12.1}$$

where RFc is a constantly adjusted risk factor,
MV is the current market value of a trade (or trades),
MTM is the difference between the original value of the trade(s) and the MV.

Obviously, as we adjust for the mark-to-market value, we also need to adjust our risk factor on a continuous basis. Since a forward trade can go out as long as six, 12 or 24 months into the future (and perhaps longer), a bank booking such a trade will see the value of the position rise or fall with currency movements. By incorporating the MTM element and constantly adjusting the risk factor downwards (as maturity draws closer) we are establishing a framework not unlike that found in the swap product, ie potential exposure is equivalent to fractional exposure (RFc above) plus actual exposure (MTM above).

Table 12.2 helps to illustrate the concept: Bank X transacts a six-month DM/$ forward with Corporation Y, $100m notional on March 1.

Table 12.2. Sample Forward Transaction

Date	MV	Risk factor	MTM	Total REE
March 1	$100m	11.0%	0	$11m
April 1	$100.2m	10.0%	($250m)	$9.8m
May 1	$100m	9.0%	0	$9m
June 1	$99m	7.0%	$1m	$7.9m
July 1	$98.5m	6.5%	$1.5m	$7.9m
August 1	$98.5m	4.5%	$1.5m	$5.9m
September 1	$98m	1.0%	$2m	$3m

As maturity draws nearer, risk factors start declining. Total REE will not necessarily decline, since market movements may be such that the bank is at greater risk as time goes by (ie the MTM value is positive in the bank's favour). However, in establishing a maximum risk factor at the start of the trade (based on our REE framework), we expect to be comfortable that the total risk exposure will rarely be more than we predict at the outset.

To put the discussion on forwards in the framework of orderly and default scenarios, consider Figure 12.1.

To summarise our discussion on spot and forward FX, a credit officer needs to establish a number of limits to control market and delivery risk. Gross limit covers the total amount of trades outstanding at any point in time with a given counterparty and delivery limit covers the total amount of trades deliverable on a single business day with a given counterparty. The credit officer must also establish a maximum risk equivalent limit which will accommodate the potential market risk of the gross limit. This risk equivalent limit is simply the product of the gross limit and the appropriate risk factor. Since different tenors and currencies will yield different risk factors, and since a limit is likely to be used for a variety of different trades, the most conservative approach is to determine the maximum maturity allowable under the limit (generally 12 months for a good counterparty) and the most volatile currency which will be traded under the gross limit. Since the risk factor is a function of both maturity and volatility of the underlying currency, the combination of these will yield a risk factor which will cover the maximum risk likely to be encountered in any trading situation; of course this may result in some overstating of the REE but not by so much that it diminishes the capacity to transact other business.

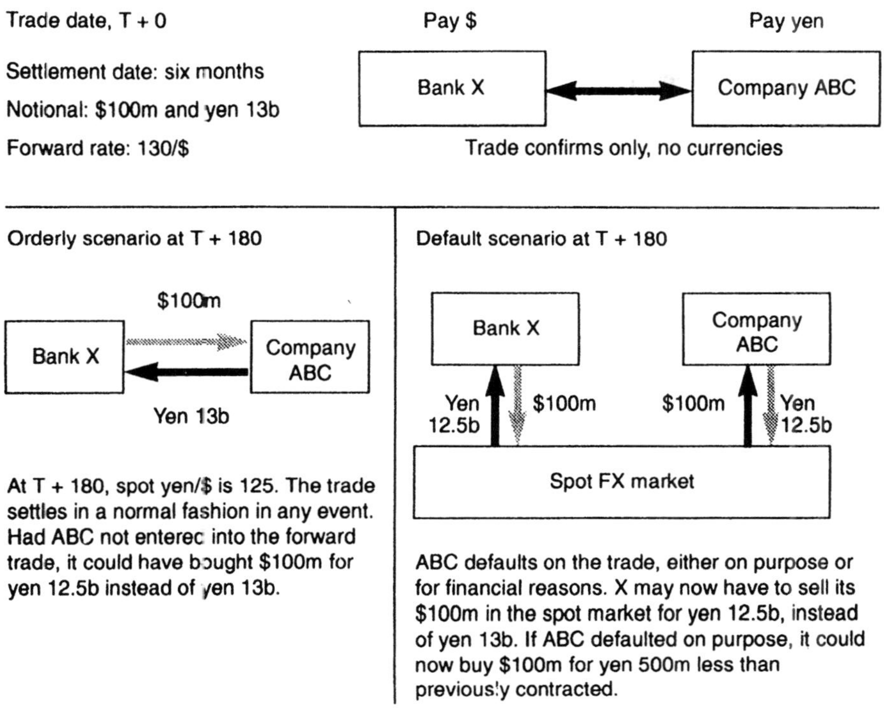

Figure 12.1. Forward Foreign Exchange, Orderly and Default Scenarios.

When these steps are completed, an analyst will have three separate guides by which to control the FX risk to a given counterparty. As an example, an analyst might determine that a strong, medium-sized, investment grade company (with hedging needs and, perhaps, some desire to take an outright speculative position from time to time) is worthy of a gross limit of $300m, a delivery limit of $100m and, based on a maximum trade maturity of 12 months, a risk-adjusted limit of $15m. These limits would then be communicated to the trading desk and the operational unit.

Reducing Risks

For an analyst especially concerned about controlling the risks incurred with a given counterparty, but still believing that some level of FX business can be transacted, the following are possible means of mitigating risk.

Establish A 'Non-delivery Limit'

Under this type of arrangement, a bank would extend only a gross limit (with its associated potential market risk) and would prohibit any delivery. Since delivery risk is equal to 100 per cent, albeit for a short time period, the bank is able to avoid potentially the riskiest portion of the trade. Under a non-delivery scheme, the counterparty has to execute an equal and opposite trade prior to maturity which closes out the original trade. By effecting such a transaction, no delivery will occur, only a net payment in one direction or another. For example, if a counterparty sells \$10m forward against receipt of yen (at ¥120/\$) in 30 days and then finds that, prior to maturity, spot yen is ¥125/\$, it will effect a trade selling ¥1.25b against \$10m. The net flows will be as shown in Table 12.3.

Table 12.3. "No-delivery" Cash flows

	Bank A	Counterparty
Trade date	Buy \$10m Sell ¥1.2b	Sell \$10m Buy ¥1.2b
Prior to close out	Sell \$10m Buy ¥1.25b	Buy \$10m Sell ¥1.25b
Net effect	−¥50m	+¥50m

The counterparty will have earned ¥50m (\$400,000 at current rates). More importantly for the bank, the trades are 'paired off' so that the dollar amounts net out to zero and the yen amounts net out to a single payment of ¥50m in the direction of the counterparty. By setting a non-delivery limit, the bank has effectively reduced its risk to one of market movement alone. Had the yen gone to ¥115/\$, the counterparty would have made a ¥50m payment to the bank; while the bank would be at risk for that amount (ie market risk), that is clearly preferable to a full delivery risk of ¥1.25b. A note on the legal aspects of netting is included at the end of this chapter.

Establish a 'Delivery Versus Payment' Scheme

Once again, if the aim of the bank is to avoid 100 per cent delivery risk, a delivery *versus* payment (DVP) arrangement can be set up. Under this arrangement, the bank's operations department is under instructions not to deliver any currency to the client until receipt of funds from the client has been verified. Thus, while the time zone factor which causes delivery risk is still in play, instructions will be such that no currency leaves the bank until it is as much as 24 hours overdue. In order to compensate the client for this loss of use of funds for 24 hours, an interest payment can be made to the client when remitting funds.

Limit Maturities and/or Currencies to be Transacted
By limiting the maturities of forward trades to one or two months the bank will reduce its risk equivalent exposure. In addition, where possible, the currencies to be traded should be limited, excluding illiquid currencies and perhaps incorporating some restrictions on those which are most volatile (eg the yen, the Australian dollar and the New Zealand dollar). This again helps to cut down on risk exposure.

Obtain Collateral to Cover Market Risk Exposure
Although taking collateral is unusual in the FX market, there are instances where a counterparty may be willing to post security to cover market risk. If the counterparty's plight is such that it must engage in FX for hedging purposes, this may be the only possibility available to it. If the currencies and maturities the counterparty is seeking to hedge are available through the exchange-traded market, this is perhaps a better solution (as the product is a margined one to begin with). However, the listed markets may not provide the flexibility required in terms of size, maturity and currency.

Market Risk on Options

We know from our past chapters that market risk on an options trade will be different from market risk on a regular extended settlement trade. Unlike other options dealt with so far, however, FX options have two distinct risk elements: the risk of delivery and the risk of market movement.

For other options transactions we know that if the bank is short (ie it is the writer, or seller, of the option), the only risk faced is non-receipt of premium. Since receipt generally occurs within five business days, the risk is equivalent to that of a cash trade. With an FX option this is not the case. Should the buyer of the option decide to exercise, the bank will be forced to deliver currency. Depending on which side is paying which currency, the bank may incur delivery risk. Thus, an FX option, whether long or short, may result in assumption of delivery risk by the bank. An analyst establishing an FX options line for a particular counterparty will be required either to establish a delivery limit (with a risk factor of 100 per cent, as detailed above) or to select a DVP or non-delivery arrangement.

Risk of market movement, as with other options, will occur only on a bank's long position, as it is the bank which is expecting performance from the counterparty. Should the counterparty default, the bank will have to cover the position in the market and may sustain a loss in the process. On a short options position it is the counterparty who is expecting performance by the bank, so the bank has no market risk exposure. In order to focus on market movement risk incurred by a bank's long position in options, we can consider equation (5.1) again:

$$\text{REE} = \text{RF} \times \text{N}$$

and adapt it easily to accommodate an option's risk by adding in the premium paid out (since a bank stands to lose this if the counterparty defaults). This yields the following:

$$\text{REE} = \text{premium paid} + (\text{RF} \times \text{N}) \tag{12.2}$$

We note below that this equation represents the standard form for valuing at-the-money puts and calls.

With this equation, we can imagine a scenario where Bank X buys a \$10m dollar/franc call struck at Ffr6/\$ (enabling Bank X to deliver Ffr60m in exchange for \$10m). Assuming the spot rate for francs is Ffr5.50/\$, the option is clearly out of the money (ie Bank X would have to deliver only Ffr55m for \$10m in the spot market, so would not want to exercise the call). Since the call is out of the money, the premium paid is a relatively modest \$100,000. If we assume the risk factor on a 90-day call to be 8.6 per cent, the associated REE is

$$\begin{aligned}\$100{,}000 + (0.086 \times \$10{,}000{,}000) &= \$100{,}000 + \$860{,}000 \\ &= \$960{,}000\end{aligned}$$

That is, if Bank X's counterparty defaults on the trade during the next 90 days, the bank stands to lose a maximum of \$960,000. The above represents a static, conservative model, which yields the maximum risk likely to be faced during the life of the trade.

Another method for calculating REE on options centres on determining how much in-the-money or out-of-the-money the option is and how the calculation changes on an ongoing basis. This discussion follows the model developed for both Treasury and MBS options in previous chapters. For those options which are at-the-money or in-the-money the risk to be faced on trade date is immediately greater, as the option has a higher intrinsic value. Those which are out-of-the-money have less value, so carry less risk. In addition, the farther out-of-the-money a given option is, the less likely is exercise and, consequently, the less reliance is placed on the counterparty for future performance; in deeply out-of-the-money options the only amount at risk is the premium paid by the buyer.

In this scenario we can refine our equation to include a component which compares the current market price (CMP) to the strike price (SP) to determine how much in-the-money or out-of-the-money the option is. For calls the comparison centres on the greater of 0 or ((CMP − SP)/CMP) and for puts it becomes the greater of 0 or ((SP − CMP)/CMP). In addition, we continue to incorporate a constantly adjusted risk factor RFc to reflect potential market movements which might yet occur during the life of the trade. The equation for calls now becomes:

$$\text{REE} = \text{premium} + 0 \vee [(\text{RFc} \times \text{N}) + \left(\left(\frac{(\text{CMP} - \text{SP})}{\text{CMP}}\right) \times \text{N}\right)] \qquad (12.3)$$

where SP is the strike price,
CMP is the current market price,
RFc is the constantly adjusted risk factor,
N is the notional amount of the trade(s).

For puts the equation is:

$$\text{REE} = \text{premium} + 0 \vee [(\text{RFc} \times \text{N}) + \left(\left(\frac{(\text{SP} - \text{CMP})}{\text{CMP}}\right) \times \text{N}\right)] \qquad (12.4)$$

where SP is the strike price,
CMP is the current market price,
RFc is the constantly adjusted risk factor,
N is the notional amount of the trade(s).

Obviously, if the strike price is far higher than the current market price in the case of a call, and *vice versa* in the case of a put, the option will be deeply out of the money and the second portion of the equation will be negative, so will subtract from the total potential exposure which might be encountered during the trade. If it is sufficiently negative, only the risk of the premium will be valued as REE. Note that as the option moves from out-of-the-money to in-the-money, risk equivalent exposure will begin to increase as the second portion of the equation becomes positive.

With these equations in mind it is helpful to examine sample trades. Consider a situation where Bank X is buying a series of European calls from a counterparty.

An Out-of-the-money Option

N = \$10m
SP = Ffr6/\$
CMP = Ffr5.75/\$

maturity is three months, RF is 8.6 per cent, premium paid is \$100,000

$$\text{REE} = \text{premium} + 0 \vee [(\text{RFc} \times \text{N}) + \left(\left(\frac{(\text{CMP} - \text{SP})}{\text{CMP}}\right) \times \text{N}\right)] \qquad (12.3)$$

$$= \$100{,}000 + 0 \text{ or } [(0.086 \times \$10\text{m}) + (((5.75 - 6)/5.75) \times \$10\text{m})]$$
$$= \$100{,}000 + 0 \text{ or } [\$860{,}000 + (-0.043 \times \$10\text{m})]$$
$$= \$100{,}000 + 0 \text{ or } [\$430{,}000]$$
$$= \$530{,}000$$

The risk faced by Bank X in this deal is initially $530,000. The astute reader will have noticed that the percentage by which the option is out-of-the-money is effectively subtracted from the original risk factor to give us the new risk factor, which is based on a comparison of strike and market prices. Although the option is 4.3 per cent out of the money, there are still three months left until maturity. Our risk equation allows for the possibility of the option ending at-the-money or in-the-money by still reflecting potential exposure of $430,000 (plus the premium paid). Since the option is only slightly out of the money and the time to expiry is long, the risk on the total trade will include both premium and the potential for the option to move into-the-money.

An At-the-money Option

N = $10m
SP = Ffr6/$
CMP = Ffr6/$

maturity is three months, RF is 8.6 per cent, premium paid is $250,000

$$\text{REE} = \text{premium} + 0 \vee [(\text{RFc} \times \text{N}) + (\left(\frac{(\text{CMP} - \text{SP})}{\text{CMP}}\right) \times \text{N})] \qquad (12.3)$$
$$= \$250{,}000 + 0 \text{ or } [(0.086 \times \$10\text{m}) + (((6 - 6)/6) \times \$10\text{m})]$$
$$= \$250{,}000 + 0 \text{ or } [\$860{,}000 + 0]$$
$$= \$250{,}000 + 0 \text{ or } [\$860{,}000]$$
$$= \$1{,}110{,}000$$

The risk faced by the bank on this transaction would be $1.11m. Once again, it is worth noting two items: first, the premium paid by Bank X for this call is higher because the option has more value (ie it is struck at the money); secondly, since the strike price and the current spot price are equal, the adjustment to the option's intrinsic value yields our original risk factor of 8.6 per cent. This is also identical to general equation (12.2) detailed above.

An In-the-money Option

N = $10m
SP = Ffr6/$
CMP = Ffr6.50/$

maturity is three months, RF is 8.6 per cent, premium paid is \$400,000

$$\text{REE} = \text{premium} + 0 \vee [(\text{RFc} \times \text{N}) + ((\frac{(\text{CMP} - \text{SP})}{\text{CMP}}) \times \text{N})] \qquad (12.3)$$

$$= \$400{,}000 + 0 \text{ or } [(0.086 \times \$10\text{m}) + (((6.5 - 6)/6.5) \times \$10\text{m})]$$

$$= \$400{,}000 + 0 \text{ or } [\$860{,}000 + (0.077 \times \$10\text{m})]$$

$$= \$400{,}000 + 0 \text{ or } [\$860{,}000 + \$770{,}000]$$

$$= \$2{,}030{,}000$$

In the final instance Bank X's risk is appreciably higher than that calculated by equation (12.2): \$2m against \$1.26m. The reason for the increase is that equation (12.3) values the in-the-money portion, while equation (12.2) does not. Bank X is purchasing an option which is 7.7 per cent more valuable than today's market and thus the resulting risk exposure is shown to be higher. Should the counterparty default tomorrow, Bank X would lose the \$400,000 premium plus the differential between the strike and the market (\$10m × Ffr.05/\$ divided by the spot rate, Ffr6.5/\$, or \$770,000). The equation also includes the potential risk equivalent exposure, \$860,000, which reflects potential losses if there is no default today but a default occurs in the future, with rates having moved the call even further into-the-money. Thus, equations (12.3) and (12.4) represent a conservative method of valuing options risk, particularly for options which are in the money.

In all the above scenarios we must remember that the risk of the options trade will be adjusted on an ongoing basis as both the risk factor RFc and the extent to which the option is in-the-money are updated.

While the put and call equations can be applied to a single trade or a series of trades, care must be taken when applying them to certain options strategies. For example, if a bank is buying strangles or straddles (as discussed above), only one portion of the trade will be exercised for a given pair of puts and calls. That being the case, it would be overstating the risk if the two separate trades were counted. Thus, any calculation of market risk for options strategies may require some 'manual' intervention from time to time to ensure that the proper risk is being attributed to the deal.

Market Risk on FRAs

From the point of view of a bank entering into an FRA, whether a purchase or a sale, with a second bank, the potential for market risk always exists. Recall that in an FRA the market rate of the future settling deal is compared with the agreed forward rate on settlement date. Depending upon the direction in which rates have moved, there may be a payment in either direction, regardless of who bought or sold the FRA. When a bank sells an FRA, it is essentially lending at a fixed rate, whereas if it buys an FRA it is borrowing at a fixed rate. If the bank sells an FRA and rates fall below the fixed rate level, it will receive a payment from its counterparty. Conversely, if the bank sells an FRA and rates rise, it will have to make a payment to the counterparty. We may consider two alternative scenarios.

Scenario One

Bank X buys a yen FRA from Bank Z, with settlement in three months and maturity in six months; the forward rate is 6 per cent and the notional is ¥3b ($23m).

Three months from now X and Z compare the forward rate (6 per cent) to the market rate, which is now 7 per cent on yen funds settling three months forward (six months from the original trade date). Under the agreement, Bank Z will have to compensate Bank X in the amount of ¥30m ($230,000), the difference between 7 per cent and 6 per cent multiplied by the notional principal.

Scenario Two

Assume that instead of buying the FRA, Bank X had sold it. The same movement in rates would result in Bank X's having to make a payment of ¥30m.

Establishing a formula

These examples demonstrate that, regardless of whether an FRA is purchased or sold, a bank can be exposed to market risk. In this respect an FRA differs from a traditional FX option, where the bank will be exposed to risk of market movement only if it buys the option.

With this rule in mind, it is now necessary to establish a formula for evaluating the risk a bank might face in buying or selling an FRA. It is helpful to refer first to the standard equation employed by all FRA dealers in the calculation of settlement amounts, as originally developed by a working committee within the British Bankers' Association (BBA). The equation is as follows:

$$\text{Settlement} = \frac{((\text{MR} - \text{FR}) \times \text{maturity} \times \text{N})}{((360 \times 100) + (\text{MR} \times \text{maturity}))} \qquad (12.5)$$

where MR is the market rate (often called settlement rate),
FR is the forward rate (often called agreed rate),
N is the notional amount of the FRA,
maturity is the period from settlement date to maturity date.

Note that 360 represents the number of days in the year; a 365-day convention can also be used. This equation is used by dealers to evaluate how much is to be paid or received at settlement date (readers are urged to refer to *Swap Financing* by Das or *Interest Rate Risk Management* by Andersen and Hasan for additional information on the standard BBA equation). For the purposes of our risk equivalency process we need make only minor changes to it.

The substitution which we must focus on involves (MR − FR). Since the difference between the market rate and the forward rate at settlement date will determine the direction and magnitude of the settlement amount, it is this potential movement which our risk factor (RF) must attempt to capture. As always, use of a risk factor will enable us to determine the maximum risk we are likely to face during the transaction. If we simply substitute (MR − FR) with RF (recalling that this is a factor which reflects the maturity between trade date and settlement date (ie the effective life of the FRA)), we obtain the following:

$$\text{REE} = \frac{((\text{RF} \times \text{N}) \times \text{maturity})}{((360 \times 100) + (\text{MR} \times \text{maturity}))} \tag{12.6}$$

The above change will yield the appropriate risk calculation REE and will give us a reasonable estimator of potential market risk on the settlement amount at the inception of the deal. On an ongoing basis, we can incorporate a mark-to-market calculation by comparing MR to FR and include a constantly adjusted risk factor (RFc) which decreases as settlement date draws nearer.

Based on this equation, we can demonstrate a sample risk calculation, assuming equation (12.6) and certain trade parameters:

three-month/nine-month dollar FRA

N = \$100m
RF = 0.4 per cent
contract maturity = 180 days
MR = 8 per cent

$$\text{REE} = \frac{((\text{RF} \times \text{N}) \times \text{maturity})}{((360 \times 100) + (\text{MR} \times \text{maturity}))} \tag{12.6}$$

$$= ((0.4 \times \$100\text{m}) \times (180))/(36{,}000 + (8 \times 180))$$

$$= (\$7.2\text{b})/(37{,}440)$$

$$= \$192{,}308$$

This is the maximum potential risk faced today by a bank entering into a three-month/nine-month \$100m FRA (note that, following the terms and equation established by the BBA, interest rates are put in as whole numbers, not as decimals). Should the counterparty fail, the bank could face a replacement cost of up to $192,308, based on our equation.

NETTING FOREIGN EXCHANGE EXPOSURES

As mentioned above, netting is a scheme which is often used in the FX markets. Under such arrangements, two counterparties agree to 'net out' amounts due on a particular forward or value date so that there is a net flow of a currency in only one direction; if it is a net position involving a forward, it will be discounted back to today's value. This has the effect of eliminating or reducing certain exposures and decreasing payment instructions and operational transactions.

Netting is currently a major topic of discussion among participants. In November 1990 the Bank for International Settlements released the so-called 'Lamfalussy Report' which discussed various aspects of netting within the markets. Among the major points addressed by the Lamfalussy Report were, first, that netting in different countries must have its foundation in a sound legal base, secondly, that the participants must have a clear understanding of the relevant netting process and procedure and, thirdly, that multilateral netting systems (ie those between several parties at the same time) must be well defined, so that credit and liquidity risks can be managed by all participants.

Part of the difficulty with netting is that different countries may have different ways in which they deal with it. Legal systems in most countries currently recognise and accept netting by novation (that is netting where, on each value date, all outstanding contracts are amalgamated and rewritten into a new, single master contract). Netting by novation is also a concept used by participants (and approved by regulators) in the swap markets, as we shall discuss in the next chapter. Although netting by novation is generally accepted from a legal standpoint in many countries, including the US, the UK, Canada, Australia and Japan, it tends to be complex and onerous to document. Other netting schemes include netting of bilateral payment flows (where net payments are made in a single currency on value date, with no impact on forward positions) and netting of forward positions (where multiple forward market risk exposures are replaced by a single legal agreement; under such a scheme, forward positions are discounted back to the present).

Regardless of the method contemplated, it is essential that it be legally sound. For example, we can imagine an arrangement where two counterparties contractually agree to net out offsetting positions on value dates (though not rewriting all existing positions into a master agreement, as in netting by novation). Although a contract may exist which satisfies the requirements of contractual law, it is possible that, in certain jurisdictions, such agreements may have no legal foundation in bankruptcy law; in a bankruptcy situation, a court may allow a receiver to 'cherry-pick' only those contracts favourable to the insolvent counterparty.

It is reasonably easy to see how a netting arrangement without a strong legal foundation and which is ultimately deemed to be non-binding on a receiver can be detrimental to participants. If a bank agrees to a netting arrangement, believing that in a worst case scenario only the net exposures will be at stake, it may transact significantly more FX with a given counterparty than it would normally consider. If default and bankruptcy of the counterparty ensue, the bank may lose more than it had originally anticipated.

From the point of view of a credit officer, netting can help reduce exposures, which may be a benefit in certain instances. However, it should be clear that any netting scheme being considered or used requires verification by a bank's legal counsel to ensure its enforceability in bankruptcy situations. In the US the Financial Institutions Reform, Recovery and Enforcement Act (FIRREA) and amendments to the US Bankruptcy Code provide substantial legal comfort that a netting arrangement, so long as it is contracted in a master agreement between the two parties, will be upheld in a bankruptcy court and that there will be no 'cherry-picking' by the bankruptcy receiver.

Table 12.4. Sample Risk Factors for Foreign Exchange and FX Options (per cent)

	One week	Two weeks	One month	Two months	Three months	Six months	12 months	24 months
Japanese yen HV = 11.1%	2.1	2.9	4.2	5.9	7.2	10.2	14.4	20.4
Australian dollar HV = 9.9%	1.9	2.6	3.7	5.3	6.4	9.1	12.9	18.2
Pound sterling HV = 12.3%	2.3	3.3	4.6	6.5	8.0	11.3	16.0	22.6
French franc HV = 13.3%	2.5	3.5	5.0	7.1	8.6	12.2	17.2	24.5
Swiss franc HV = 13.1%	2.4	3.5	4.9	6.9	8.5	12.0	17.0	24.1
Deutschmark HV = 13.9%	2.6	3.7	5.2	7.4	9.0	12.8	18.1	25.6
Italian lira HV = 12.9%	2.4	3.4	4.8	6.8	8.4	11.9	16.8	23.7

RISK FACTORS

As with other instruments we have dealt with so far, the REE calculation for FX spot, forward and options requires use of the risk factor (RF). Based on historical volatility studies and applying a 90 per cent confidence level to a lognormally distributed sample, Table 12.4 shows representative risk factors for selected currencies against the US dollar for a variety of trade maturities.

Note that risk factors for FRAs do not conform to the grid on Table 12.4, as FRAs represent single currency instruments and their associated rate movements, whereas the Table shows dual currency volatilities. The most accurate risk factor measure for FRAs would focus on single currency interest rate movements over the period in question, ie trade date to settlement date, as discussed above, since these ultimately determine the settlement amount.

13: Swaps and Swap Derivatives

DEFINITION

The swap in its simplest form can be described as a periodic exchange (or 'swap') of payments between two counterparties for a specified period of time; the exchange is generally based on interest rates, currency rates or commodity prices. The actual exchange of payments is governed by a contractual agreement between the participants and is reflected as an off-balance sheet exposure.

The nature and risk of these periodic exchanges is dependent upon the underlying type of obligation being exchanged and will be described more fully in the section below. Although the range of swaps is broad, the underlying motivation for a swap is the same: for reasons of absolute and comparative economics each party involved in the swap can achieve an economic goal that would not be achievable otherwise; this goal may be to lower a funding rate (sometimes referred to as a 'liability swap') or to increase an investment rate (sometimes referred to as an 'asset swap').

The following represents a general example of a swap; Table 13.1 shows sample funding costs for two borrowers.

Note that Corporation X has a comparative advantage in raising floating rate funds and can do so at LIBOR + 60, while Bank A has a comparative advantage in raising fixed rate funds and can do so at 7 per cent. Thus, Bank A has a 10 basis point absolute advantage in raising funds: it can borrow at 50 basis points less than the corporation in the fixed rate market and 40 basis points more in the floating rate market.

Given the absolute and comparative advantages enjoyed by each party, the 'swapped' flow of funds can be represented as in Figure 13.1.

Numerically, Figure 13.1 yields the results shown in Table 13.2.

Table 13.1. Sample Funding Costs

Current financing costs	Bank A	Corporation X
Floating	LIBOR + 100	LIBOR + 60
Fixed	7.00 per cent	7.50 per cent

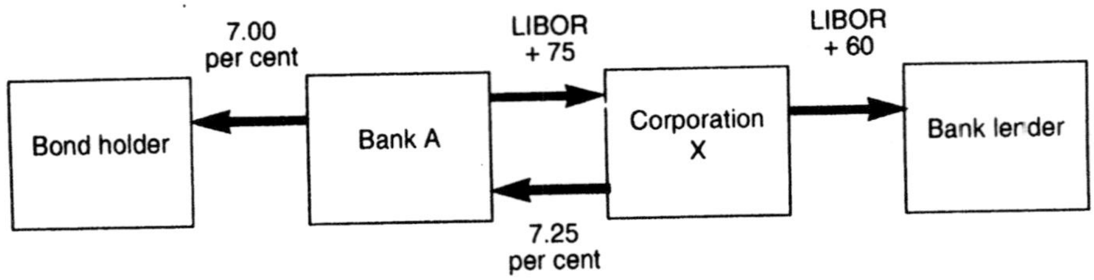

Figure 13.1. Funds Flow Diagram.

Table 13.2. Borrowing Costs After Swap

	Bank A	Corporation X
Direct cost		
– fixed	(7.00 per cent)	
– floating		(LIBOR + 60)
Swapped receive/(cost)		
– fixed	7.25 per cent	(7.25 per cent)
– floating	(LIBOR + 75)	LIBOR + 75
All-in cost*	LIBOR + 50	7.10 per cent
Comparable cost	LIBOR + 100	7.50 per cent
Total savings**	50 bp	40 bp

* All-in cost defined as ((fixed receive – fixed pay) – floating pay) or ((floating receive – floating pay) – fixed pay).
** Total savings defined as comparable cost – all-in cost.

After entering into the swap transaction outlined above, Bank A would find itself saving 50 basis points a year on its funding cost, while Corporation X would be saving 40 basis points a year. Note that these savings may be split in different proportions, depending upon such things as relative credit quality, the presence of a swap dealer acting in a particular capacity and so on. The numbers above are for illustrative purposes only.

Although the swap market has been in existence in some form for a few decades (primarily through the parallel and back-to-back loans markets), major growth did not occur until the 1980s, with much of it being fuelled by the explosive increase in general debt financings during much of that decade. In addition, more active asset and liability management by a larger number of corporations and financial institutions has led to growth in the market, since swaps and derivatives represent a key tool in the management of balance sheet risks. Swaps outstanding, in notional terms, are today estimated at approximately \$3.9 trillion (\$3.1 trillion in interest rate swaps and \$800b in cross-currency swaps).

Market Participants

Participation in the market is broad, particularly among major financial institutions which act as agents, intermediaries or principals in these transactions. If acting as an agent, a bank simply brings two counterparties together for a fee and each counterparty takes the other's credit risk. The agent bank has no further role once the parties are matched and will assume neither market nor credit risk. If acting as an intermediary, the bank will take credit risk on both sides of the transaction by standing between the two counterparties; if the swap is already perfectly matched, the dealer incurs credit risk but not market risk. If acting as a principal, the bank is essentially acting for its own book; it will transact a swap with a counterparty and assume credit risk, while attempting to match the other side of the transaction at some future date; until that second leg is matched, it will generally hedge its position to avoid (or at least minimise) market risk. When the second leg is found, the bank will then unwind its hedge and face the second party's credit risk. The roles of the swap dealer are illustrated in Figure 13.2.

Maturities

Maturities for transactions in the swap market effectively range from about one year to 10 years, with virtually all activity in this area. Certain financial institutions are becoming increasingly involved in the market for swaps of over 10 years, which involve a special set of considerations and risks. Credit risk and market risk intensify, given respectively the very long time horizon with which the credit officer must deal in assessing future performance of the counterparty and the fact that accurate hedging in that area of the yield curve is exceedingly difficult, if not impossible. In today's environment current credit quality constraints among major market participants are also a deterrent to swaps of over 10 years, as there are few remaining AAA counterparties who are able to face each other without altering the structure of the deal by incorporating options to terminate, taking collateral, etc.

Certain institutions have created special AAA-rated swap and derivative subsidiaries to assist in capturing a larger portion of the long-term market. The ratings are obtained through overcollateralisation levels, restrictions on ratings of counterparties, maximum market and credit risk levels and so on.

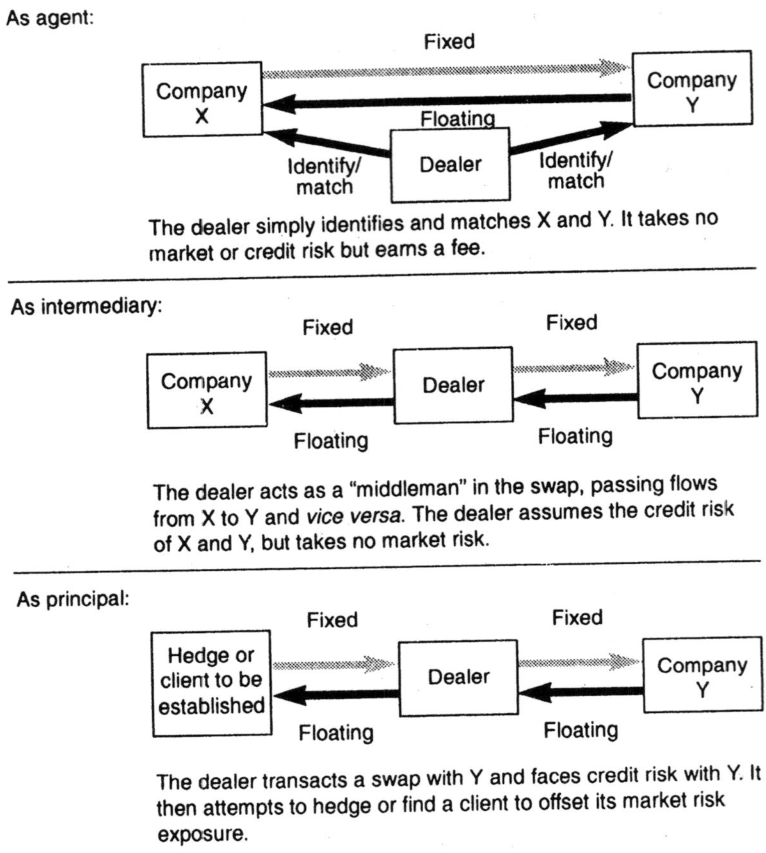

Figure 13.2. The Dealer's Position in Swap Transactions.

Although the product variation in the swap market is broad and always changing, it is possible for the purposes of our discussion to narrow the product description and risk analysis into the following categories: interest rate swaps, cross-currency swaps and swap derivatives (including swap options, callable/puttable swaps, caps, floors, collars, corridors and forward swaps, commodity swaps)

Interest Rate Swaps

The interest rate swap (IRS), and most specifically the 'plain vanilla' structure, represents the fundamental building block of the swap market. An IRS can be defined as an exchange of two payments based on different underlying interest rate measures, both in the same currency; the typical exchange involves a fixed rate payment for a floating rate payment. It is important to note that in an IRS the underlying notional amount is not exchanged; the only cash flows being swapped are the interest payments. The frequency of exchanges can range from monthly to annual but is most commonly semi-annual.

The classic 'plain vanilla' structure, also known as a 'coupon swap', occurs when Company A pays a fixed rate against receipt of a floating rate from Company B on a matched basis (ie each makes a payment every six months, for example) for a period of time. In practice, if a swap is executed on a matched basis, only one party will make a payment every period, net of the proceeds it expects to receive from its counterparty; that is, the party owing the larger amount on a given payment date will pay the market value of the rate (fixed or floating) times the notional principal less the amount to be received from the other party. As an example, consider the payments listed in Table 13.3, made under a swap with the following parameters: Bank A pays six-month LIBOR + 50 bp, Corporation X pays 7 per cent fixed; payments are semi-annual over a three-year maturity and the notional principal is $100m.

Table 13.3. Payments Under Swap

	Six-month LIBOR (per cent)	Bank A	Corporation X	Net payment
Six months	7.50	$4m	$3.5m	$500,000 by A
12 months	8.00	$4.25m	$3.5m	$750,000 by A
18 months	8.00	$4.25m	$3.5m	$750,000 by A
24 months	6.50	$4.25m	$3.5m	0
30 months	6.00	$3.25m	$3.5m	$250,000 by X
36 months	5.00	$2.75m	$3.5m	$750,000 by X

In the first period Bank A, paying floating, must pay $4m ($100m × ((7.5 per cent + 0.5 per cent)/2)). It is expecting, however, to receive $3.5m ($100m × (7 per cent/2)) from Corporation X. Thus, Bank A will make a net payment of $500,000. By the fifth payment date, if LIBOR has dropped to 6 per cent, making the all-in payment rate 6.5 per cent, Bank A will expect to receive a net payment of $250,000 from Corporation X. When discrepancies exist in payment frequency, preventing netting of payments, risk increases substantially, as we shall explore later in this chapter.

Cross-currency Swaps

In cross-currency swaps (CCSs) the exchanges taking place between the parties involve currencies rather than interest rates, although the interest rate exchange is implicit in the currency rates being swapped. A standard CCS functions just as an IRS would, with the primary exception being actual exchange of the underlying notional principal.

Consider the following example: Company Y has a Deutschmark liability on its books, requiring a DM interest payment every year. Because of its view on exchange rates, Company Y would rather convert its effective liability into an annual dollar payment: the company feels that the dollar will weaken against the Deutschmark, making its effective interest cost once swapped lower in dollar terms. Company Z has a dollar liability requiring a dollar payment and would like to convert the obligation into a DM payment because its own view of likely exchange rate movements is that the dollar will strengthen against the Deutschmark.

In this particular situation Company Y would sell its Deutschmark notional obligation for an equivalent amount of dollars, while entering into a contractual agreement to sell the required dollars forward at maturity date and repurchase the Deutschmark obligation (not unlike a forward foreign exchange contract). Company Z would do exactly the opposite on trade date. This effectively represents an exchange of principal on day one. Company Z would be able to service the Deutschmark obligation as it had desired, by making annual Deutschmark payments, as outlined above, and Company Y would be able to service the dollar obligation as it had desired.

An outline summary of the flow of payments is given in Table 13.4. It assumes a five-year final maturity, a Deutschmark coupon of 6 per cent and a dollar coupon of 8 per cent; the Deutschmark liability is worth DM180m and the dollar liability is worth $100m; there is a constant exchange rate of DM1.8/$.

With the final payment in year five, which includes the exchange of principal, both Y and Z have returned to their original positions. Obviously, the principal exchanges at inception and maturity represent the largest difference (and the largest risk) between IRSs and CCSs. This will be discussed in the risk section. Note that, in addition to CCSs with principal exchange, banks also transact CCSs without principal exchange, where only periodic currency coupon payments are made.

Swap Derivatives

As swap market participants have grown more sophisticated and as new financial needs have developed, financial institutions have pioneered addi-

Table 13.4. A Deutschmark/Dollar Swap

Original position	Company Z $100m	Company Y DM180m
Payments by	Z	Y
Trade date	$100m	DM180m
Year 1	DM10.8m	$8m
Year 2	DM10.8m	$8m
Year 3	DM10.8m	$8m
Year 4	DM10.8m	$8m
Year 5	DM190.8m	$108m
Final position	$100m	DM180m

tional swap-based derivative products, grouped in this section under the title of 'swap derivatives'. The products described below very often provide much the same protection or yield enhancement as IRSs and CCSs but can often be executed by the client at a fraction of the cost associated with swaps. In addition, there are some specific derivatives which have been developed because the precise results required are not available in the traditional swap market.

Swap Options

Swap options (also known as swaptions) are a relatively recent derivative of a standard swap. As the name suggests, a swaption is a combination of a swap and an option; in its basic form a swap option gives the buyer of the option the right, but not the obligation, to buy (call) or sell (put) a swap. In that sense an option on a swap is no different in concept from an option on any other instrument.

As an example, if Bank A sells Corporation X a six-month American call swaption, then Corporation X has two choices available to it once it has paid Bank A the premium. Sometime during the next six months it can either enter into the regular swap underlying the swaption, receiving a predetermined fixed rate, or cash-settle the option at the prevailing mark-to-market price.

Recall that, if Bank A had sold Corporation X a European call, the company would have been able to exercise this choice only on the expiry date of the option and not before.

If Bank A sells Corporation X a put swaption, Corporation X, similarly, may choose to enter into the regular swap underlying the swaption, paying a predetermined fixed rate, or to cash-settle the option at the prevailing mark-to-market price.

Callable/Puttable Swaps

Callable and puttable swaps are designed to let the buyer terminate a swap at some point in the future with no economic penalty (ie the swap will terminate at zero value to both parties). In exchange for the right to terminate without penalty, the purchaser will effectively pay the other party a premium for the privilege. Such a premium is payable in two forms: an upfront payment, such as one might see in a traditional option, or an alteration to the underlying fixed rate being paid or received such that it is advantageous to the party granting the option to terminate.

A callable swap is one where the fixed rate payer can terminate without penalty, while a puttable swap is one where the fixed rate receiver can terminate without penalty.

Caps/Floors/Collars/Corridors

These derivative products are treated together primarily because they are all related to one another in some way: a floor is the reverse of a cap, a collar comprises a cap and a floor and a corridor comprises two caps. The basic definitions of each are given below.

CAP

This is an option which provides the buyer with interest rate protection on the upside. The seller, or 'writer', of a cap contracts with the buyer to pay the differential between the market rate and the strike rate once the market rate exceeds the strike rate. Using

sc = strike rate of the cap
m = market rate
N = notional

the cap has value to the buyer when m is greater than sc and the payment the buyer will expect to receive will be $(m - sc) \times N$. If m is less than or equal to sc, no payment is required for that particular period. The differential between the strike and market rates is evaluated on a prearranged periodic schedule for a set amount of time (eg every quarter for three years). In return for the protection being provided, the buyer pays the seller a premium. The premium payment is dependent upon how far out of the money the strike rate is against the prevailing market rate; the further out of the money the cap is, the smaller are the chances of its being needed for protection and, accordingly, the lower the premium to be paid. A cap written at the money or in the money is almost certain to be exercised, so the seller will demand a much greater premium.

FLOOR

As one might expect, a floor is the reverse of a cap transaction: it is an option which provides the buyer with interest rate protection on the downside. The writer contracts with the buyer to pay the differential between the market rate and the strike rate once the market rate falls below the strike rate. Using

sf = strike rate of the floor
m = market rate
N = notional

the floor has value to the buyer when m is less than sf and the payment the buyer will expect to receive will be (sf − m) × N. If m is greater than or equal to sf, no payment is required for that particular period. All other characteristics are the same as the cap described above.

COLLAR

A collar is a combination of a cap and a floor, with each party involved in selling the other a portion of the transaction. For example, Bank A, as seller of the cap, may be willing to provide protection on the upside in exchange for receipt of a premium and at the same time will be receiving protection on the downside from Bank B in return for payment of a premium. Conversely, Bank B, as the seller of the floor, is providing downside protection to Bank A in return for premium income and is expecting upside protection from Bank A in exchange for a premium payment. Depending upon how far in the money or out of the money the separate 'legs' are, one party may be paying more premium than the other. A 'zero-cost collar', as the name implies, occurs when the theoretical premium payment is the same for each party and neither incurs an upfront cost in entering into the arrangement. Apart from using one side of the transaction to assist in asset and liability management, the primary motivation for entering into a collar is to receive premium income or to defray the cost of receiving a certain type of interest rate protection. Using

sf = strike rate of the floor
sc = strike rate of the cap
m = market rate

no payments will be made when sf is less than or equal to m which is less than or equal to sc; Bank A will provide protection when m is greater than sc; and Bank B will provide protection when m is less than sf.

CORRIDOR

A corridor is a combination of the purchase of a cap and the sale of a second cap with a higher strike rate. In this type of structure Bank A purchases from Bank X a cap at some strike rate sc; Bank X provides Bank A with upside protection in exchange for a premium. Bank A then writes a cap at sc + x (where x is an additional spread) to Bank Z, which pays it a premium for protection when the market rate exceeds sc + x. As with a collar, one of the primary motivations is to receive additional premium income to defray the cost of the purchase of the original cap at strike rate sc. By definition a corridor cannot be a costless transaction, since the lower strike cap will always be closer to the market rate than the higher strike cap (ie it will always be closer to the money and, therefore, more expensive). Using

sc = strike rate of the cap
x = additional spread
m = market rate

in a corridor Bank A will receive, but not have to pay, when m is greater than sc, but is less than sc + x.

Forward Swaps

A forward swap is a swap which, instead of beginning on trade date, begins at some specified date in the future, although all terms and conditions are contracted on the trade date for future use.

One of the primary reasons for the use of forward swaps is that one of the parties swapping against an underlying debt obligation may not require the use of the swap until a future event occurs. The underlying debt financing may, for example, include a call or put provision, a step-up clause or some type of convertibility clause, which will alter the nature of the obligation to be swapped. Alternatively, assume that the party involved will be a payer of fixed rates and a receiver of LIBOR on a swap starting in three years. He may believe that LIBOR rates will continue to fall for the next three years but will rise dramatically thereafter. In a forward swap he will be able to take advantage of any drop in rates for the next three years (if there is any) and then be in a position to lock in at the fixed rate contracted today.

Commodity Swaps

A commodity swap involves the exchanging of cash flows based on an underlying commodity price or index and seems a logical step to follow the exchange of interest and currency rates. Although market participation in general is still quite narrow compared with the traditional swap market, it is clear that a certain sector of the market has a use for these swaps. A typical commodity swap generally involves the producer of the underlying commodity as a floating payer against receipt of fixed from a swap dealer or bank. For example, an oil company might wish to hedge a certain amount of its production forward, given that it anticipates very volatile markets in the near future. It can elect to hedge *via* the listed options and futures market or it can enter into an oil swap. The terms of the trade might be: Bank A will pay Oil Company X $23 a barrel fixed on 10,000 barrels of oil a month for one year.

Oil Company X, in exchange for receiving a fixed flow every month, will pay Bank A a floating price based on the average monthly price of West Texas Intermediate (WTI) crude as traded on the New York Mercantile Exchange (NYMEX).

Consider the following price scenarios: if spot oil prices rise to $30 a barrel, Oil Company X will have to pay out a greater amount to Bank A under the terms of the swap. The company does not find this unacceptable because it will be making more income on its unhedged production and, as a result, will welcome the increased oil prices. Alternatively, if spot oil prices fall to $18 a barrel, Oil Company X will receive a greater amount from Bank A than it is paying out on a floating basis. Although it will receive more of an economic benefit, it will lose on the unhedged production it is being forced to sell at spot price.

Recall from Part I that the above is the definition of a hedge: a gain on one side of the position will be partially or completely offset by a loss on the other side; the net effect is that the hedger will not be affected economically and should be indifferent to price movements.

The simple example above is representative of how a commodity swap can be utilised to hedge certain amounts of a producer's underlying commodity production. As an over-the-counter transaction, the commodity swap has an inherent advantage over the listed futures and options market in that it can be tailor made to coincide with both the producer's and the dealer's specific requirements and need not be constrained by standard contract size, strike price or strike dates.

A Final Note

The list of 'refinements' to both traditional swaps and the special derivatives listed above is seemingly never ending. There are many other structures which have been created over the past few years: options on caps, swaps in arrears, superfloater swaps, amortising swaps, equity derivative swaps (with such novel intricacies as knockout options, lookback options, digital options, etc) and so on. Each of these products has its own description and its own risks; some will survive and become important financial instruments, while others will have served a specific purpose at a point in time and then faded away. For those credit analysts who will be exposed to some or all of the above, an obvious word of caution is to make certain that the nature of the product and/or strategy is fully understood, so that the appropriate risk level can be assigned and the correct credit decision made.

GENERAL CREDIT CONSIDERATIONS

We return once more to our credit decision-making framework.

Risk

On an unsecured basis swaps and derivatives are typically medium to high risk transactions. There is no risk, however, on a bank's short cap, floor or cash-settling swaption positions. The BIS risk weightings on swaps and swap derivatives is 50 per cent, though local regulators may elect to go as high as 100 per cent; the figure is lowered to 20 per cent if qualifying collateral is used.

Return

Return on plain vanilla structures with medium quality counterparties is low. Swap derivatives and more esoteric structures command medium to high returns. Although in most countries the BIS risk weighting is only 50 per cent (and can be lower), capital charge spreads are reasonably significant, given the higher risk factors associated with term business. For cross-currency swaps and zero coupon structures, capital charge spreads are higher still.

Maturity

Most swap activity is medium- to long-term in nature.

Motivation

Swaps can be executed for hedging, speculation, yield enhancing and arbitrage.

Enhancement

Standard swap transactions carry no enhancement. However, taking collateral for deals with sub-investment grade counterparties is widely practised, as is altering the underlying structure to produce additional credit protection. These items are discussed at length below.

Creditworthiness

A swap is a long-term exposure, though not in the sense of a long-term bank loan or term credit. In those instances very rigid structures and documentation make it more difficult, if not impossible, for a bank to extricate itself from the lending relationship once a loan is drawn.

With a swap, however, that is not necessarily the case. At a given point in time a bank may decide to reduce or eliminate its term swap exposure to a given counterparty. In order to do this, it can go into the market and sell off a swap (or swaps) to a third party. Although the bank will probably lose some basis points in doing so (depending on the current level of rates and the perceived condition of the underlying credit) and will require the approval of the counterparty in order to assign the swap, we must recall that a swap, particularly a plain vanilla structure, is a reasonably liquid instrument with a defined market value at today's rates. Thus, although the analyst must focus on the fact that the approval of a multi-year swap exposes the bank to a term exposure, in theory it is not an exposure that need be on the bank's books until maturity.

In practice, most swaps do run their course until maturity and are then removed from the bank's books. That is the correct way of viewing the process. An analyst should approve a given transaction only if it is his credit judgement that the counterparty will be able to perform for the duration of the swap. It would be folly to approve a five-year transaction for a weak credit on the assumption that six months or a year later the desk can sell it off, if required. At the same time an analyst should be aware that a swap does not have to be on the books for the entire life of the deal.

In our earlier grids we commented that medium and high risk transactions, and medium- and long-term maturities, were generally suitable only for medium and high quality credits. This effectively suggests that the lower tier of counterparties (ie those rated below investment grade) should be completely eliminated from the decision-making framework when dealing with a standard, unsecured swap.

While an unsecured swap with no collateral or other risk-limiting devices is acceptable only for investment grade companies, 'secured' swaps can be transacted with lower rated counterparties. These structures must incorporate some type of security so that the bank extending the swap will be willing to assume the exposure. Examples of ways to limit (or eliminate) risk and still transact a swap with a lower rated client are discussed here.

Collateral

The client can post a certain amount of collateral with the bank providing the swap. Collateral tends to be in the form of cash, Treasury or agency securities, high quality corporate paper, bank letters of credit or third party guarantees. The amount the client will have to place with the bank varies depending upon the type of mark-to-market procedure being used: if there is no marking to market during the life of the swap, collateral posted should be equal to the potential exposure (as defined in the risk quantification section below). If a periodic marking to market is incorporated, a fraction of the potential exposure should be posted. If periodic marks to market and lower collateral are selected. operational controls need to be in place.

Option to Terminate
Under an option to terminate the bank reserves the right to terminate the swap at any point in time at the prevailing mark-to-market (MTM) value. The effect of incorporating this type of option is to reduce the maximum maturity of a deal. If, for example, a weaker client wanted to do a three-year swap but the bank was unwilling to go out beyond one year, an agreement could be reached whereby the bank would retain the right to cancel the swap at market at any point after the first year. By structuring this option into the deal, the bank would face the client for one year, although the deal's pricing and risk would be based on three-year rates.

Non-standard Cash Flows
A bank can arrange a swap where it receives a year's worth of interest payments upfront, while not making any payments itself until some point after that. The idea is to establish a cash 'buffer' which provides protection. An extreme example of this would be a zero coupon structure where the client makes periodic payments during the life of the swap but receives nothing from the bank until maturity, when it is due a single bullet payment. There is thus no incentive for the client to default during this period as it has paid out cash and has received nothing in return, so the MTM value of the swap is in its favour and the bank has no exposure it need be concerned about. Zero coupon swaps and their associated risks are covered in the section below.

RISK QUANTIFICATION

Swaps and swap derivatives are affected by currency and/or interest rate movements. As such. they are considered market risk products and must be risk-adjusted in order to determine the true value of risk exposure.

As with other market risk products, if Company ABC enters into a swap with Securities Firm X, the swap will have a MTM value which changes over time, depending upon the direction of rates and the remaining cash flows to be made. If Company ABC defaults three years into a five-year swap, the potential loss which X will face is represented by the MTM value. If it is in X's favour, X has exposure to ABC and will attempt to recover what it is owed; before doing so it will have to replace the swap in the market at rates less favourable to it. If the MTM value of the swap is in ABC's favour, then X has no exposure to ABC and can replace the swap transaction in the market at rates much more favourable to it.

As one might suspect, the ongoing MTM value is not the best measure of total swap risk to the client, as it captures the value of the swap at only one point in time. It cannot tell us at the inception of a swap the total risk we might face (the MTM value at inception is zero, as rates will not yet have moved) or the risk we have during the life of the swap and how much risk will remain at any point. To understand what the best measure is (and why) it is important to establish some definitions relating to swap risk (note that different institutions may have slightly different names for the same concept and that these definitions are used generically in the discussion of interest rate swaps but are equally applicable to currency swaps).

Potential exposure is defined as fractional exposure plus actual exposure. Fractional exposure represents the maximum anticipated market risk exposure over the life of the transaction, based on the potential future movement of rates, and actual exposure is the current MTM value plus any accrued interest receivable. Potential exposure (or PE) can be thought of in general terms as the maximum risk exposure, both anticipated and actual, a bank must allocate to the swap transaction.

Actual Exposure

We have already discussed mark-to-market value: it is the market value of a swap at a given point in time, based on the differential between contracted rates and actual market rates multiplied by the notional amount of the transaction. In order to account for the time value of money and the remaining life of the deal, the present value of the amount is taken at the new market rate for the remaining life of the swap. It represents, in other words, the value of the swap in the market on a given day and can be positive (implying exposure) or negative (implying no exposure).

On a practical level we can consider the following: if Corporation X is a payer of LIBOR flat (originally contracted at 7 per cent but today worth 8 per cent) and Bank A is a payer of 7 per cent fixed on a swap with a notional principal of \$100m and two years remaining to maturity, then Corporation X's annual payments are currently \$8m and Bank A's are \$7m. The difference in interest payments today equals \$1m and is in Bank A's favour (Bank A is expecting a net inflow from Corporation X based on today's rates). The present market value (discounted at 8 per cent over a two-year period) equals:

$$\$1,783,264 = \frac{\$1,000,000}{(1.08)^1} + \frac{\$1,000,000}{(1.08)^2}$$

If Corporation X defaults on the swap, Bank A must replace the transaction. If Bank A goes into the market to attempt to cover the swap, it will find it is more expensive to do so because rates have risen by 100 basis points since the original swap was booked. That is, Bank A will have to contract with Company EFG to pay it a 7 per cent fixed flow (as it was with Corporation X) in an environment where floating rates are already above that. Obviously, the bank will have to make the deal more attractive to EFG and, as a result, will have to accept less or pay more; in either event, it will represent an economic loss to the bank. The present market value above of $1.78m is a discounted annuity of the amount which Corporation X owes to Bank A and represents the economic loss which the bank will sustain in replacing the swap. If a default occurs, the bank will become an unsecured creditor of the company and will attempt to receive all, or a portion of, the amount it is owed.

Accrued interest receivable, the second component of actual exposure, takes into account any differential which might occur between the payment of interest and the receipt of interest. In an obvious case we can imagine a scenario where Bank A pays three-month LIBOR on a quarterly basis against receipt of a fixed coupon every six months. The bank is therefore making an extra interest payment every six months and is exposed to the counterparty for a certain amount Table 13.5 illustrates the accrued interest receivable on a swap with a notional principal of $100m where Bank A pays three-month LIBOR quarterly and Corporation X pays fixed 7 per cent semi-annually.

Table 13.5. Accrued Interest Receivable

Payment	Three-month LIBOR (per cent)	Bank A	Corporation X	Accrued Interest receivable
First quarter	8.00	$2m	None	$2m
Second quarter	8.50	$2.13m	$3.5m	Flat
Third quarter	6.00	$1.5m	None	$1.5m
Fourth quarter	6.00	$1.5m	$3.5m	Flat

Note that, while Bank A makes four payments a year, Corporation X makes only two. Accrued interest receivable applies only to those periods where there is a true mismatch in receipt and payment of interest; it does not consider the market value of the payments being made, since that is reflected in the mark-to-market calculation. Hence, every time a larger semi-annual payment comes in to offset the two smaller quarterly payments, the accrued interest receivable s said to be 'flat' again. However, we can see that in quarters one and three there is additional exposure of $2m and $1.5m. These are amounts which cannot be ignored, since they represent substantial actual exposure for the party receiving the less frequent payments. If default were to occur during one of the mismatch periods, there would be interest receivable exposure in addition to the MTM value of the swap. It is for this reason that the receivable is included as part of the actual exposure calculation. A methodical approach for dealing with the risk of mismatches appears below.

It should be stated at this point that, although various institutions have different ways of approaching the risk equivalency calculation, many which use a model encompassing actual exposure use the concepts detailed above. The calculation of both a mark-to-market component and an accrued interest receivable component is standard in the industry.

Fractional Exposure

In calculating fractional exposure we are essentially calculating the risk equivalent exposure (REE) we have discussed throughout this book. We have stated that RF is a representation of the maximum risk we are likely to face during the life of the trade as calculated today, at the inception of the trade. Our calculation of fractional (or anticipated) exposure yields precisely the same information. Although we continue to use RF in the calculation of exposure, the derivation of RF for swaps is more complex than the model employed for other products.

The calculation of the fractional exposure of a swap varies from institution to institution, as statistical methods, simulations of market movements and formulaic procedures differ. However, a general guideline is presented below. In addition, a specific model for approaching the issue is included as a point of reference.

In order for a calculation of fractional exposure to be effective two items must be considered: a simulation of likely future rates and the calculation of a replacement cost. The general model must contain some estimation of future rates. Since the value of the swap (and the level of perceived risk) at some point in the future will depend on the actual level of those future rates, the establishment of this parameter is vital. The number of ways in which future rates can be simulated is quite large. Some institutions elect to use a Monte Carlo simulation (a random generation of samples involving certain models and probability distributions); others choose to focus on regression analysis of historical market movements and so forth. There is no single, correct way to simulate likely future rates but this step represents an important part of the process.

The model must also consider some replacement cost. As the name implies, replacement cost is the price that a bank will be required to pay should a client default on a swap in the future. Naturally, when a default does occur, the existing MTM value will dictate how much the bank will have to pay to replace the swap in the current market. However, at the inception of a swap, before any market movements have taken place, the anticipated replacement cost must be calculated. This cost is today's estimate of how much a bank will have to pay if a client defaults on a swap at some point in the future under certain rate scenarios.

The calculation of a replacement cost tends to follow a general pattern and is somewhat intuitive in nature. Just as in a mark-to-market calculation, the replacement cost at a point in the future is simply the difference between entering into a swap at a future point (t + 1) and the original point (t); if one assumes rates at (t + 1) will be higher than at (t) for a fixed rate payer, this implies that the difference between the original coupon and the new coupon will be positive. Under most replacement cost models the difference between the two coupons is discounted for all remaining periods until maturity by the new rate being faced. Some models will go further and discount that result back to the present using the originally contracted swap rate; that will yield a cost which is to be faced at the specified point in the future but discounted back to today's environment. Note that the new rates being used in replacement cost equations are derived from the simulated future rates discussed above.

A More Specific Model

Since we have outlined in general terms the main components of a fractional exposure framework, we need to highlight a more specific model to put the above into practice. We begin by developing a method to simulate future rates and will then turn to a discussion of replacement costs.

In order to develop a model which simulates possible future rates, we draw heavily on certain statistical and mathematical models employed in the pricing of stocks, options and bonds. A mathematical approach known as the Markov process is especially helpful for a model such as the one we are considering, since it presumes that only the present level of prices (or rates) is relevant to the future estimate; that is, past movements are irrelevant both in dictating how rates got to their present state and in determining how they might move in the future. The actual approach we choose to take in applying the Markov process is through a discrete time stochastic model. We are attempting to simulate a rate which is changing continuously (stochastic) but at specific time intervals, such as at every swap coupon payment date (discrete time).

For the purposes of our discussion we adapt a procedure known as the Rendleman and Bartter Model, which provides a method of valuing interest rate movements in an environment of constant growth and volatility (readers interested in reviewing the original equations are urged to refer to *The Pricing of Options on Debt Securities* by Rendleman and Bartter, *Journal of Financial and Quantitative Analysis*, volume 15, March 1980). Rendleman and Bartter is a binomial model which estimates upward and downward movements in rates and also takes into account probabilities associated with such movements (note that the Rendleman and Bartter Model is itself an adaptation of Cox, Ross and Rubenstein's binomial model first presented in their work *Option Pricing: A Simplified Approach*, *Journal of Financial Economics*, October 1979. In the article they linked the Black-Scholes option pricing model to a binomial pricing framework). In this text we will not focus on the probability portion of the model, since we opt for a conservative approach and assume that rates will always move in the direction most detrimental to the current swap exposure; that is, rates will move such that fractional exposure is always increasing, implying a 100 per cent probability of upward or downward movement, depending upon the side on which the swap's fixed rate is paid. With the Rendleman and Bartter Model we focus on the upward movement of rates for fixed rate payers (which is when risk increases) and downward movement of rates for fixed rate receivers (which is also when risk increases). By the original equation, upward movements are captured by:

$$u = e^{(s\sqrt{\Delta t})}$$

where s is the standard deviation of rates,
delta t is the period time interval.

Downward movements in rates are captured in a similar equation:

$$d = e^{(-s\sqrt{\Delta t})}$$

These equations contain parameters which should by now be familiar to the reader. The time component the Rendleman and Bartter Model terms 'delta t' represents the time change in small intervals (ie from semi-annual period to semi-annual period). In a Markov process a long interval becomes T, which is precisely equal to the T we use in Part II of this text and represents a cumulative, not period, timeframe. The appropriate standard deviation measure in a stochastic Markov model is equal to sigma. By way of comparison, we know from Part II that the standard deviation of rate movements over time is the historical volatility of rate movements HV. Using our own terminology, we can adjust the two equations as follows:

Upward movements:

$$u = e^{(HV\sqrt{T})}$$

Downward movements:

$$d = e^{(-HV\sqrt{T})}$$

We take one further step and set new rates equal to the original rates times the upward (or downward) movement estimated by the equations above. This yields, for a fixed rate payer, the following simulated future rate scenario:

$$r_n = r_0 \times e^{(HV\sqrt{T})} \tag{13.1}$$

and, for a fixed rate receiver:

$$r_n = r_0 \times e^{(-HV\sqrt{T})} \tag{13.2}$$

As an example, if we assume original rates today to be 10 per cent and the historical volatility of interest rates to be 16 per cent (lognormally distributed and adjusted to a 90 per cent confidence level), we obtain the results shown in Table 13.6.

Table 13.6. Possible Future Interest Rates (per cent)

Time	r(0)	r(n) (up)	r(n) (down)
0.5	10.00	11.19	8.93
1.0	10.00	11.74	8.52
1.5	10.00	12.16	8.22
2.0	10.00	12.54	7.97
2.5	10.00	12.88	7.76
3.0	10.00	13.19	7.57
3.5	10.00	13.49	7.41
4.0	10.00	13.77	7.26
4.5	10.00	14.04	7.12
5.0	10.00	14.30	7.00
5.5	10.00	14.55	6.87
6.0	10.00	14.80	6.76
6.5	10.00	15.00	6.65
7.0	10.00	15.27	6.55
7.5	10.00	15.50	6.45
8.0	10.00	15.72	6.36
8.5	10.00	15.94	6.27
9.0	10.00	16.16	6.19
9.5	10.00	16.37	6.10
10.0	10.00	16.58	6.02

We have just established the initial part of our fractional exposure framework using the Rendleman and Bartter Model. There are, of course, other forms for modelling interest rates but the above approach is both intuitively simple and mathematically powerful.

The above equations can be incorporated into a broader Monte Carlo simulation, where we examine varying historical volatilities and original rates in order to produce a data set from which to derive a new future rate. Monte Carlo simulations involve the repeated, and random, generation of data within a defined set of parameters, any or all of which can be altered to augment the data set. For example, using our basic equations above, we might run a Monte Carlo simulation which produces sample rates for constant historical volatilities but varying original rates. Or we may elect to have a simulation which alters the historical volatilities along with the original starting rates. As the simulation values are calculated, each one representing a random sample, they are stored for later use in the calculation of an arithmetic average. The central point behind a Monte Carlo is that a large number of repeated, random sample calculations will yield an average value from the set of all possible values, which can then be used in the relevant equation (such as the ones we have above). Monte Carlo models are widely used by institutions employing a method to simulate future rates.

Under our assumptions, the general equation employed to run a Monte Carlo simulation for a fixed rate payer would be as follows:

$$f = E\,[r_0 \times e^{(HV\sqrt{T})}] \tag{13.3}$$

where we are attempting to simulate the value of new rates (r(n)) based on our original rates (r(0)). E is the expected value of r(n) in a non-risk neutral world. Once sufficient values have been simulated, E(r(n)) will be estimated through an arithmetic average. In the above simulation we can establish different trials, holding HV constant while varying r(0) or *vice versa* or altering both variables at once. As one might suspect, the more variables altered in a given equation, the more complex the simulation.

Having developed a means by which to derive new rates, we focus on our replacement cost calculation. As mentioned above, the replacement cost equation sums the difference between the new coupon on the swap (r(n)) and the original coupon on the swap (r(0)) over the number of periods remaining until maturity, discounted back by the new coupon rate (ie the coupon rate in existence at the time of default); this process is similar in theory to a standard mark-to-market calculation. The equation provides an estimate of how much it will cost to replace a swap in the future (at the time of default), using simulated future rates. Most replacement cost calculations are quite standard and are patterned after the general form below; this is used for a swap paying semi-annually, hence the division by two. We term this the calculated replacement cost:

$$r_d = \text{calculated replacement cost} = \sum_{x=1}^{p} \left(\frac{\frac{(r_n - r_0)}{2}}{(1 + \frac{r_n}{2})} \right)^p \tag{13.4}$$

where r_n is the new rate in period x,

r_0 is the original rate,
p is the number of periods until maturity.

Very often the calculated replacement cost will be discounted back to today's terms using r(0). This can be detailed as:

$$r = \text{discounted replacement cost} = \frac{r_d}{(1 + r_0)^q} \tag{13.5}$$

where q is the period in which the default occurs.

If we were to examine the results produced by the above equations, we would be able to see the maximum replacement cost we are likely to face at any point during the swap's life. It is, effectively, the risk factor RF for a swap with that maximum maturity and those particular initial rate and volatility characteristics (see the last section of this chapter for representative risk factors).

Having developed both the simulated future rates and the replacement cost calculation (which can be implemented *via* the calculated or discounted equation), it is helpful to review a full example of how risk factors are developed for a five-year fixed/floating interest rate swap, with 16 per cent historical volatility, 10 per cent original rate for the fixed payer and semi-annual payments. Our simulated new rates are given in Table 13.7.

Table 13.7. New Simulated Interest Rates (per cent)

Time	r(0)	r(n) (up)
0.5	10.00	11.19
1.0	10.00	11.74
1.5	10.00	12.16
2.0	10.00	12.54
2.5	10.00	12.88
3.0	10.00	13.19
3.5	10.00	13.49
4.0	10.00	13.77
4.5	10.00	14.04
5.0	10.00	14.30

Using the simulated rates above in the calculated replacement cost equation (recalling that we compare r(n) with r(0) at each semi-annual period), we obtain a discounted calculation for each semi-annual period of the five-year swap (see Table 13.8).

Table 13.8. Discounted Replacement Costs at Each Period

	Individual r(d) terms (per cent)								
	Number of periods remaining in swap life								
n	1	2	3	4	5	6	7	8	9
0.5	.37	.39	.41	.43	.46	.48	.51	.54	.57
1	.55	.58	.62	.65	.69	.73	.77	.82	
1.5	.72	.76	.81	.86	.91	.96	1.0		
2	.88	.94	.99	1.06	1.12	1.2			
2.5	1.05	1.12	1.19	1.27	1.35				
3	1.24	1.32	1.41	1.50					
3.5	1.44	1.53	1.64						
4	1.65	1.76							
4.5	1.89								
5	0.00								

If we sum the individual calculated replacement cost terms above for each time period, we get a total calculated replacement cost. Discounting back using r(0) yields the discounted replacement cost, r. These are shown in Table 13.9.

Table 13.9. Total Discounted Replacement Costs

n	r(d) (per cent)	r(per cent)
0.5	4.1	4.0
1	5.4	4.9
1.5	6.0	5.2
2	6.2	5.1
2.5	6.0	4.7
3	5.5	4.1
3.5	4.6	3.3
4	3.4	2.3
4.5	1.9	1.2
5	0.0	0.0

Note that the maximum discounted replacement cost is 5.2 per cent occurring in year 1.5. This information indicates that the maximum replacement cost (and hence the maximum risk) we are likely to face under the above scenario is 5.2 per cent of the notional amount of the swap. We can say, therefore, that our risk factor RF for a five-year, 10 per cent fixed pay swap is 5.2 per cent.

If one plots the maturity of the swap transaction on the x-axis of a graph and the replacement cost along the y-axis, an interesting observation can be made. Because of the interaction of two distinct effects, typically referred to as the 'diffusion' effect and the 'amortisation' effect, the maximum risk facing the bank will occur not at the beginning or end of the swap but at some point in between.

The reason for this is relatively easy to explain: simulated future rates used in the calculation of replacement cost will not have had a chance to move sufficiently in the early periods to pose the greatest economic loss (diffusion effect); yet insufficient payments remain to be made towards the end of the swap to pose the greatest economic loss (amortisation effect). As a result, the greatest economic loss will occur at some point in between, when rates have had a chance to move and when there are still enough swap payments remaining to involve significant extra cost. Depending on the historical volatility used, the maximum replacement cost will occur between one-third of the way and halfway through the life of the swap. We can see in the example above that the maximum point on the five-year swap under 16 per cent volatility conditions is reached in year 1.5, one-third of the way through the life of the transaction.

Figure 13.3 demonstrates the interaction of the diffusion and amortisation effects in creating the replacement curve for both five- and 10-year swaps. It also allows the reader to see graphically where the risk factor on a swap with certain rate and maturity parameters comes from.

Once the equations above have been used to produce the series of replacement costs (discounted to today's value), it is relatively easy to create a table for risk factors (RF) to be used for easy calculation of swap risk. The procedure entails creating data tables with a range of fixed rates, say 5 per cent to 12 per cent. It is then necessary to create a range of maturities, from one year to 10 or 15 years. This encompasses a normal range of likely swap rates and maturities; for each rate and each maturity, the maximum replacement cost calculated becomes the risk factor for that maturity. This risk factor (or replacement cost) is then multiplied by the notional principal to obtain REE, as in our original equation (5.1)

$$\text{REE} = \text{RF} \times \text{N}$$

We considered above a five-year swap with 10 per cent rates and a 16 per cent historical volatility and found the maximum replacement cost and our RF to be 5.2 per cent, occurring in year 1.5. A 10-year swap with 10 per cent rates would have a maximum replacement cost of 10.7 per cent in year 3. Thus, a \$100m swap, where the bank pays 10 per cent fixed for 10 years

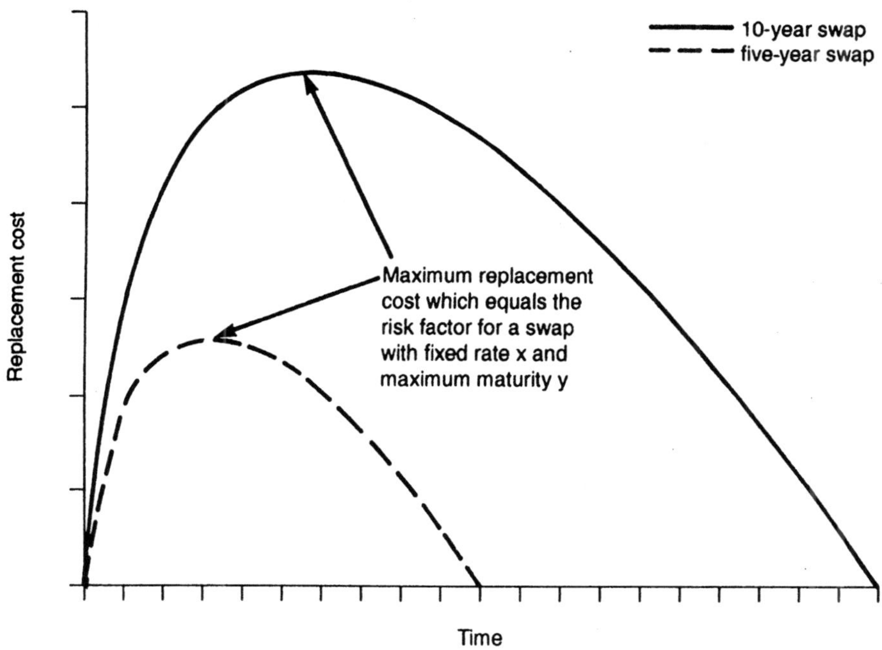

Figure 13.3. Swap Replacement Costs.

against receipt of LIBOR, will result in REE of \$10.7m (ie \$100m × 10.7 per cent). A full table of risk factors appears at the end of this chapter. Figure 13.4 demonstrates the replacement cost/risk factor calculation for the above swaps.

An Example of Swap Risk

Having defined both actual and fractional exposure, and knowing that the sum of the two equals potential exposure, we can create an example which demonstrates why potential exposure is the best measure of swap risk at inception, during the transaction and at maturity. Consider our 'plain vanilla' swap:

$$n = \$100m$$

Bank A is payer of 10 per cent fixed, semi-annually
Corporation X is payer of six-month LIBOR, semi-annually
maturity is 5 years, payments are matched

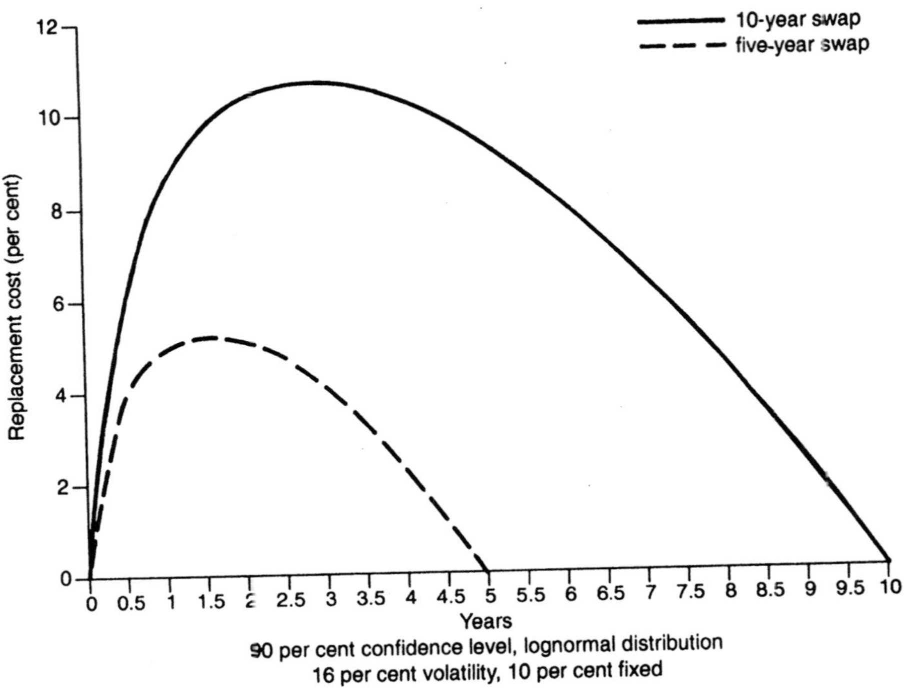

Figure 13.4. Swap Replacement Costs, 16 per cent Volatility, 10 per cent Fixed Rate.

Under this example we isolate the values of PE, FE and AE at different points in time, as shown in Table 13.10.

Bank A's maximum risk equivalent exposure attributable to the transaction can now be calculated:

$$\text{REE} = \text{RF} \times \text{N}$$
$$\$5.2\text{m} = 5.2 \text{ per cent of } \$100\text{m}$$

Several items can be noted from the above. First, we know that on trade date the MTM value and the accrued interest receivable (AIR) will both equal zero. Since rates will not have moved at trade date, the market value of the swap will not have changed. Likewise, since there has been no exchange of interest payments (matched or mismatched) on trade date, there can be no interest receivable. Consequently, the value of AE at trade date will always equal zero. Note that in the example above we have elected to use matched payments on a semi-annual basis; as a result, the interest receivable will always equal zero. Secondly, at inception, when the analyst approves the

Table 13.10. Risk Equivalent Exposure Calculation (Dollar Millions)

	Six-month LIBOR (per cent)	PE	=	FE	+	AE (MTM	+	AIR)
Trade date	10.00	0.0	=	0.0	+	0	+	0
Year 0.5	10.00	4.0	=	4.0	+	0	+	0
Year 1	10.00	4.9	=	4.9	+	0	+	0
Year 1.5	9.50	3.74	=	5.2	+	(1.46)	+	0
Year 2	9.50	3.82	=	5.1	+	(1.28)	+	0
Year 2.5	10.00	4.98	=	4.7	+	0	+	0
Year 3	10.50	4.65	=	4.1	+	0.88	+	0
Year 3.5	11.00	3.68	=	3.3	+	0.35	+	0
Year 4	11.50	1.9	=	2.3	+	1.38	+	0
Year 4.5	11.50	.75	=	1.2	+	.71	+	0
Year 5	11.50	1.5	=	0.0	+	.75	+	0

deal, the maximum risk which can be assigned to the swap will be the amount represented by FE (ie $5.2m). Thirdly, at the maturity of the swap, in five years, there is no more fractional exposure to consider, since there can be no more future rate movements which will affect the deal. Consequently, potential exposure at the end of the deal is always equal to actual exposure. Finally, the credit analyst at Bank X, evaluating the deal prior to trade date, cannot know how much risk to assign to the transaction without having a measure such as fractional exposure. With the deal data on hand and a swap risk grid indicating the appropriate fractional exposure factor to use against this swap, the analyst can assign a maximum risk figure prior to the inception of the swap (in our model it would be a 5.2 per cent factor against the notional amount of $100m, yielding a risk equivalent exposure on the transaction of $5.2m).

The example above in fact yields a maximum risk (FE + AE) of nearly $5m in the latter half of year three. The maximum actual MTM peak on this swap is nearly $1.4m in year four. Both measures fall within the amount of risk initially allocated to the transaction.

In order to highlight further the notion of a swap default, we turn to Figure 13.5. This simple example demonstrates the loss a bank could suffer if a counterparty defaulted while rates were in the bank's favour.

Risks Inherent in Other Swaps

Cross-currency Swaps

A traditional CCS combines elements of market risk which are slightly different from those found in an interest rate swap. Whereas in the IRS case

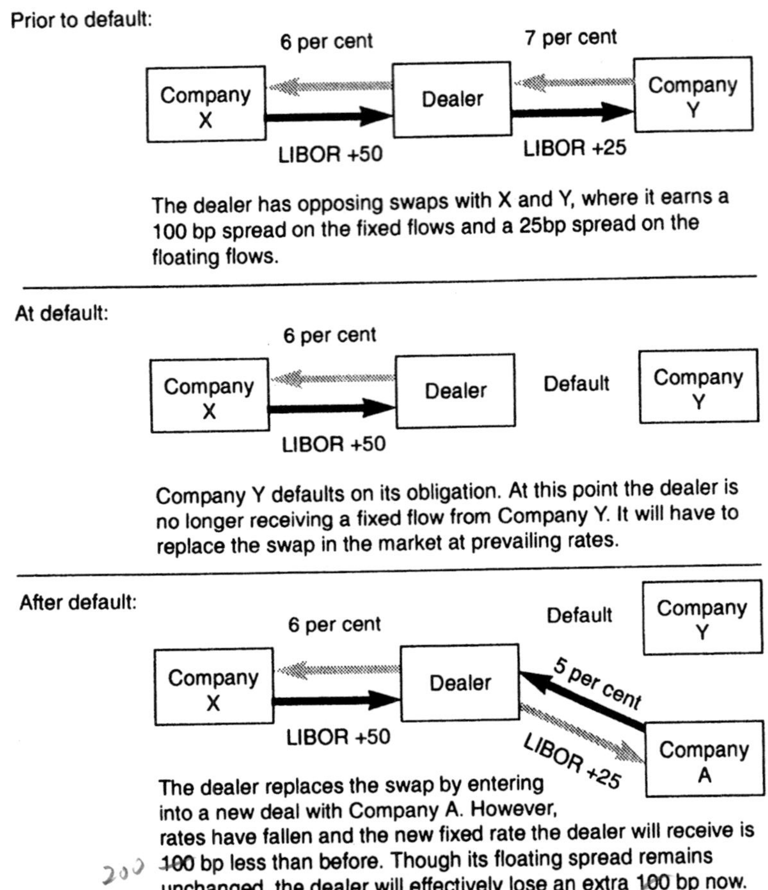

Figure 13.5. Loss to a Bank in the Event of Swap Default.

the focus was on the movement of interest rates, a CCS will focus on the movement of currency rates. In most risk evaluation models the risk attributable to market movement of currency rates far outweighs that of interest rates. The historical volatility of currencies since floating rates were introduced has shown substantial movement in a number of exchange rates against the US dollar (eg the yen, several European currencies and the Australian dollar).

The concept of actual exposure discussed above is still applicable to the evaluation of CCS risk: depending upon the movement of currency rates and whether or not a mismatch exists, a swap will always carry some actual exposure, whether positive or negative. Likewise, fractional exposure is still a key measure, with interest rate data replaced by currency rate data.

Understanding that currency volatilities are much greater than interest rate volatilities offers the conclusion that fractional exposures found in currency swaps will be greater than those found in interest rate swaps for corresponding maturities.

In addition to the slight difference found in the calculation of fractional exposure, a standard CCS with principal exchange carries with it an additional element of risk: since the two parties are literally swapping the notional currency obligations at trade date and at maturity date, there will be delivery risk involved in the transaction (see Chapters 4 and 12). For a period of perhaps 24 hours one party will be exposed in an amount equal to 100 per cent of the notional principal while it awaits receipt of the currency due to it. This obviously adds significantly to the risk of the transaction, if only for a short while (note that the same risk is assumed on every coupon payment date, although the amounts are smaller). The need to make a final currency payment at some distant future point is the single largest risk element in a standard CCS.

A currency coupon swap, with no principal exchange, will carry no delivery risk on the full notional amount but will do so on the coupon payments. The risk calculation in such scenarios focuses on single current interest rate movements plus a component to value the volatility of the currency. This may be achieved by using the correct fixed pay interest rate swap factor and adding the currency movement factor for the same maturity (see Chapter 12).

Special Derivatives

SWAP OPTIONS Recalling that a swaption is a hybrid which includes both an option and a swap, both instruments must be considered in the calculation of risk. For the writer of a swaption no risk exists on the option portion of the trade, since it is the purchaser of the option who is expecting performance on the underlying contract. Should a swaption be exercised by the purchaser, requiring the writer to enter into the swap transaction and not cash-settle at market, the writer would then face normal swap risk as outlined above. Thus, a short swaption with cash settlement involves no risk to the seller, while a non-cash-settling swaption implies normal swap risk. These two choices can be highlighted as follows:

$$\text{REE} = \{0 \vee (\text{RF} \times \text{N})\} \tag{13.6}$$

where RF is a standard swap risk factor,
N is the notional.

The purchaser of a swaption is expecting performance on the contract and, if exercised, on the swap as well. In entering into a swaption the purchaser will have paid a premium, so is initially at risk for the amount of premium paid out. In addition, should the purchaser choose to exercise the option to enter into the swap, it faces risk of default if the option writer reneges on the deal. At that point, the purchaser will most certainly be facing market risk, as it is unlikely that the option would be exercised if it were not in the money.

The amount of risk at that point will be equal to the MTM value of the potential swap transaction which the writer refuses (or is unable) to honour. The purchaser will therefore be out by the premium it has paid plus any market loss sustained by having to enter into a new swap transaction at less favourable rates. Should the option be exercised to cash-settle a position (as opposed to entering into a swap), the purchaser will once again be subject to market risk as calculated by the market value.

The above is accurate once the deal is in progress but it does not indicate the potential risk on the deal prior to execution (which is ultimately the value the analyst requires to make the correct decisions). For that we must consider a normal potential exposure framework. In the simplest form one can simply view the amount of premium paid as the risk of the deal, since this is the amount a purchaser stands to lose upfront. Should an option be exercised and a swap transacted, risk attributable to the deal will then be equal to that of a standard swap. A conservative model would value the risk as the premium paid out plus fractional exposure derived from the swaption contract (eg if the option allowed the purchaser to enter into a five-year, 8 per cent fixed/floating swap, the appropriate risk factor representing fractional exposure would be used). From a credit officer's point of view this covers all elements of risk which can possibly be encountered in the deal; this approach is rather conservative in that it views the exercise of the option into a swap as a certain event, which it is not. The equation would be written as follows:

$$\text{REE} = \text{premium paid} + (\text{RF} \times \text{N}) \tag{13.7}$$

where RF is the risk factor for the underlying swap,
N is the notional.

CALLABLE/PUTTABLE SWAPS In the case of callable and puttable swaps, we need to consider the differences between buying and selling. When selling either structure, a bank will receive either an upfront premium or a preferential rate embedded in the swap. From a risk point of view, the bank can remove the premium and focus solely on the normal risk associated with the swap. As an upfront payment it is relatively easy to isolate and to ignore. If the rate is embedded, the bank has to subtract the benefit derived from the preferential rate to yield the current swap par rate. At that point the bank will attribute only normal swap risk to the transaction, since counterparty default may still occur. Some institutions elect to subtract premium received from the normal swap exposure, since it ostensibly helps to 'defray' the risk. The risk equation reflecting both scenarios is:

$$\text{REE} = (\text{RF} \times \text{N}) - 0 \vee \text{premium received} \qquad (13.8)$$

A bank buying a puttable or callable swap will be facing a twofold risk, namely the option premium paid out plus the normal swap risk. If the counterparty defaults, the bank will be out by the premium paid as well as by any normal replacement cost associated with the underlying swap. The risk is therefore once again as expressed in equation (13.7).

CAPS AND FLOORS In the case of both caps and floors the buyer of the option pays a premium in return for a contractual obligation on the part of the writer to provide interest rate protection at certain levels. The buyer is thus exposed to the writer in the same fashion as the buyer of a swaption: it carries an exposure equal to the premium paid and, in instances where the cap or floor has moved into the money, is at risk to the writer in an amount equal to the in-the-money portion of the transaction (ie its market value).

If the writer of a cap defaults on its obligation to provide protection at 8 per cent when market rates have moved to 10 per cent, the buyer of the cap will be exposed to the 2 per cent differential it believed it had covered in entering the cap agreement. It will have to attempt to contract with another party to cap at 8 per cent, when market rates are already 200 basis points above, implying a very expensive in-the-money option with a high premium, or it will have to remain exposed to the market rates and cover the costs without protection. In either event, it is clear that the buyer faces an economic loss equal to the differential between the strike level and current market rates.

The writer of a cap or floor carries no risk in the transaction. Since it has received premium income from the buyer, it is the one which must perform on its part of the contractual obligation.

Generally, the most basic way to approach the risk calculation of the cap or floor is once again to focus on the premium paid out by the buyer of the option. The buyer pays out the premium today and, assuming immediate default by the cap or floor writer (prior to rates moving), it is the most to which the buyer will ever be exposed. On an ongoing basis, as the cap or floor moves into the money (if it ever does), some risk models will focus on the new differential between market and strike rates as the appropriate risk level (ie the market exposure the buyer now faces).

As with swaptions, the most conservative approach looks at some combination of the premium paid out and the exposure based on the strike rate and maturity of the cap or floor. A useful starting point in this effort is use of the swap risk grid. If a bank buys a two-year cap at 10 per cent in an 8 per cent market (ie the cap is 20 per cent out of the money), an analyst could take the two-year, 8 per cent swap risk factor and adjust it for the portion which is out of the money. Assuming that the swap risk factor is 1.3 per cent, an adjustment of 20 per cent would yield a new risk factor of 1.04 per cent. This, added to the premium paid out, would represent the risk on the cap. Note that this concept follows generally the treatment we applied to Treasury, MBS and FX options in previous chapters. In equation form we would obtain:

$$\text{REE} = \text{premium} + (\text{RF}_{\text{mkt}} \times \left[\frac{\text{mc}}{\text{sc}}\right] \times \text{N}) \tag{13.9}$$

where RF_{mkt} is the swap risk factor for the market rate,
sc is the strike rate of the cap,
mc is the market rate of the cap,
N is the notional.

For a floor, we would reverse one term of the equation:

$$\text{REE} = \text{premium} + (\text{RF}_{\text{mkt}} \times \left[\frac{\text{sf}}{\text{mf}}\right] \times \text{N}) \tag{13.10}$$

where RF_{mkt} is the swap risk factor for the market rate,
sf is the strike rate of the floor,
mf is the market rate of the floor,
N is the notional.

Note that the above equations will value the in-the-money portion by increasing the underlying risk factor; this occurs, obviously, once the ratio of mc/sc or sf/mf is above 1.

COLLARS AND CORRIDORS Recalling that collars and corridors are combinations of caps and floors, the easiest way to view the risk of the entire deal is to look at the different components of the transaction. In the case of a collar (X sells a cap to Y and buys a floor from Y) the most conservative approach would be for X to ignore the sale of the cap and focus solely on the purchase of the floor. Although X is expecting receipt of premium from the sale of the cap (which will help defray the premium it is paying on the floor), it can effectively ignore this and focus only on the obligation it is expecting Y to perform when it purchases the floor from it. In this scenario X will take the role of an option buyer detailed above.

Perhaps a more realistic scenario is one which would allow for the risk calculation to account for the receipt of premium as a means of defraying premium being paid out. In the case of a zero-cost collar there is no exchange of premium. This does not imply that there is no risk on the transaction; in these instances the focus of the risk equation might turn solely to either a market-based calculation (ie how much the 'long' leg of the collar is in the money) or a fractional exposure calculation based on the strike and maturity of the long portion.

In the instance of a corridor (X buys a cap from Y and simultaneously sells it a higher strike cap) the discussion is much the same: the risk focus can be isolated to the long portion of the transaction, while the short portion can be ignored (although once again the premium received from the sale of the higher cap can be factored into the calculation). Recall that a corridor can never be at zero cost. As with a collar, other models might focus on MTM value or a fractional exposure calculation as appropriate.

FORWARD SWAPS A forward swap is a unique instrument in that it involves two contract periods, one at the trade date of the underlying commitment and one at the inception of the swap. For example, a counterparty might enter today (trade date) into a two-year swap to begin in four years (inception date of swap). Although the underlying risk of the transaction should be no different from that of any other IRS (it has both actual and fractional exposures which change during the life of the deal), the important point to note is the rate benchmark used. In the example above our underlying risk factor cannot be based on two-year rates, since we are not contracting to start the swap today. Four years from now, when the deal actually hits the books, the floating rates we will face might be very different from those we see today.

In order to capture the potential difference in where rates may actually be, it is more logical to approach the calculation as follows: a forward swap in which Bank X pays 10 per cent fixed in four years for two years and Corporation Y pays LIBOR in four years for two years can be broken into two separate swaps. Under swap 1 Corporation Y receives 10 per cent for six years and pays LIBOR; under swap 2 Corporation Y pays 10 per cent for four years and receives LIBOR. Of course, Bank X would be on the opposite side of both of the above. The next step would be to subtract the flows. Since Corporation Y pays and receives LIBOR above, these flows cancel out. We are left with Corporation Y receiving 10 per cent for two years in four years, which is precisely the composition of our forward swap. The risk that can be assigned to the transaction follows the same logic: swap 1, based on the swap risk grid, might be a 4 per cent factor, while the risk on the second portion might only be 2 per cent: the risk on the deal would then be 2 per cent. The risk on a normal four-year swap according to the grid, in contrast, would be closer to 1.5 per cent. We can reflect the above in a simple equation:

$$\text{REE} = \{ (\text{RF}_1 \times \text{N}_1) - (\text{RF}_2 \times \text{N}_2) \} \qquad (13.11)$$

where RF1 is the risk factor attributable to a swap with maturity equal to both the forward period and the normal swap period,

N1 is the notional principal associated with the first swap,
RF2 is the risk factor attributable to a swap with only the normal swap period (not the forward period),
N2 is the notional principal associated with the second swap.

COMMODITY SWAPS A commodity swap model retains all the elements of our original IRS model: actual exposure (which is based on a mark-to-market calculation, although there are no receivables involved, since a standard commodity swap calls for net matched payment of obligations) and fractional exposure, with the historical volatilities reflecting movement of commodity prices, not interest or currency rates.

When commencing an oil swap, for example, oil prices will not have moved, so the actual exposure will be zero. Fractional exposure will be an amount calculated from the historical movement of oil prices within a certain statistical confidence level and will reflect anticipated exposure over a certain period. In practice most commodity swaps call for settlement every quarter. If Bank X is paying fixed oil at $23 a barrel and receiving from Company Y the average floating price on NYMEX as calculated one month prior to settlement date, one of the two will be making a net payment to the other at the end of each quarter. The swap will then 'begin' again for the second period, after which a further net payment will be made, and so on. This process has the effect of not allowing the MTM value (or actual exposure) to build up too far during the life of the swap, thus lessening the overall risk of the transaction.

Of course there are commodity swaps where no periodic marking to market and settlement occur; the risk in these will naturally be higher. Most commodity swaps tend to be in the short end of the maturity spectrum (six months to three years), since that is where most of the liquidity in the underlying commodity markets actually is. At the same time, however, commodity prices can be extremely volatile, even in the short run, so that there are still substantial risks in transacting this type of business. The movements in oil prices during the second half of 1990 and early 1991 are an excellent example of what can happen to commodity prices within a 12-month period.

Non-standard Swaps

The discussion above has centred on swap transactions which are considered 'standard', swaps where the periodic cash flows travel in a regular fashion, with no severe mismatches or uneven flows, and/or where the contracted fixed rate is equal to the current market rate. There are, as one might expect, instances where the frequencies and rates are executed at uneven intervals or off-market levels. In most situations the risk evaluation needs to be adjusted to accommodate these parameters.

PAYMENT MISMATCHES A swap may have payment mismatches, which can generally take three different forms: payment frequency mismatch, day count mismatch and reset mismatch.

In the case of payment frequency mismatch a bank may be paying semi-annually but receiving only annually. This, as we have seen, has the net effect of building up the accrued interest receivable, which is a key component in our potential exposure calculation (see above). It is simple to adapt our risk to account for a payment mismatch scenario; the adjustment is dependent upon the frequency of both payment and receipt. For practical purposes, we can consider the scenarios outlined in Table 13.11.

Table 13.11. Payment Mismatches

Frequency of payments	Frequency of receipts	Extra payments each period
Monthly (12)	Quarterly (4)	2
Monthly (12)	Semi-annually (2)	5
Monthly (12)	Annually (1)	11
Quarterly (4)	Semi-annually (2)	1
Quarterly (4)	Annually (1)	3
Semi-annually (2)	Annually (1)	1

The above extra payment calculation indicates how many additional payments the bank will make between receipts. The next step is to quantify the amount the bank will be paying out during these extra periods; this is accomplished by dividing the actual swap coupon by the payment frequency. This figure is multiplied by the extra payment calculation above and is then added to our normal RF to yield the REE for a mismatched swap against a bank. Note that a bank can reduce REE if the mismatch is in its favour, although it may choose to be conservative and ignore the favourable flows. The form of the equation is:

$$\text{REE} = \left(\frac{\text{coupon}}{\text{payment frequency}} \times \text{extra payments} + \text{RF}\right) \times \text{N} \quad (13.12)$$

For example, if Bank Q is going to pay 7 per cent quarterly and receive LIBOR annually for five years on $100m, it will face the following risk:

$$\text{REE} = (0.07/4 \times 3 + 0.041) \times \$100\text{m} = \$9.35\text{m}$$

From a practical standpoint the higher risk makes sense. Every quarter Bank Q will be paying $1.75m. By the time its counterparty makes a payment at the end of the fourth quarter, three periods will have elapsed, meaning the accrued interest receivable will be $5.25m. If the counterparty defaults before making its payment in the fourth quarter, Bank Q will be out $5.25m plus the amount it costs to replace the swap in the current market (which is captured by the 4.1 per cent risk factor included in the equation). Note that this pattern will be repeated every year for five years. These types of payment mismatch, which are relatively common, add very significant amounts of risk to a transaction and should not be ignored.

The most extreme example of a payment mismatch is one where the bank pays its coupon semi-annually or annually but receives no inflow until the maturity of the swap; this is known as a zero coupon swap.

Consider the following example: Bank A contracts to pay Company Z 7 per cent fixed on $50m notional for the next four years. In return, Company Z will make no floating payments until maturity, when it will advance Bank A the full amount owed it (based on 12-month LIBOR rates in existence at each anniversary, no compounding). The flows over the next four years, given certain assumptions about 12-month LIBOR, will be as shown in Table 13.12.

Table 13.12. Zero Coupon Swap

Period	12-months LIBOR (per cent)	Payments by Bank A	Payments by Company Z
Year 1	6 per cent	$3.5m	$0
Year 2	7 per cent	$3.5m	$0
Year 3	9 per cent	$3.5m	$0
Year 4	7 per cent	$3.5m	$14.5m
Total		$14m	$14.5m

For the first three years Bank A is extending a loan to Company Z for an eventual total of $10.5m. The bank is effectively an unsecured lender in this situation, with a full $10.5m at risk. In this extreme form of payment frequency mismatch, every dollar of interest paid out is at risk, since it is not being offset by inflows until some distant future date. In addition to this amount, the bank faces normal swap risk associated with a four-year, 7 per cent fixed/floating interest rate swap (approximately 3 per cent, according to the risk factors at the end of this chapter). That would imply an additional $1.5m, bringing total REE to $12m. We must always consider the second element because, if Company Z defaults at some point during the life of the transaction, Bank A faces not only the loss of funds already paid out but the possible replacement cost associated with its swap transaction. The form of the risk equation for zero coupon swaps, then, is:

$$\text{REE} = \Sigma \text{ unsecured payments} + (\text{RF} \times \text{N}) \qquad (13.13)$$

Recall further that the larger risk exposure will require additional capital support which, in turn, places additional profit pressure on the bank. The vital point to stress in any zero coupon structure is that the actual exposure on a transaction will be positive, and large, throughout. A great deal of care must be taken when considering such swaps.

Day count mismatch results from the count used to value the coupon payments. Depending upon the underlying index being used as a reference, day counts may be actual/365, actual/360, 30/360, actual/actual and so on. Although day count mismatches represent a change to the generic swap structure, they will not significantly alter the risk on a deal.

Reset mismatch occurs when a floating index is reset at a time other than its regular reset date. As an example, if the bank is paying six-month LIBOR, one would normally expect the LIBOR rate to be reset every six months. In a reset mismatch the six-month LIBOR rate would be changed every month or every quarter; this might have an impact on the coupon being paid to, or received from, the counterparty. Again, from a risk perspective, such a mismatch will not materially alter the risk encountered on a given trade.

NON-PAR SWAPS Non-par swaps are those which are contracted at rates other than current market rates. In such instances an upfront payment is likely to be made in one direction or the other. If a bank contracts to receive 10 per cent fixed in a market where fixed rates are only 9 per cent, it is booking a non-par swap. Since it is slated to receive a rate which in today's terms is advantageous, it will pay an upfront fee to the counterparty; this is known as a premium swap. If a bank agrees to receive 9 per cent in a 10 per cent market, it will expect a fee and is said to be booking a discount swap. From a risk perspective the primary concern comes with a premium swap; discount swaps typically carry normal swap risk, as we shall demonstrate below.

The primary item to consider in a premium swap is the immediate, built-in, mark-to-market exposure which the bank will incur. Since the swap will be 100 basis points above market in our example, any failure by the counterparty once the transaction has commenced will leave the bank with positive actual exposure. While we normally have to wait for a period of time before rates move and the mark-to-market exposure on a swap builds up, it should be apparent that such exposure will occur immediately with a premium swap. In exchange for the preferential rate, the bank will have paid a fee equivalent to the mark-to-market amount at inception.

Consider the following example: Bank Y enters into a \$25m three-year premium swap, paying 12-month LIBOR against receipt of 10 per cent fixed in a 9 per cent market (and paying its counterparty \$632,000 for the benefit). The mark-to-market exposure the day the swap is booked is

$$\$632{,}000 = \frac{\$250{,}000}{(1.09)^1} + \frac{\$250{,}000}{(1.09)^2} + \frac{\$250{,}000}{(1.09)^3}$$

Note that this figure is substantial compared with a mark to market of zero at inception date on standard transactions; since this is the MTM value of the swap, it is also equal to the fee being paid out. Our total risk must also include a standard risk factor applied against the notional principal to give us a potential market movement calculation. The total risk on this transaction is, therefore, \$1.26m, substantially higher than the \$625,000 attributable to a swap done under normal market rates. To capture the above in an equation, we can consider the following:

$$\text{REE} = \text{upfront payment} + (\text{RF} \times \text{N}) \tag{13.14}$$

with upfront payment equal to the initial MTM calculation.

As one might expect, if a bank is executing a discount swap the scenario is somewhat different. The bank will receive an upfront payment from the counterparty which can be used to defray the risk on the transaction if desired. This represents a payment to the bank for the privilege of paying a lower fixed rate in a higher fixed rate environment. Although the bank will be receiving less than the market rate, it incurs no exposure beyond normal REE. Should the counterparty default while the above arrangement is in place, one of two situations will result: if fixed rates have risen to 11 per cent at the time of default, the bank can rebook the transaction and receive 200 basis points more than it was previously receiving (and it would still have the fee it had obtained from the company); if rates have fallen to 8 per cent, the bank will have to replace the swap at a lower fixed rate and will sustain a loss. However, this difference should be captured in our potential exposure allocation, so should be viewed as normal swap risk. There is no additional swap risk incurred in transacting a discount swap. Our formula, therefore, is

$$\text{REE} = (\text{RF} \times \text{N}) - \text{upfront payment} \tag{13.15}$$

Ancillary Issues

The BIS Approach and Capital Considerations

While we have presented one approach to calculating swap risk, other institutions and regulators have their own approaches. In the BIS study of July

1988 entitled *The International Convergence of Capital Measurements and Capital Standards* (referred to in Part I) the BIS provided its methodology for calculating risk for swap and swap derivative products.

The BIS report includes two separate methods for calculating swap credit risk, the current exposure method (CEM) and the original exposure method (OEM). Under the CEM the relevant risk calculation is the replacement cost (similar to actual exposure above, ie MTM value, although the BIS approach makes no explicit mention of accrued interest) plus potential future credit exposure (which we term potential exposure in our model). Under future credit exposure the BIS recommends factors of 0.5 per cent for IRSs over one year and 5 per cent for CCSs over one year. Under the OEM no replacement cost is considered (the BIS ignores the ongoing MTM value of the transaction) but future credit exposure factors are higher: 0.5 per cent for IRSs under one year (2 per cent for CCSs), 1 per cent for IRSs from one to two years (6 per cent for CCSs) and an extra 1 per cent for each year an IRS exceeds two years (4 per cent a year for CCSs). The BIS indicated that institutions (with their regulators' permission) could choose between the CEM and OEM methods at the outset but, once selected, the method could not be changed. The Bank of England opted for the CEM, the Federal Reserve Bank required use of the CEM, the Reserve Bank of Australia allowed a choice of either the CEM or OEM and Canada's Office of the Superintendent of Financial Institutions allowed the OEM until October 1992 and the CEM thereafter.

Although certain other off-balance sheet items received a 100 per cent risk weighting under the BIS guidelines, swaps and derivatives initially received a 50 per cent variable weighting, on the assumption that the most active counterparties in the business are highly rated international banking institutions. However, the BIS has expressly reserved the right to alter the risk weighting in the future, if required. In order to determine the amount of capital to be allocated to a given CEM swap transaction, a bank would need to apply the following general formula (assuming it were targeting an 8 per cent capital ratio, the minimum required by the BIS):

$$\text{Captial ratio} = \frac{k}{(\text{MTM} + (\text{CEM}_{\text{factor}} \times \text{N}) \times \text{RW})} \qquad (13.16)$$

where Capital ratio is an institution's target BIS ratio,
k is the capital required to support a transaction (and represents an unknown to be solved),
MTM is the current mark-to-market value of the swap,
$\text{CEM}_{\text{factor}}$ is the appropriate current exposure method factor,
N is the notional,
RW is the risk weighting.

Placing the above in the form of an example, let us assume the following parameters: a \$100m notional swap with a two-year maturity, indicating a CEM(factor) of 0.5 per cent, no MTM value as yet, an 8 per cent BIS capital ratio and 50 per cent risk weighting. Solving for k, we obtain

8 per cent = k/(0 + (0.5 per cent × \$100m) × 50 per cent)
8 per cent = k/\$250,000
k = \$20,000

Accordingly, the swap desk would have to allocate \$20,000 of capital in support of this transaction under BIS CEM requirements. Note that this would represent a cost to the desk, as it is effectively 'renting' a portion of the bank's equity base; such cost would be transferred to the client in the pricing mechanism. Assuming that the bank's cost of capital is 10 per cent, the swap desk would pass on \$2000 a year to the client in the form of 'capital charges'.

We can modify the formula slightly to reflect the OEM method. Under this scenario we would have:

$$\text{Capital ratio} = \frac{k}{((\text{OEM}_{\text{factor}} \times N) \times RW)} \tag{13.17}$$

where Capital ratio is an institution's target BIS ratio,
k is the capital required to support a transaction (and represents an unknown to be solved),
$\text{OEM}_{\text{factor}}$ is the appropriate original exposure method factor,
N is the notional,
RW is the risk weighting.

Using the example above, the reader can easily calculate the capital required to support a swap under the BIS's OEM as \$40,000 or double that of the CEM. However, \$40,000 is the maximum that will ever be allocated, regardless of the ongoing value of the swap.

It should be pointed out that while the above BIS methods and capital requirements are applicable to all banks in countries such as the US, Canada, Germany, the UK, Australia and Japan, they are not applicable to other financial institutions in those countries. For example, the Federal Reserve does not regulate securities firms and insurance companies in the US, both of which are heavily involved in the swap business. While the SEC (which regulates securities firms) has capital requirements for securities firms (and has imposed a 100 per cent 'haircut' on swap transactions in determining net capital requirements), most major firms have transferred their swap business out of the registered broker dealers into other financial structures, so do not face such explicit capital requirements.

Swaps and Netting

One of the dominant topics of discussion in the swap market is the applicability of netting in bankruptcy situations. The BIS, in drawing up its swap methodology and weighting policy, allowed for netting by novation but not by close-out. Netting by novation is a procedure by which every time a swap payment is made the entire portfolio of swap contracts between two parties is amalgamated and rewritten into a new master transaction; this procedure is generally thought to be onerous as it calls for constant changes to documentation between counterparties. Netting by close-out, in contrast, is simply a netting arrangement where, in the event of default, contracts can be accelerated and the sum total of the actual exposures netted down to one payment in a single direction. In such cases a bankruptcy receiver would be unable to 'cherry-pick' those contracts which had value to the bankrupt company, since they would be included under one master swap contract or agreement. The concept of netting obviously has substantial appeal to most swap participants as it would allow for lower credit limits and/or a higher amount of business without incurring additional charges. In addition, in a bankruptcy situation, an institution facing the bankrupt counterparty would no longer have to be at the mercy of the receiver.

While the BIS has left netting by close-out open for future discussion, regulators in most countries have continued to allow explicitly only netting by novation (the UK, Canada, Japan and Australia all come into this category). The one exception is the US, where the Financial Institutions Reform, Recovery and Enforcement Act of 1989 (FIRREA) paved the way for netting by close-out. Under FIRREA a bank facing a bankrupt bank with which it has swap contracts can terminate the contracts, exercise its right to liquidate any collateral which might be available in support of any contract and offset, or net out, all contracts. There can be no 'cherry-picking' by the receiver or trustee and swap payments cannot be deemed preference items (in bankruptcy law so-called 'clawbacks' may occur if a payment is determined to be a preference item; that is, if a payment effected 90 days or less before bankruptcy results in the recipient's gaining more than it would have done as a creditor, it must be repaid to the trustee or receiver).

In addition to FIRREA, the US Bankruptcy Code has also been amended where corporations and other financial institutions not covered by FIRREA would have the same protection. Specifically, the US Bankruptcy Code amendment now states that there is an exemption from the automatic stay which will allow parties to use collateral to cover amounts due under a transaction, there is a right to net out all outstanding contracts and swap payments cannot be deemed preference items.

Generally speaking, most swap participants use the International Swap Dealers' Association (ISDA) master swap agreement as a means to document swaps between two parties. The ISDA documentation contains a number of legal definitions and details, including events of default, termination events, calculation of swap values in the event of early termination, cross-default, credit event upon merger and so on. It is generally considered that all swaps transacted under an ISDA master agreement are a single transaction, thus countering 'cherry-picking' under FIRREA and the US Bankruptcy Code. Such a single agreement structure helps to prevent receivers from honouring only contracts favourable to a bankrupt company.

The concept of netting by close-out is powerful and has important implications. Aside from not having to be concerned about a receiver's actions during bankruptcy, an institution can effectively lower the credit limits required to support swap transactions. The true measure of swap risk will now be a 'net', not a 'gross', potential exposure. If a counterparty is active on both sides of the market (ie paying fixed on some swaps and receiving fixed on others), by definition the net potential exposure will be lower. Consider Table 13.13, an example from the perspective of Bank Y.

Table 13.13. Bank Y's Swaps

	Pay fixed		Receive fixed		Gross	Net
	PE	AE	PE	AE	PE	PE
Bank A	$100m	$25m	($50m)	($40m)	$100m	$50m

Bank Y has a portfolio of pay fixed swaps with Bank A, with potential exposure of $100m. It also has receive fixed swaps with potential exposure of ($50m); since the MTM is heavily in A's favour ($40m), it more than offsets any effects remaining from the fractional exposure component. In a non-netting situation Bank Y would measure the potential risk of the swaps at $100m. If it had previously established a $100m REE limit for swaps with A, it could no longer accommodate any transactions. However, since netting by close-out is allowable in the US, we know that the true PE is only $50m, which would allow a further $50m of swaps to be booked with A.

The second point we highlight occurs if A files for bankruptcy. Under a regime of no close-outs, and assuming a competent receiver, Bank Y would be forced to pay $40m to Bank A and receive nothing in return. That is, the receiver would 'cherry-pick' the contracts with value to A, with a total AE of ($40m), and dismiss those contracts detrimental to A, with a total AE of $25m. Using close-outs, Y would make a payment to A of only $15m, or ($40m) + $25m, which is the amount it was expecting to pay out.

While netting by close-out has not been resolved on a global basis, there is a strong expectation by market professionals that an agreement on an approach will be reached soon; the exact form of the approach remains to be seen. Until that time, however, any institution not operating solely in the US is likely to be prudent in applying gross exposures against limits.

Swaps in a Portfolio Framework: Individual Counterparties

We have developed a framework for looking at the risk of each swap as it is added to a bank's books. We know that, in transacting the next swap, we will incur a certain amount of additional risk, identified as fractional exposure. An issue worth exploring, particularly as the swap and derivatives business grows, is how much incremental risk a bank assumes in transacting the next deal.

If we consider an extreme example, where our bank has a portfolio of 10 interest rate swaps with Company X, evenly split between pay fixed and receive fixed and all booked on a par basis on the same day, we can come to an important initial conclusion: we cannot suffer increasing exposure (and potential losses) on all swaps at the same time, if only because we are on both sides of the transactions.

Although we have allocated fractional exposure to each individual transaction (eg a total of $10m), we know that the maximum amount we can be exposed to and could potentially lose must be some amount less than $10m. When rates rise, our pay fixed swaps will increase in exposure. When rates fall, they will decrease in exposure. At the same time, our receive fixed swaps will react in the opposite way. Thus, rate movements will be beneficial to our exposure on some swaps and detrimental to our exposure on others. Depending on one's view of netting in the swap market, the actual amount at stake could be less than $5m. When we add another swap, we assume some increased level of risk but it cannot be equal, on an ongoing basis, to the full fractional risk exposure we assign to the deal.

Consider Table 13.14, which is a portfolio simulation for Counterparty X. Under this approach, all interest rate swaps booked with X are combined together and identified as fixed pay or receive (we could also incorporate other interest rate products, such as caps, floors and swaptions). We include our original fixed rate level, as well as the current par fixed rate which would be required to duplicate a given swap in today's market. These two items can be used to determine our current mark-to-market exposure (or actual exposure AE; for the purposes of this exercise we simplify the concept and assume that there are no payment mismatches causing an accrued interest receivable).

As a next step, we simulate fixed rates from today to the end of a given swap's maturity. Using the Rendleman and Bartter Model discussed earlier in this chapter, we can simulate both upward and downward movements in rates, where our starting rate is the current par fixed rate, not the original fixed rate. We then calculate the simulated MTM values (AEs) for both up and down scenarios. The actual MTM values are based on a default at the

Table 13.14. Portfolio Simulation: counterparty X As at: 6/92

Historical volatility 16 per cent, 90 per cent confidence level, lognormal distribution

Swap #	Start	End	Co. pay	Notional	Orig fixed (per cent)	Curr par fixed (per cent)	Simul fixed up (per cent)	Simul fixed down (per cent)	Init FE	Curr AE	Simul AE up	Simul AE down
1	6/90	6/93	fix	$100m	6.00	7.10	8.33	6.05	2.10	−1.03	0.00	−0.05
2	12/88	12/98	flt	$75m	7.25	7.60	11.43	6.48	7.00	1.39	8.53	0.00
3	9/90	6/95	fix	$30m	6.25	7.22	9.53	6.15	0.90	−0.76	0.00	0.03
4	6/87	6/93	fix	$30m	7.50	7.15	8.39	6.09	1.62	0.10	0.00	0.39
5	5/89	5/93	flt	$40m	7.00	7.11	8.29	6.06	1.20	0.04	0.25	0.00
6	6/90	12/92	fix	$35m	6.00	7.08	7.93	6.03	0.53	−0.37	0.00	0.00
7	12/89	12/95	flt	$50m	7.00	7.22	9.74	6.15	2.55	0.38	1.25	0.00
Counterparty X totals:									15.90	−0.25	10.03	0.37
						no netting:				1.91	10.03	0.42

Where columns are defined as follows:
Co-pay: counterparty pays fixed or floating
Orig fixed: originally contracted fixed rate
Curr par fixed: current fixed rate required to book a new par swap with a given original deal's parameters
Simul fixed: simulated fixed rate, based on Rendleman and Bartter Model, reflecting current par fixed rate and time left to maturity
Init FE: initial fractional exposure allocated in the transaction (ie RF × N)
Curr FE: current fractional exposure based on ever reducing risk factors
Curr AE: current actual exposure, or mark-to-market value plus accrued interest
Simul AE up: simulated mark-to-market values when rates rise (detrimental to bank when fixed rate payer)
Simul AE down: simulated mark-to-market values when rates fall (detrimental to bank when fixed rate receiver)
MTM is defined as sum of cash flows (simulated coupon – original coupon × notional) discounted at simulated fixed rate, from one-third through remaining maturity to maturity.
The one-third assumption is used since the maximum exposure we are likely to face will occur one-third of the way through the remaining swap, based on 16 per cent historical volatility.
Note: original, current and simulated rates are for illustrative purposes only.

point when rates have moved to their maximum or minimum. We already know that, with a 16 per cent historical volatility (90 per cent confidence level, lognormal distribution), the worst point will occur one-third of the way through the remaining term. With that as the worst point, we take a mark-to-market calculation from that point to the end of the swap. This will be the maximum AE a bank would face under the new simulated rates.

Since we know that rising rates will be detrimental to the bank's exposure if it is a fixed rate payer on certain swaps, the opposite scenario must by definition equal zero; therefore, we set our simulated AE in a down market to zero when the bank is a fixed payer. It will also, of course, be true that when a bank is a fixed rate receiver its simulated AE in a down market will increase as rates fall and will be set at zero in a rising environment. As a result, the ongoing simulated mark-to-market exposure is going to be less than our initially calculated fractional exposure. In our example the simulated AE in a market moving up is $10m, against an initial FE of $16m. When rates are moving down the bank's exposure is even less, since only two of the smaller and shorter swaps present the chance for substantial movements.

This exercise could be repeated on a quarterly basis for every counterparty, with new simulated rates being projected based on new quarterly current par fixed rates. As new swaps are added and old swaps mature, we would expect to see overall changes in the total portfolio exposure. Likewise, if netting were applicable, total exposure would be lower; if an institution elected not to use netting, it could adjust its simulation techniques accordingly.

For currency swaps a similar approach could be taken by grouping opposing currency pairs within a given simulation framework. For example, a bank could group its DM/$ swaps against its $/DM swaps, under the same assumption that a movement of Deutschmark against the $ cannot hurt both positions simultaneously. In addition, it could also elect to include currencies which are very closely correlated with the Deutschmark (eg the ECU and the Dutch guilder).

The central point to emphasise in this process is that a portfolio treatment of swaps with a given counterparty has some very legitimate uses. It can more effectively value incremental swap exposure on an ongoing basis and will generally not overstate a bank's exposure to a given counterparty in the same way that a strict summation of fractional exposures will. While simulation techniques can vary, it should be clear that the result will be a lower, and ultimately more accurate, exposure figure. Naturally, an analyst initially considering a swap transaction must still rely on a fractional exposure calculation to make his or her decision, hence the value and use of the framework we have developed. However, on an ongoing basis, when considering the effects of an incremental deal, an analyst could find the portfolio approach of use.

Swaps in a Portfolio Framework: All Counterparties

Some institutions elect to look at a portfolio in its entirety, across counterparties. The underlying rationale for doing so is that risk of default on swaps is unsystematic, ie there is no correlation between one counterparty's default and a second counterparty's default. With that assumption in mind, one might believe that the greater the number of swaps in a portfolio, the lower the risk of default, so long as the dealer is active on both sides of the market, which is a reasonable assumption. This, of course, is no different from diversification in a securities portfolio.

One way in which to develop a view of the whole portfolio is as follows: first, we assume that a swap dealer, based both on the overall credit quality of its portfolio and on its study of bond default rates for entities with the same credit quality, assigns a 2 per cent likelihood of default, in the first year, to swaps in the portfolio; the likelihood of default attributable to the second year is 3 per cent. This is a figure which may be revised every six or 12 months as the average credit quality of the entire portfolio changes or as new bond default information becomes available. Note that actual swap default percentages may not be relevant, since the number of defaults to date is very low; bond defaults offer a very conservative proxy.

Secondly, the dealer calculates the average REE of a typical swap to be \$1m (again, this is a parameter which might vary over time). Using these assumptions, the expected value of default in the first year is \$1m x 2 per cent or \$20,000. The default risk for each swap is calculated as the standard error of the expected value of the default, which is simply a statistical calculation. This is denoted as follows:

$$EV_{\mu} = \frac{ED_d}{\sqrt{n}} \tag{13.18}$$

where EV_d is \$20,000,
n is the number of swaps in the portfolio.

If we assume that the bank has 10 swaps in the portfolio, the risk of default per swap is \$6324. As the portfolio increases, and recalling that swaps are written on both sides of the market and swap defaults are uncorrelated, the risk of default per swap continues to fall (see Table 13.15).

The above could be repeated for a portfolio of swaps by examining the probability of default in the second and subsequent years. This is represented graphically in Figure 13.6.

This is a theoretical framework and relies on certain underlying assumptions such as average REE and probabilities of default. Its primary application is likely to come in a complete risk management framework, so that an institution is able to estimate generally how risk is reduced or increased in a

Table 13.15. Risk of Default

n	EV(u) (year 1)
10	$6324
20	$4472
30	$3641
40	$3162
50	$2828
60	$2581

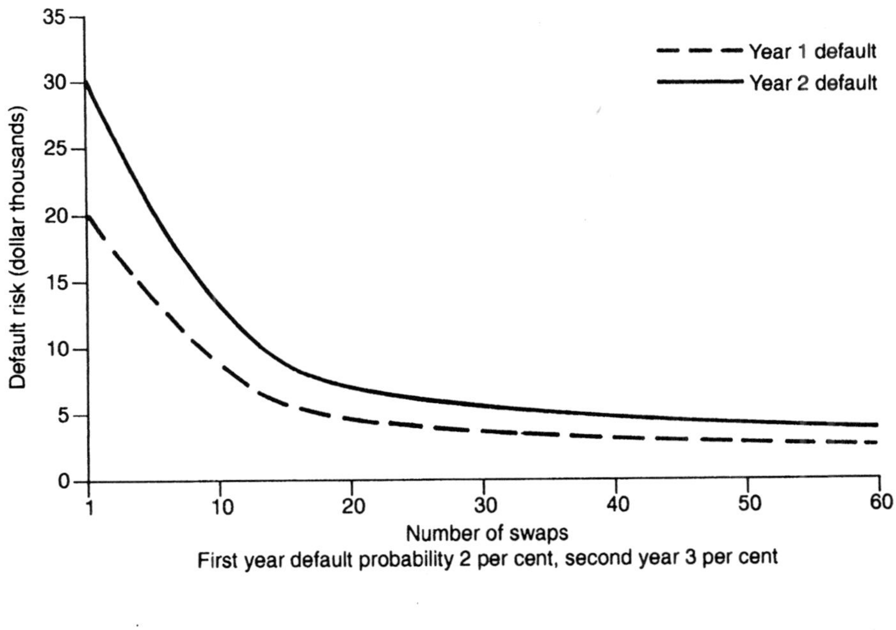

Figure 13.6. Swap Portfolio Risk Across Counterparties.

total portfolio of swaps as it grows (or shrinks). It is obviously less relevant when we are considering exposures to specific counterparties, since there we must constrain ourselves to individual legal entities and the risks associated in dealing with specific credit qualities and probabilities of default.

A Note on Swap Defaults

While the above discussion attempts to quantify risks which might be encountered should a counterparty default on a swap, the reality is that there have not been many major defaults in the market to date. As indicated in Chapter 1, in a recent survey by Arthur Andersen of banks and dealers controlling 70 per cent of the swap market only $385m in losses were reported as having occurred since the inception of the market (the actual figure may be slightly higher, since 30 per cent of the market is not included in the survey, but it is unlikely to be much more). According to the survey, the losses came from exposure to the UK local authorities ($178m), US and foreign financial institutions ($83m), non-financial corporations ($90m) and other governmental authorities ($3m). On a gross mark-to-market basis, which is the most accurate form for risk measurement since it indicates actual risk exposure without the benefit of netting, this equates to losses of 0.5 per cent. In a market which is close to $4 trillion notional in size, with a gross mark to market of $77.5b, the loss figure is low.

As indicated above, nearly half of the losses recorded in the survey are attributable to the case where several major banks holding in-the-money swap contracts with UK local authorities, principally Hammersmith & Fulham, had their contracts (and claims) deemed unenforceable. In the early 1980s Hammersmith, and up to 77 other local authorities, began transacting swap and swap derivative transactions. At its peak Hammersmith's own portfolio reached approximately $10b notional in size. Eventually many of these contracts turned against the authorities, which elected not to pay. In the ensuing legal cases the courts declared that the local authorities had been acting *ultra vires* (outside the scope of their powers) in entering the swap contracts and judged them unenforceable.

There have been several instances where counterparties have declared bankruptcy with substantial swap portfolios outstanding but the process of transferring existing deals has been relatively smooth. When Bank of New England filed for bankruptcy it had over $7b notional in swaps with a net positive mark to market of $200m. The entire portfolio was transferred to the FDIC and was subsequently sold to Fleet Norstar. In a further instance the failure of British and Commonwealth Holdings (a financial services conglomerate) left a swap portfolio of nearly $4b notional outstanding through its subsidiary, British and Commonwealth Merchant Bank. Once again a smooth transfer was effected by the sale of the entire portfolio to Barclays Bank. Similar problem-free transfers were accomplished with the swap portfolios of both DFC (which had swaps outstanding of NZ $4b notional) and Drexel Burnham Lambert (with $30b notional).

Despite several instances of clean portfolio transfers and reasonably low default and loss experience to date, it should be obvious that this might not always be the case. There is a need to quantify and manage the actual and anticipated risk on all swap transactions.

Hedging Swap Exposure

For swap market makers to be able to transact business they must be able to hedge their positions; this is true primarily when an institution seeks to act as a dealer. The swap dealer's ability to hedge a given transaction ultimately adds to the liquidity of the market. If a bank were unable to hedge effectively, it would find itself acting as an agent or intermediary, not as a principal. If that were the case, the volume and turnover of business would be lower, as banks would simply wait until they found the opposite side of a given trade, rather than taking the position onto their own books, hedging it and finding the opposite transaction at some future point. It is vital, then, that dealers be able to hedge.

In general terms, if a bank is a fixed rate payer (floating rate receiver), it hedges by having a cash position exactly opposite to the flows generated by the swap, in other words by receiving a fixed rate flow and paying a floating rate flow. To accomplish this, the bank can go long a 'like' bond with a fixed rate coupon and short a bond with a floating rate coupon. Alternatively, it can use the futures markets, so long as they have contracts on the underlying instruments required for the hedge. While the theory sounds straightforward, in reality a hedge is a much more complex (and often less than perfect) proposition. The ongoing correlation between the coupons of the swap and the coupons of the instrument(s) being used to hedge will ultimately determine the effectiveness of that hedge. A less than perfect hedge, however, is generally better than no hedge at all.

In the dollar interest rate swap market, particularly with standard structures, effective hedging is possible by several means. A dealer paying a fixed rate and receiving floating can do a reverse repo with 'like' US Treasuries (same maturity, same coupon), which will cause it to be long Treasuries and to receive a fixed Treasury rate which either duplicates or approximates the fixed rate being paid on the swap. Recall that most fixed rate dollar swaps are priced at a spread to Treasuries. Alternatively, if the dealer is receiving fixed and paying floating, it will want to be short Treasuries, so will repo them out.

Eurodollar futures can also be used to create a hedge. If a dealer is paying fixed and receiving floating, it will want to be long Eurodollar futures: such a position will allow it to receive fixed while paying out LIBOR. The reverse is obviously true: if the bank is paying floating and receiving fixed, it will go short Eurodollar futures. In practice the process is more difficult, as the dealer has to combine strips of Eurodollar futures to coincide with the various interest payment dates. Since a dealer is at the mercy of the standard futures contract dates, this type of hedging can be more difficult to accomplish.

It is generally true that Eurodollar hedging can be effective at the short end of the yield curve but as contract maturities and volumes thin out in the intermediate part of the curve futures are less effective and a US Treasury hedge is more useful. It makes sense that as the swaps become more complex the hedging becomes more involved and, perhaps, less effective. This is a principal reason why complex structures generally yield more income to the swap dealer and are much less liquid.

In the currency swap market hedging is considerably more difficult, primarily as a result of lower, or non-existent, liquidity in instruments normally associated with hedging, such as government bonds and futures instruments. Because of the difficulty and costs involved in hedging currency transactions as effectively as IRS transactions, the liquidity of the non-dollar market is much lower.

If there is an active government bond market, as in the UK, Germany, Japan, Italy, etc, the bank may short the underlying government obligation if it is a fixed rate receiver of that country's currency, sell the proceeds spot into the currency of which it is a payer and invest the proceeds in a Eurodeposit in the same currency.

Alternatively, if the above is not possible or is deemed to be too expensive, a dealer may elect not to attempt to match or hedge the swap in one piece. Rather, it will seek to match it up in sections. If it is to receive fixed Dutch guilders and pay out floating dollars, it can undertake two different swaps: a guilder IRS (where the bank receives floating guilders and pays fixed guilders) and a dual-currency LIBOR swap (where the bank pays floating guilders and receives floating dollars). This process again is not perfect but may be easier or cheaper to achieve. The dealer may also use the foreign exchange market, particularly long-dated transactions, to achieve its hedge.

At this point it is probably obvious that hedging can be difficult and often cannot guarantee that a dealer will not lose at least some money before the second side of a transaction is matched up. No hedge is perfect, since even in attempting to execute the structures above it is unlikely that all reset dates will be perfectly matched, that the market of the hedging instrument will always be perfectly in alignment with the swap market and so on. Nonetheless, it should be clear that not having a hedge in place can be potentially disastrous to the dealer.

RISK FACTORS

Table 13.16 gives sample risk factors based on the model discussed earlier in this chapter. The factors are based on Treasury rates with a 16 per cent historical volatility (after being adjusted to a 90 per cent confidence level, lognormal distribution). Factors are shown for fixed rates from 5 per cent to 12 per cent and for maturities from one year to 10 years. This range of rates and maturities encompasses the most likely scenarios to be encountered by an analyst approving a transaction. As explained earlier in the chapter, the risk factor for a given swap with fixed rate x and final maturity y is simply the maximum replacement cost of a swap with those characteristics when the adjusted historical volatility is 16 per cent. For example, in applying the model presented in this chapter, a 10-year, 10 per cent fixed rate swap will have a maximum replacement cost of 10.7 per cent, occurring in year three. Therefore, the relevant factor to encompass the maximum point of risk is 10.7 per cent. An analyst or credit committee seeking to approve a $100m swap with such parameters would assign an REE of $10.7m to the transaction.

Table 13.16. Sample Risk Factors for Interest Rate Swaps and Derivatives (per cent) (Fixed Payer)

Rate/Year	1	2	3	4	5	6	7	8	9	10
5 per cent	0.3	0.8	1.0	1.5	2.3	3.9	4.9	5.8	7.2	7.6
6 per cent	0.3	1.0	1.8	2.7	3.6	4.6	5.6	6.6	8.1	8.5
7 per cent	0.4	1.1	2.1	3.0	4.1	5.1	6.2	7.3	8.8	9.3
8 per cent	0.4	1.3	2.3	3.4	4.5	5.6	6.7	7.8	9.4	9.9
9 per cent	0.5	1.4	2.5	3.7	4.9	6.1	7.2	8.3	9.9	10.4
10 per cent	0.5	1.5	2.7	3.9	5.2	6.4	7.6	8.7	10.3	10.7
11 per cent	0.6	1.7	2.9	4.2	5.5	6.8	8.0	9.1	10.6	11.1
12 per cent	0.6	1.8	3.1	4.5	5.8	7.1	8.3	9.4	10.9	11.3

No risk factors have been included for currency swaps. The methodology employed to calculate such factors is identical to that illustrated, except that volatility on Treasury rates would be replaced by volatility on the relevant currency rate. See Chapter 12 for volatilities of major currencies.

Appendix 1: Alternative Method for Computation of Calculated Replacement Cost and Discounted Replacement Cost

INTRODUCTION

The customary methodology involved in the computation of calculated and discounted replacement costs is described and illustrated in Chapter 13. Essentially it features stepwise calculation, for a specified time, of the increment of the calculated replacement cost corresponding to each discount time interval. The summation of these incremental rates provides the total calculated replacement cost for the specified time during the term of the contract.

Although this procedure yields the desired information, computation can be lengthy and tedious. An alternative method of calculation is presented below. This method involves less computation and is just as accurate as the customary method already dealt with. In addition, the determination of the points of maximum differential rate and replacement rate is not difficult to obtain with this alternative method.

The author wishes to thank Dr Robert B. Banks for his valuable contribution to this section.

DEFINITIONS

t	time(years)
$r_d = f_t$	calculated replacement cost
$r = g_t$	discounted replacement cost, $r = \dfrac{r_d}{(1 + r_0)^t}$
r_0	original rate (per cent)
r_n	new rate (per cent), $r_n = r_0 \times e^{HV\sqrt{T}}$
HV	historical volatility (per cent)

T	maturity period (years)
D	discount interval (years)

DERIVATION OF THE ALTERNATIVE METHOD

In concise mathematical form, the formula to compute the calculated differential cost r(d) by the customary method is shown as

$$r_d = (r_n - r_0) \sum_{i=1}^{\frac{(T-t)}{d}} \frac{D}{(1 + r_n D)^i} \tag{A.1}$$

where r(n) is defined above. For example, if T = 10 years and D = 0.5 years, this expression becomes equation

$$\frac{r_d}{(r_n - r_d)} = \frac{1}{2\,(1 + \frac{r_n}{2})} + \frac{1}{2\,(1 + \frac{r_n}{2})^2} + \ldots + \frac{1}{2\,(1 + \frac{r_n}{2})^{2(10-t)}} \tag{A.2}$$

When t = 1 year this equation contains 18 terms; when t = 5 it contains 10 terms and so on.

We shall omit most of the mathematical details concerning the derivation of the final desired result. The main point is that in equation A.2 use is made of the infinite series

$$(1 + x)^{-n} = 1 - n\,x + \frac{n\,(n+1)}{2\,!}\,x^2 - \frac{n\,(n+1)\,(n+2)}{3\,!}\,x^3 + \ldots$$

This series can be utilised for our purposes so long as x = r(n)D is less than 1. If x is small or very small compared to 1, so much the better; the series converges even more rapidly. From equations A.1 and A.2, the final result is

$$r_d = (r_n - r_0) \sum_{i=1}^{N} \left(- \frac{1^{i-1}}{i\,!}\, r_n^{i-1} \prod_{j=1}^{i} [T + (j-1)\,D - t] \right) \tag{A.3}$$

where i! is the factorial of i (eg 4! = 4 × 3 × 2 × 1 = 24). The sigma symbol of course refers to addition, the pi symbol to multiplication; the quantity N is an integer. In most instances the series quickly converges; accordingly, N need be no larger than about 6 or 7.

Although equation A.3 looks rather formidable, it is in fact quite user-friendly. The first few terms of this are shown as

$$r_d=(r_n - r_0)\left((T-t) - \frac{r_n}{2}(T - t)(T + D - t) + \frac{r_n^2}{6}\right.$$
$$\left.(T - t)(T + d - t)(T + 2D - t) - \ldots\right) \quad \text{(A.4)}$$

The calculated replacement cost r(d) is calculated from this expression. The discounted replacement cost r is computed from

$$r = \frac{r_d}{(1 + r_0)^t} \quad \text{(A.5)}$$

NUMERICAL EXAMPLES

The computed results of two numerical examples are presented in Tables A1 and A2 and are shown in graphical form in Figures A1 and A2.

Table A1. Calculated Replacement Cost r(d) and Discounted Replacement Cost r for v=16 Per Cent, r(0)=10 Per Cent, T=10 Years, D=0.5 Years

t	r(d)	r
1	9.49	8.63
2	12.60	10.41
3	14.31	10.75
4	15.00	10.29
5	15.00	9.31
6	14.10	7.96
7	12.32	6.32
8	9.51	4.44
9	5.49	2.33
10	0.00	0.00

Table A2. Calculated Replacement Cost r(d) and Discounted Replacement Cost r for v=14.5 Per Cent, r(0)=10 Per Cent, T=Five Years, D=0.5 Years

t	r(d)	r
1	4.89	4.44
2	5.54	4.58
3	4.90	3.68
4	3.06	2.09
5	0.00	0.00

FURTHER REMARKS

The time and magnitude corresponding to the maximum calculated replacement cost can be determined by iterated solutions of equation A.4. In a similar way the time and magnitude of the maximum discounted replacement cost can be calculated by using equation A.5.

In the limiting case D = 0 we have the situation of instantaneous discounting. In this instance equation A.4 reduces

$$r_d = (r_n - r_0)(T - t)\left(1 - \frac{r_n}{2}(T - t) + \frac{r_n^{\,2}}{6}(T - t)^2 \ldots\right) \quad (A.6)$$

As might be anticipated from the well known result of instantaneous compounding, the value of r(d) calculated from equation A.6 is slightly larger than that computed from equation A.4.

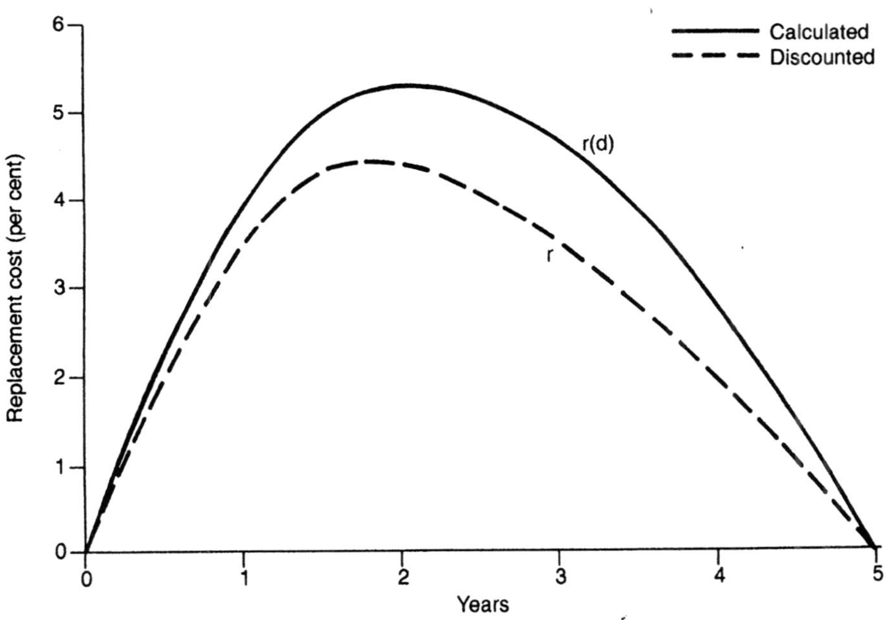

Figure A1.1. Calculated Replacement Cost r(d) and Discounted Replacement Cost r for V= 16 Per Cent, r(0) = 10 Per Cent, T = 10 Years, D = 0.5 Years.

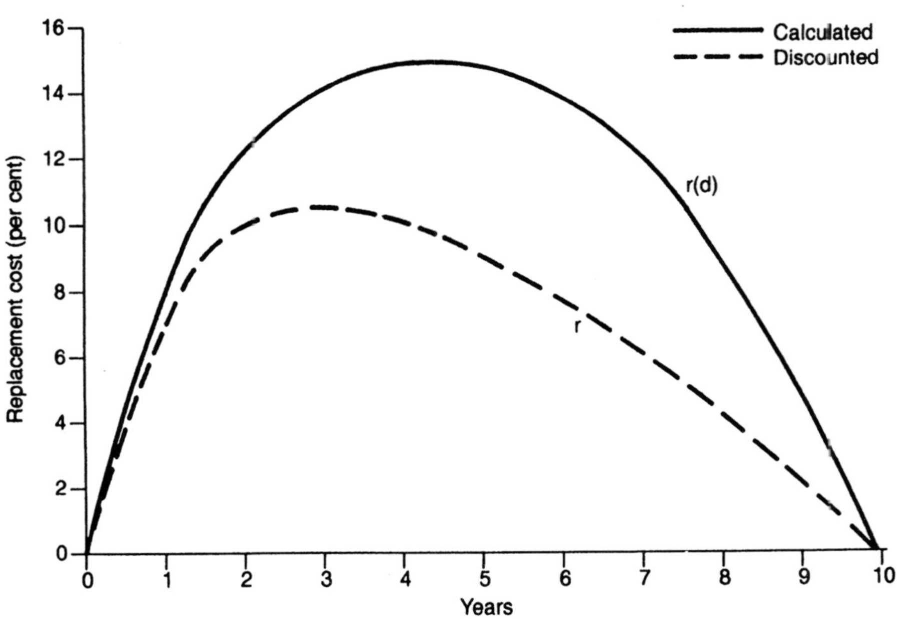

Figure A1.2. Calculated Replacement Cost r(d) and Discounted Replacement Cost r for V = 14.5 Per Cent, r(0) = 10 Per Cent, T = Five Years, D = 0.5 Years.

Appendix 2: Graphical Representation of Swap Replacement Costs

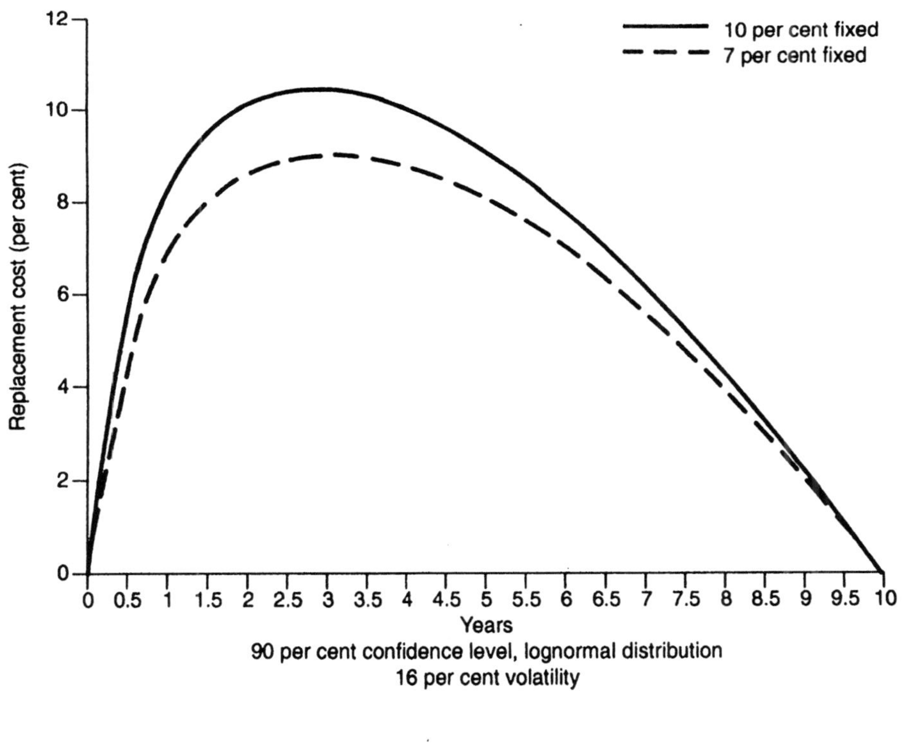

Figure A2.1. Swap Replacement Costs, 16 Per Cent Volatility

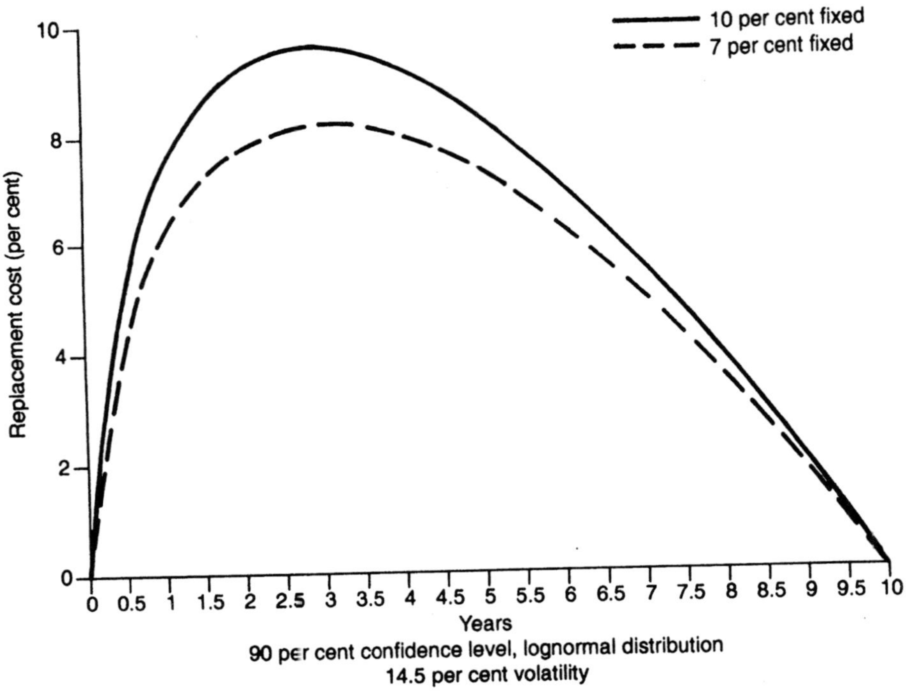

Figure A2.2. Swap Replacement Costs, 14.5 Per Cent Volatility

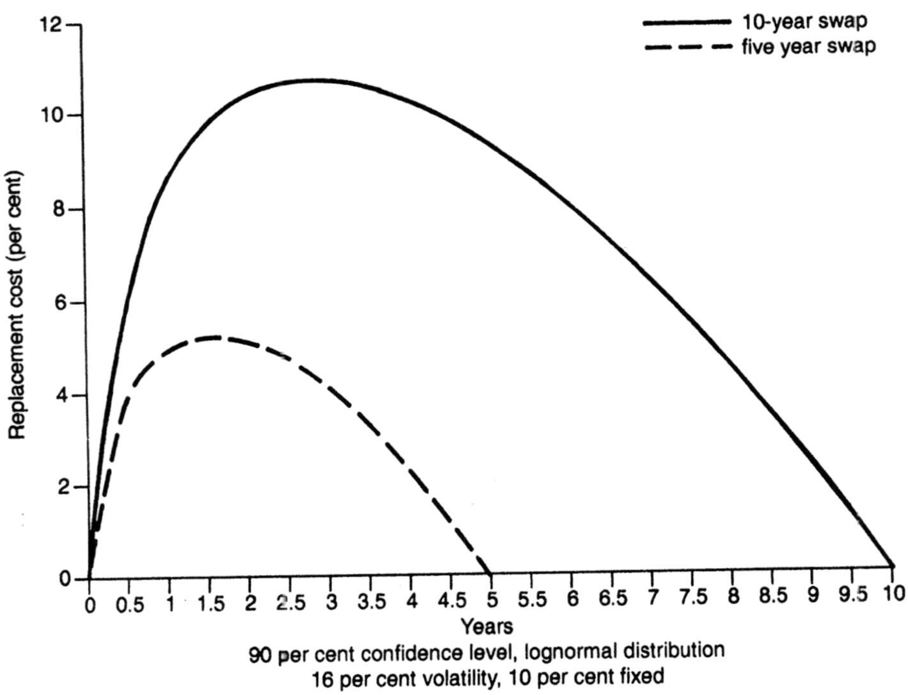

Figure A2.3. Swap Replacement Costs, 16 Per Cent Volatility, 10 Per Cent Fixed

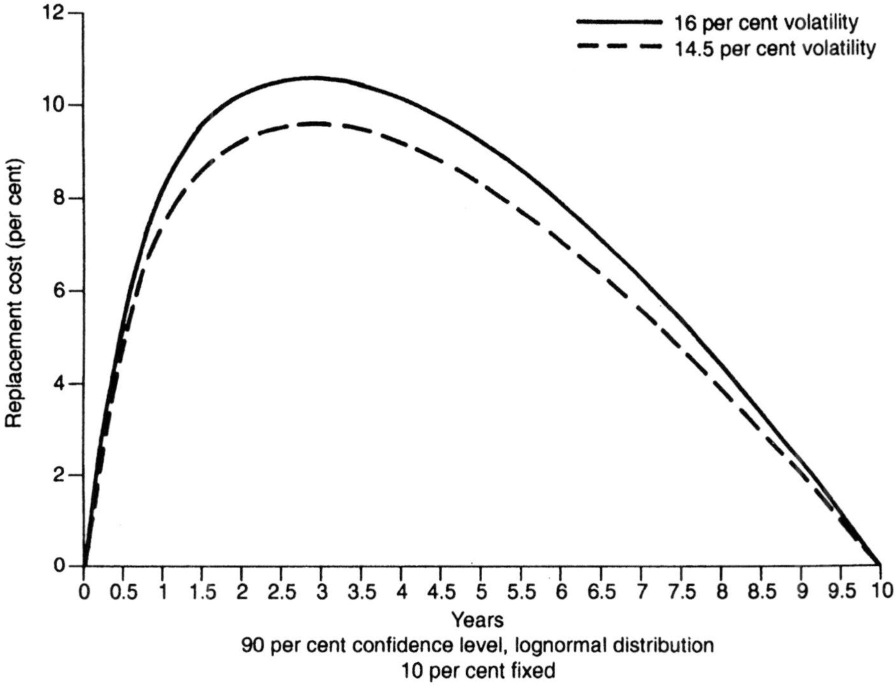

Figure A2.4. Swap Replacement Costs, 10 Per Cent Fixed

Appendix 3: Tabular Representations of Swap Replacement Costs

Swap Replacement Costs (Per Cent)

Historical volatility: 14.50 per cent

Orig rate (per cent)	Period	New rate (per cent)	Calculated replacement cost (per cent)	Number of periods remaining in swap life: 1	2	3	4	5	6	7	8	9	10	11	12	13	14	15	16	17	18	19	Discounted replacement cost (per cent)
7.00	0.5	7.76	5.0	0.183	0.191	0.198	0.206	0.214	0.222	0.230	0.239	0.249	0.258	0.268	0.279	0.290	0.301	0.312	0.325	0.337	0.350	0.364	4.8
7.00	1	8.09	6.9	0.267	0.278	0.290	0.301	0.313	0.326	0.339	0.353	0.367	0.382	0.398	0.414	0.430	0.448	0.466	0.485	0.504	0.525		6.4
7.00	1.5	8.36	8.2	0.339	0.353	0.368	0.383	0.399	0.416	0.433	0.452	0.470	0.490	0.511	0.532	0.554	0.577	0.602	0.627	0.653			7.4
7.00	2	8.59	9.1	0.406	0.424	0.442	0.461	0.481	0.501	0.523	0.546	0.569	0.593	0.619	0.645	0.673	0.702	0.732	0.764				7.9
7.00	2.5	8.80	9.8	0.473	0.493	0.515	0.538	0.562	0.586	0.612	0.639	0.667	0.696	0.727	0.759	0.793	0.827	0.864					8.2
7.00	3	9.00	10.2	0.540	0.564	0.589	0.616	0.643	0.672	0.703	0.734	0.767	0.802	0.838	0.876	0.915	0.956						8.3
7.00	3.5	9.18	10.5	0.609	0.636	0.666	0.696	0.728	0.762	0.797	0.833	0.871	0.911	0.953	0.997	1.043							8.3
7.00	4	9.35	10.6	0.680	0.712	0.745	0.780	0.817	0.855	0.895	0.937	0.981	1.027	1.075	1.125								8.1
7.00	4.5	9.52	10.6	0.756	0.792	0.829	0.869	0.910	0.954	0.999	1.047	1.096	1.149	1.203									7.8
7.00	5	9.68	10.4	0.835	0.876	0.918	0.963	1.009	1.058	1.109	1.163	1.219	1.278										7.4
7.00	5.5	9.84	10.1	0.920	0.966	1.013	1.063	1.115	1.170	1.227	1.288	1.351											7.0
7.00	6	9.99	9.6	1.011	1.061	1.114	1.170	1.228	1.290	1.354	1.422												6.4
7.00	6.5	10.13	9.0	1.108	1.164	1.223	1.285	1.350	1.418	1.490													5.8
7.00	7	10.27	8.3	1.212	1.274	1.339	1.408	1.481	1.557														5.2
7.00	7.5	10.41	7.3	1.324	1.393	1.465	1.542	1.622															4.4
7.00	8	10.55	6.3	1.445	1.521	1.601	1.686																3.6
7.00	8.5	10.68	5.0	1.575	1.659	1.748																	2.8
7.00	9	10.81	3.5	1.717	1.810																		1.9
7.00	9.5	10.94	1.9	1.870																			1.0
7.00	10	11.07	0.0	0.000																			0.0

Where columns are defined as follows:

Orig rate = original rate at which swap was booked
Period = semi-annual period at which default occurs
New rate = simulated future rate based on equation of orig rate × e ^ (HV × SQRT(period))
Calculated replacement cost = sum of differences between original rate and new rate, discounted by new rate
Columns 1–19 = individual coupon differentials period by period, required for calculation of calculated replacement cost
Discounted replacement cost = calculated replacement cost discounted by original rate to express maximum replacement cost in current terms

Swap Replacement Costs (per cent)

Historical volatility: 14.50 per cent				Number of periods remaining in swap life																			
Orig rate (per cent)	Period	New rate (per cent)	Calculated replacement cost (per cent)	1	2	3	4	5	6	7	8	9	10	11	12	13	14	15	16	17	18	19	Discounted replacement cost (per cent)
10.00	0.5	11.08	6.2	0.194	0.205	0.216	0.228	0.240	0.254	0.268	0.283	0.298	0.315	0.332	0.351	0.370	0.391	0.412	0.435	0.459	0.485	0.512	6.0
10.00	1	11.56	8.6	0.284	0.300	0.317	0.336	0.355	0.376	0.398	0.420	0.445	0.471	0.498	0.526	0.557	0.589	0.623	0.659	0.697	0.738		7.8
10.00	1.5	11.94	10.2	0.362	0.384	0.407	0.431	0.457	0.484	0.513	0.544	0.577	0.611	0.647	0.686	0.727	0.770	0.816	0.865	0.917			8.8
10.00	2	12.28	11.4	0.439	0.466	0.494	0.525	0.557	0.591	0.627	0.666	0.707	0.750	0.796	0.845	0.897	0.952	1.010	1.072				9.4
10.00	2.5	12.58	12.3	0.516	0.549	0.583	0.620	0.659	0.700	0.744	0.791	0.841	0.894	0.950	1.009	1.073	1.140	1.212					9.7
10.00	3	12.85	12.9	0.597	0.635	0.676	0.719	0.766	0.815	0.867	0.923	0.982	1.045	1.113	1.184	1.260	1.341						9.7
10.00	3.5	13.12	13.4	0.682	0.727	0.775	0.826	0.880	0.937	0.999	1.064	1.134	1.209	1.288	1.372	1.462							9.6
10.00	4	13.36	13.6	0.774	0.826	0.881	0.940	1.003	1.070	1.141	1.217	1.299	1.385	1.478	1.577								9.3
10.00	4.5	13.60	13.6	0.873	0.933	0.996	1.064	1.136	1.213	1.296	1.384	1.478	1.579	1.686									8.9
10.00	5	13.83	13.5	0.981	1.049	1.122	1.199	1.282	1.371	1.465	1.567	1.675	1.791										8.4
10.00	5.5	14.05	13.2	1.099	1.176	1.259	1.348	1.442	1.544	1.652	1.768	1.892											7.8
10.00	6	14.26	12.7	1.229	1.316	1.410	1.511	1.619	1.734	1.858	1.990												7.2
10.00	6.5	14.47	12.0	1.371	1.471	1.577	1.691	1.813	1.945	2.085													6.4
10.00	7	14.68	11.0	1.529	1.641	1.761	1.891	2.029	2.178														5.7
10.00	7.5	14.88	9.9	1.703	1.829	1.966	2.122	2.269															4.8
10.00	8	15.07	8.5	1.896	2.039	2.192	2.357																4.0
10.00	8.5	15.26	6.8	2.110	2.271	2.444																	3.0
10.00	9	15.45	4.9	2.348	2.529																		2.1
10.00	9.5	15.63	2.6	2.613																			1.1
10.00	10	15.82	0.0	0.000																			0.0

Where columns are defined as follows:

Orig rate = original rate at which swap was booked
Period = semi-annual period at which default occurs
New Rate = simulated future rate based on equation of orig rate × e (HV × SQRT(period))
Calculated replacement cost = sum of differences between original rate and new rate, discounted by new rate
Columns 1–19 = individual coupon differentials period by period, required for calculation of calculated replacement cost
Discounted replacement cost = calculated replacement cost discounted by original rate to express maximum replacement cost in current terms

Swap Replacement Costs (per cent)

Historical volatility: 16.00 per cent				Number of periods remaining in swap life																			
Orig rate (per cent)	Period	New rate (per cent)	Calculated replacement cost	1	2	3	4	5	6	7	8	9	10	11	12	13	14	15	16	17	18	19	Discounted replacement cost (per cent)
7.00	0.5	7.84	5.5	0.202	0.210	0.218	0.227	0.236	0.245	0.254	0.264	0.275	0.285	0.297	0.308	0.320	0.333	0.346	0.359	0.374	0.388	0.403	5.4
7.00	1	8.21	7.6	0.294	0.306	0.319	0.332	0.346	0.360	0.375	0.390	0.406	0.423	0.440	0.458	0.477	0.497	0.517	0.538	0.560	0.583		7.1
7.00	1.5	8.52	9.0	0.373	0.389	0.405	0.423	0.441	0.459	0.479	0.499	0.521	0.543	0.566	0.590	0.615	0.641	0.669	0.697	0.727			8.2
7.00	2	8.78	10.1	0.447	0.467	0.487	0.508	0.531	0.554	0.578	0.604	0.630	0.658	0.687	0.717	0.748	0.781	0.816	0.851				8.8
7.00	2.5	9.02	10.8	0.520	0.543	0.568	0.594	0.620	0.648	0.678	0.708	0.740	0.773	0.808	0.845	0.883	0.922	0.964					9.1
7.00	3	9.24	11.3	0.594	0.622	0.650	0.680	0.712	0.745	0.779	0.815	0.852	0.892	0.933	0.976	1.021	1.068						9.3
7.00	3.5	9.44	11.7	0.670	0.702	0.735	0.770	0.806	0.844	0.884	0.926	0.970	1.016	1.063	1.114	1.166							9.2
7.00	4	9.64	11.8	0.750	0.786	0.824	0.864	0.906	0.949	0.995	1.043	1.093	1.146	1.201	1.259								9.0
7.00	4.5	9.83	11.8	0.834	0.875	0.918	0.964	1.011	1.061	1.113	1.167	1.225	1.285	1.348									8.7
7.00	5	10.01	11.6	0.924	0.970	1.019	1.070	1.123	1.179	1.238	1.300	1.365	1.434										8.3
7.00	5.5	10.19	11.3	1.019	1.071	1.126	1.183	1.243	1.306	1.373	1.443	1.516											7.8
7.00	6	10.36	10.8	1.121	1.179	1.240	1.305	1.372	1.443	1.518	1.597												7.2
7.00	6.5	10.53	10.1	1.231	1.296	1.364	1.436	1.511	1.591	1.675													6.5
7.00	7	10.69	9.3	1.350	1.422	1.498	1.578	1.662	1.751														5.8
7.00	7.5	10.85	8.2	1.478	1.558	1.643	1.732	1.826															5.0
7.00	8	11.01	7.0	1.617	1.706	1.800	1.899																4.1
7.00	8.5	11.16	5.6	1.768	1.866	1.970																	3.2
7.00	9	11.31	4.0	1.932	2.041																		2.2
7.00	9.5	11.46	2.1	2.110																			1.1
7.00	10	11.61	0.0	0.000																			0.0

Where columns are defined as follows:

Orig rate = original rate at which swap was booked
Period = semi-annual period at which default occurs
New Rate = simulated future rate based on equation of orig rate × e (HV × SQRT(period))
Calculated replacement cost = sum of differences between original rate and new rate, discounted by new rate
Columns 1–19 = individual coupon differentials period by period, required for calculation of calculated replacement cost
Discounted replacement cost = calculated replacement cost discounted by original rate to express maximum replacement cost in current terms

Swap Replacement Costs (per cent)

Historical volatility: 16.00 per cent				Number of periods remaining in swap life																			
Orig rate (per cent)	Period	New rate (per cent)	Calculated replacement cost (per cent)	1	2	3	4	5	6	7	8	9	10	11	12	13	14	15	16	17	18	19	Discounted replacement cost (per cent)
10.00	0.5	11.20	6.9	0.213	0.225	0.237	0.251	0.265	0.279	0.295	0.312	0.329	0.347	0.367	0.387	0.409	0.432	0.456	0.482	0.509	0.537	0.567	6.6
10.00	1	11.74	9.5	0.311	0.329	0.348	0.369	0.390	0.413	0.438	0.463	0.491	0.519	0.550	0.582	0.616	0.652	0.691	0.731	0.774	0.819		8.6
10.00	1.5	12.16	11.3	0.397	0.421	0.446	0.474	0.502	0.533	0.565	0.600	0.636	0.675	0.716	0.759	0.806	0.855	0.907	0.962	1.020			9.8
10.00	2	12.54	12.6	0.480	0.510	0.542	0.576	0.612	0.650	0.691	0.734	0.781	0.829	0.881	0.937	0.995	1.058	1.124	1.195				10.4
10.00	2.5	12.88	13.6	0.564	0.601	0.639	0.681	0.724	0.771	0.821	0.874	0.930	0.990	1.054	1.121	1.194	1.270	1.352					10.7
10.00	3	13.19	14.3	0.653	0.696	0.742	0.791	0.843	0.899	0.958	1.021	1.088	1.160	1.237	1.318	1.405	1.498						10.7
10.00	3.5	13.49	14.8	0.747	0.797	0.851	0.908	0.970	1.035	1.105	1.179	1.259	1.344	1.435	1.531	1.635							10.6
10.00	4	13.77	15.1	0.848	0.906	0.969	1.036	1.107	1.183	1.265	1.352	1.445	1.544	1.651	1.764								10.3
10.00	4.5	14.04	15.1	0.958	1.025	1.097	1.174	1.257	1.345	1.439	1.540	1.648	1.764	1.888									9.9
10.00	5	14.30	15.0	1.078	1.155	1.238	1.326	1.421	1.523	1.632	1.748	1.873	2.007										9.3
10.00	5.5	14.55	14.7	1.210	1.298	1.392	1.494	1.602	1.719	1.844	1.978	2.122											8.7
10.00	6	14.80	14.1	1.355	1.456	1.563	1.679	1.803	1.937	2.080	2.234												8.0
10.00	6.5	15.04	13.3	1.516	1.630	1.753	1.885	2.026	2.179	2.342													7.2
10.00	7	15.27	12.3	1.695	1.824	1.963	2.113	2.275	2.448														6.3
10.00	7.5	15.50	11.1	1.893	2.040	2.198	2.368	2.552															5.4
10.00	8	15.72	9.5	2.114	2.280	2.460	2.653																4.4
10.00	8.5	15.94	7.7	2.361	2.549	2.752																	3.4
10.00	9	16.16	5.5	2.637	2.850																		2.3
10.00	9.5	16.37	2.9	2.946																			1.2
10.00	10	16.59	0.0	0.000																			0.0

Where columns are defined as follows:

Orig rate = original rate at which swap was booked
Period = semi-annual period at which default occurs
New rate = simulated future rate based on equation of orig rate × e (HV × SQRT (period)
Calculated replacement cost = sum of differences between original rate and new rate, discounted by new rate
Columns 1–19 = individual coupon differentials period by period, required for calculation of calculated replacement cost
Discounted replacement cost = calculated replacement cost discounted by original rate to express maximum replacement cost in current terms

Swap Replacement Costs (per cent)

Historical volatility: 14.50 per cent

Orig rate (per cent)	Period	New rate (per cent)	Calculated replacement cost	Number of periods remaining in swap life: 1	2	3	4	5	6	7	8	9	Discounted replacement cost (per cent)
10.00	0.5	11.08	3.7	0.332	0.351	0.370	0.391	0.412	0.435	0.459	0.485	0.512	3.6
10.00	1	11.56	4.9	0.498	0.526	0.557	0.589	0.623	0.659	0.697	0.738		4.4
10.00	1.5	11.94	5.4	0.647	0.686	0.727	0.770	0.816	0.865	0.917			4.7
10.00	2	12.28	5.6	0.796	0.845	0.897	0.952	1.010	1.072				4.6
10.00	2.5	12.58	5.4	0.950	1.009	1.073	1.140	1.212					4.2
10.00	3	12.85	4.9	1.113	1.184	1.260	1.341						3.7
10.00	3.5	13.12	4.1	1.288	1.372	1.462							3.0
10.00	4	13.36	3.1	1.478	1.577								2.1
10.00	4.5	13.60	1.7	1.686									1.1
10.00	5	13.83	0.0	0.000									0.0

Where columns are defined as follows:

Orig rate = original rate at which swap was booked
Period = semi-annual period at which default occurs
New rate = simulated future rate based on equation of orig rate × e (HV × SQRT (period)
Calculated replacement cost = sum of differences between original rate and new rate, discounted by new rate
Columns 1–9 = individual coupon differentials period by period, required for calculation of calculated replacement cost
Discounted replacement cost = calculated replacement cost discounted by original rate to express maximum replacement cost in current terms

Swap Replacement Costs (per cent)

Historical volatility: 16.00 per cent				Number of periods remaining in swap life									
Orig rate (per cent)	Period	New rate (per cent)	Calculated replacement cost	1	2	3	4	5	6	7	8	9	Discounted replacement cost (per cent)
10.00	0.5	11.20	4.1	0.367	0.387	0.409	0.432	0.456	0.482	0.509	0.537	0.567	4.0
10.00	1	11.74	5.4	0.550	0.582	0.616	0.652	0.691	0.731	0.774	0.819		4.9
10.00	1.5	12.16	6.0	0.716	0.759	0.806	0.855	0.907	0.962	1.020			5.2
10.00	2	12.54	6.2	0.881	0.937	0.995	1.058	1.124	1.195				5.1
10.00	2.5	12.88	6.0	1.054	1.121	1.194	1.270	1.352					4.7
10.00	3	13.19	5.5	1.237	1.318	1.405	1.498						4.1
10.00	3.5	13.49	4.6	1.435	1.531	1.635							3.3
10.00	4	13.77	3.4	1.651	1.764								2.3
10.00	4.5	14.04	1.9	1.888									1.2
10.00	5	14.30	0.0	0.000									0.0

Where columns are defined as follows:

Orig rate = original rate at which swap was booked
Period = semi-annual period at which default occurs
New rate = simulated future rate based on equation of orig rate × e (HV × SQRT (period)
Calculated replacement cost = sum of differences between original rate and new rate, discounted by new rate
Columns 1–9 = individual coupon differentials period by period, required for calculation of calculated replacement cost
Discounted replacement cost = calculated replacement cost discounted by original rate to express maximum replacement cost in current terms

Appendix 4: Sample Risk Factors at Various Volatility Levels

Sample Risk Factors at Various Volatility Levels

Sample risk factors (RF) in %

General formula: HV *SQRT (time) *CLF, where

HV = historical volatility

CLF = confidence level factor

time = maturity of trade

Annual Historical Volatility*	Maturity of Trade								
	1 week	2 week	4 week	2 month	3 month	6 month	12 month	24 month	36 month
10.00%	1.85%	2.61%	3.69%	5.22%	6.40%	9.05%	12.80%	18.10%	22.17%
10.50%	1.94%	2.74%	3.88%	5.49%	6.72%	9.50%	13.44%	19.01%	23.28%
11.00%	2.03%	2.87%	4.06%	5.75%	7.04%	9.96%	14.08%	19.91%	24.39%
11.50%	2.12%	3.00%	4.25%	6.01%	7.36%	10.41%	14.72%	20.82%	25.50%
12.00%	2.22%	3.14%	4.43%	6.27%	7.68%	10.86%	15.36%	21.72%	26.60%
12.50%	2.31%	3.27%	4.62%	6.53%	8.00%	11.31%	16.00%	22.63%	27.71%
13.00%	2.40%	3.40%	4.80%	6.79%	8.32%	11.77%	16.64%	23.53%	28.82%
13.50%	2.49%	3.53%	4.99%	7.05%	8.64%	12.22%	17.28%	24.44%	29.93%
14.00%	2.58%	3.66%	5.17%	7.31%	8.96%	12.67%	17.92%	25.34%	31.04%
14.50%	2.68%	3.79%	5.36%	7.58%	9.28%	13.12%	18.56%	26.25%	32.15%
15.00%	2.77%	3.92%	5.54%	7.84%	9.60%	13.58%	19.20%	27.15%	33.26%
15.50%	2.86%	4.05%	5.73%	8.10%	9.92%	14.03%	19.84%	28.06%	34.36%
16.00%	2.95%	4.18%	5.91%	8.36%	10.24%	14.48%	20.48%	28.96%	35.47%
16.50%	3.05%	4.31%	6.10%	8.62%	10.56%	14.93%	21.12%	29.87%	36.58%
17.00%	3.14%	4.44%	6.28%	8.88%	10.88%	15.39%	21.76%	30.77%	37.69%
17.50%	3.23%	4.57%	6.47%	9.14%	11.20%	15.84%	22.40%	31.68%	38.80%
18.00%	3.32%	4.70%	6.65%	9.40%	11.52%	16.29%	23.04%	32.58%	39.91%
18.50%	3.42%	4.83%	6.84%	9.67%	11.84%	16.74%	23.68%	33.49%	41.01%
19.00%	3.51%	4.96%	7.02%	9.93%	12.16%	17.20%	24.32%	34.39%	42.12%
19.50%	3.60%	5.09%	7.21%	10.19%	12.48%	17.65%	24.96%	35.30%	43.23%
20.00%	3.69%	5.23%	7.39%	10.45%	12.80%	18.10%	25.60%	36.20%	44.34%
25.00%	4.62%	6.53%	9.24%	13.06%	16.00%	22.63%	32.00%	45.25%	55.43%
30.00%	5.54%	7.84%	11.08%	15.67%	19.20%	27.15%	38.40%	54.31%	66.51%

* based on a 250 trading day year

The above factors are calculated at a 90% confidence level, lognormal distribution

References

Abken, P, *Interest Rate Caps, Collars, and Floors, Federal Reserve Bank of Atlanta Economic Review*, November–December 1989, pp 3–23

Andersen, T, *Euromarket Instruments*, New York: New York Institute of Finance (1990)

Andersen, T and R Hasan, *Interest Rate Risk Management*, London: IFR Publishing (1989)

Antl, B, editor, *Swap Finance*, Volume 1, London: Euromoney Publications (1986)

Antl, B, editor, *Swap Finance*, Volume 2, London: Euromoney Publications (1986)

Arak, M, L Goodman and A Rones, *Credit Lines for New Instruments: Swaps, Over-the-counter Options, Forwards and Floor-ceiling Agreements*, from Proceedings of the Conference on Bank Structure and Competition, Federal Reserve Bank of Chicago, May 1986, pp 437–56

Arthur Andersen & Co, *ISDA Default Survey*, New York, July 1992

Auerbach, J and S Hayes, III, *Investment Banking and Diligence*, Boston: Harvard Business School Press (1986)

Bank for International Settlements, *International Convergence of Capital Measurement and Capital Standards*, Basle, Switzerland, July 1988

Bartko, P, *BIS Plugs the Holes in Netting*, *Euromoney*, May 1991, pp 101–102

Bartlett, W, *Mortgage-Backed Securities*, New York: New York Institute of Finance (1989)

Baxter, N, *The Commercial Paper Market*, Boston: Bankers Publishing Company (1966)

Beidelman, C, editor, *Cross Currency Swaps*, Homewood, Illinois: Business One Irwin (1992)

Beidelman, C, *Financial Swaps*, Homewood, Illinois: Dow Jones Irwin (1985)

Beidelman, C, editor, *Interest Rate Swaps*, Homewood, Illinois: Business One Irwin (1991)

Bhala, R, *Perspectives on Risk Based Capital*, Tokyo: Toppan Co (1992)

Bishop, P and D Dixon, *The Foreign Exchange Handbook*, New York: McGraw Hill (1992)

Brady, S, *Eurobond Markets Get Trigger Happy*, *Euromoney*, March 1992, pp 34–40

Brady, S, *The Ref Gets Rough*, *Euromoney*, April 1992, pp 25–31

Breeden, R and E Corrigan, *Proposed Minimum Capital Rules for Banks and Securities Firms*, *World of Banking*, March 1992, p 9

Brown, S and M Kritzman, editors, *Quantitative Methods for Financial Analysis*, Homewood, Illinois: Dow Jones Irwin (1992)

Bullock, G, *Euronotes and Eurocommercial Paper*, London: Butterworths (1987)

Carter, H and I Parington, *Applied Economics in Banking and Finance*, 2nd edition, Oxford: Oxford University Press (1981)

Charlton, W, *The Pricing Effects of the Risk-based Capital Regulations*, *Journal of Commercial Bank Lending*, April 1991, pp 29–34

Chiriniko, R and G Guill, *A Framework for Assessing Credit Risk in Depository Institutions: Toward Regulatory Reform*, *Journal of Banking and Finance*, September 1991, Volume 15, pp 785–804

Chorafas, D, *Risk Management in Financial Institutions*, London: Butterworths (1990)

Cook, T and B Summers, editors, *Instruments of the Money Market*, 5th edition, Richmond, Virginia: Federal Reserve Bank of Richmond (1981)

Cooper, I and A Mello, *The Default Risk of Swaps*, *Journal of Finance*, June 1991, Volume XLVI, Number 2, pp 597–620

Cox, J, R Hillman *et al*, *Securities Regulation*, Boston: Little, Brown and Company (1991)

Das, S, *Swap Financing*, Sydney: The Law Book Company (1989)

Davis, K and I Harper, *Risk Management in Financial Institutions*, Sydney: Allen and Unwin Australia (1991)

Doherty, N, *Corporate Risk Management*, New York: McGraw Hill (1985)

Donaldson, J and T Donaldson, *The Medium Term Loan Market*, London: Macmillan (1982)

Donaldson, T, *Credit Risk and Exposure in Securitization and Transactions*, London: St Martin's Press (1989)

Donaldson, T, *International Lending by Commercial Banks*, New York: John Wiley (1979)

Farrant, R, *Swap Markets: A Central Bank Perspective*, *World of Banking*, January 1992, pp 14–32

Fabozzi, F and F Modigliani, *Capital Markets Institutions and Instruments*, Englewood, New Jersey: Prentice Hall (1992)

Fabozzi, F, editor, *The Handbook of Fixed Income Options*, Chicago: Probus Publishing Company (1989)

Fabozzi, F and I Pollack, editors, *The Handbook of Fixed Income Securities*, Homewood, Illinois: Dow Jones Irwin (1987)

Fabozzi, F, editor, *The Handbook of Mortgage Backed Securities*, revised edition, Chicago: Probus Publishing Company (1988)

Felgran, S, *Interest Rate Swaps: Use, Risk and Prices*, *New England Economic Review*, November–December 1987, pp 22–32

Felix, R, editor, *Commercial Paper*, London: Euromoney Publications (1987)

Fisher, F, *Eurobonds*, London: Euromoney Publications (1988)

Flom, J, B Garfield *et al*, editors, *Disclosure Requirements of Public Companies and Insiders*, New York: Practising Law Institute (1967)

Fons, J, A Kimball and D Girualt, *Corporate Bond Defaults and Default Rates 1970–1991*, *Moody's Special Report*, Moody's Investor Service, January 1992

Fons, J and A Kimball, *Defaults and Orderly Exits of Commercial Paper Issuers 1972–1991*, *Moody's Special Report*, Moody's Investor Service, February 1992

Gibson, R, *Option Valuation*, New York: McGraw Hill (1991)

Gilbert, A, *Implications of Netting Arrangements for Bank Risk in Foreign Exchange Transactions*, *Federal Reserve Bank of St Louis Review*, January 1992, pp 3–15

Haley, C and L Schall, *The Theory of Financial Decisions*, Tokyo: McGraw Hill International (1979)

Heller, L, editor, *Eurocommercial Paper*, London: Euromoney Publications (1988)

Henderson, S and J Price, *Currency and Interest Rate Swaps*, London: Butterworths (1988)

Hull, J, *Introduction to Futures and Options Markets*, Englewood, New Jersey: Prentice Hall (1991)

Hull, J, *Options, Futures and Other Derivative Securities*, Englewood, New Jersey: Prentice Hall (1989)

James, J *Risk Management in Banking*, Washington, DC: American Bankers Association (1979)

Kapner, K and J Marshall, *The Swaps Handbook*, New York: New York Institute of Finance (1990)

Kaufold, H and M Smirlock, *The Impact of Credit Risk on Pricing and Duration of Floating Rate Notes, Journal of Banking and Finance*, February 1991, Volume 15, pp 43–53

Lagayette, P, *A Central Banker's Perspective on Risk and Innovation, World of Banking*, January 1991, pp 21–24

Lee, P, *Securities Houses Face Capital Clampdown, Euromoney*, April 1992, pp 32–43

Levonian, M, *Have Large Banks Become Riskier? Recent Evidence from the Option Markets, Federal Reserve Bank of San Francisco Economic Review*, Fall 1991, Number 4, pp 3–17

Logue, D, editor, *Handbook of Modern Finance*, Boston: Warren, Gorham and Lamont (1990)

Maisel, S, *Risk and Capital Adequacy in Commercial Banks*, Chicago: University of Chicago Press (1981)

Mann, C A, *The Evolution of the CMO and its Influence on the Structuring of Derivative Mortgage Products, Mortgage Backed Securities Research*, New York: Drexel Burnham Lambert, September 1987

Meyer, S and W Stevens, *An Introduction to Stripped Mortgage Backed Securities, Mortgage Backed Securities Research*, New York: Drexel Burnham Lambert, April 1987

Morgen, K, *Balancing Financial Innovation and Exposure, World of Banking*, January 1991, pp 12–14

Muehring, K, *Derivatives – Who Do You Trust?, Institutional Investor*, May 1992, pp 51–55

Muffet, M, *Modeling Credit Exposure on Swaps*, from Proceedings of the Conference on Bank Structure and Competition, Federal Reserve Bank of Chicago, May 1987, pp 473–496

OECD, *Systemic Risks in the Securities Markets*, Paris, OECD: (1992)

Park, Y S, *Eurobond Market: Function and Structure*, New York: Praeger Publishers (1974)

Ratner, D, *Securities Regulation*, St Paul, Minnesota: West Publishing (1988)

Rendleman, R and B Bartter, *The Pricing of Options on Debt Securities, Journal of Financial and Quantitative Analysis*, March 1980, Volume 15, pp 11–24

Riehl, H and R Rodriguez, *Foreign Exchange and Money Markets*, New York: McGraw Hill (1983)

Sacks, P and S Crawford, *New Products, New Risks*, New York: Harper Business (1991)

Sarwal, A, editor, *KPMG International Handbook of Financial Instruments and Transactions*, London: Butterworths (1989)

Schwartz, R and C Smith, Jr, editors, *The Handbook of Currency and Interest Rate Risk Management*, New York: New York Institute of Finance (1990)

Securities Act of 1933, Chicago: Commerce Clearing House (1985)

Securities Exchange Act of 1934, Chicago: R R Donnelley (1990)

Soderquist, L, *Securities Regulation*, 2nd edition, Westbury, New York: Foundation Press (1988)

Soderquist, L, *Understanding the Securities Laws*, New York: Practising Law Institute (1987)

Stigum, M, *The Money Market*, Homewood, Illinois: Dow Jones Irwin (1983)

Stigum, M, *The Repo and Reverse Markets*, Homewood, Illinois: Dow Jones Irwin (1989)

Sutton, W, *Trading in Currency Options*, New York: New York Institute of Finance (1988)

Swary, I and B Topf, *Global Financial Deregulation*, Cambridge, Massachusetts: Blackwell Publishing (1992)

Tiner, J and J Conneely, *Managing International Treasury Transactions*, New York: New York Institute of Finance (1992)

Veale, S, *Handbook of US Capital Markets*, New York: Harper Brothers (1991)

Wall, L and J Pringle, *Interest Rate Swaps: a Review of the Issues, Federal Reserve Bank of Atlanta Economic Review*, November–December 1988, pp 22–37

Walmsley, J, *The Foreign Exchange Guide*, New York: John Wiley (1983)

Walmsley, J, *The New Financial Instruments*, New York: John Wiley (1988)

Walter, I, editor, *Deregulating Wall Street*, New York: John Wiley (1985)

Welch, J, editor, *The Regulation of Banks in the Member States of the EEC*, London: Graham and Trotman (1981)

Index

accrued interest receivable (AIR) 218
actual exposure 207–209
actual market risk (AMR) 58, 65
Alton Box v Goldman Sachs 151
AMR, see actual market risk
arbitraging 45, 46, 48, 49, 170–171, 204
Arthur Andersen 11, 240
asset-backed securities 5, 6, 87

Bank for International Settlements (BIS) 14, 17, 38, 40, 89, 123, 174, 190, 204, 230–1
bank lines 135–6
Bank of Credit and Commerce International (BCCI) 16, 178
Bank of England (BOE) 13–14, 16, 231
Bank of Japan 14–16
Bank of New England (BNE) 11–12, 16, 240
Bankers' Acceptances 15, 134
bankruptcy 9, 12, 32, 62, 95, 144–5, 150–151, 164–5, 191, 233–4, 240
Banque de France 14
Barclays Bank 240
Basle Committee 17, 40
BCCI, see Bank of Credit and Commerce International
Bevill, Bresler and Schulman 95
Big Bang 5
BIS, see Bank for International Settlements
BNE, see Bank of New England
BOE, see Bank of England
bond 10–11, 43, 46, 62, 73, 89, 155–168
bond characteristics 158–160
bond indenture 155
bond underwriting 5, 160–161, 163, 166–8
bonds with warrants 8
Bretton Woods Agreement 3, 4, 13
British and Commonwealth plc 12, 16, 240

calculated replacement cost 215, 244–8
callable swaps 196, 200–203, 222–4
Campeau Corp 163
cap 196, 200–202, 204, 223–5
capital asset pricing model 36
cash settlement 100–101, 170
CDs, see certificates of deposit
CEM, see current exposure method
certificates of deposit (CDs) 15, 86, 134, 141–2, 146
CFTC, see Commodities and Futures Trading Commission
Chase Manhattan 94
Chicago Board Options Exchange 171
Christiania Bank 16
CMOs, see collateralised mortgage obligations
collar 196, 200–202, 224–5
collateral 21, 31, 40–42, 49–50, 67, 85–7, 90, 92–3, 95, 175, 183, 204–206
collateralised mortgage obligations (CMOs) 8, 87, 96–7, 119–120, 123
Colorado Ute 10, 151
Columbia Gas 10–11, 32, 151
Comark 95
commercial mortgage 115, 117
commercial paper (CP) 5, 15, 62–3, 134–8, 140–141, 146–152, 167
Commissioner of Public Debt 86
committed lines 136
Commodities and Futures Trading Commission (CFTC) 14
commodity swap 196, 202–203, 226
Conditional Prepayment Rate (CPR) 117
confidence level 37, 69, 73, 77–80, 191, 212, 226, 236
conforming pools 116
conforming whole loans 87
convertible bonds 157–8, 162, 168
corporate bond 5, 15, 16
corporate settlement 100
corridor 196, 200–202, 224–5
counterparty risk 8, 9, 26, 29–30, 33, 55–6, 64–6, 163
covenant 136
CP, see commercial paper
CPR, see Conditional Prepayment Rate
credit analysis 27, 29, 31
credit enhancement 25, 50, 118
credit risk 17, 26, 33–5, 38, 67, 174–6, 195, 203–248

credit spread 35, 37–9
cross currency swap (CCS) 33, 44, 196, 198, 219–222
cross rates 169
currency derivatives 169–192
currency swap 8, 16, 207, 243
current exposure method (CEM) 231–2
current ratio 28

debt underwriting 6
default 9–12, 22, 30, 49, 62, 64, 71, 86–7, 90, 94, 104, 144, 152, 164, 238–240
delivery risk 57–9, 65, 174, 177–8
delivery versus payment (DVP) 31, 50, 121, 182
Den norske Bank 16
Department of Housing and Urban Development (HUD) 117
Deutsche Bundesbank 14
Development Finance Corporation of New Zealand (DFC) 10, 12, 32, 140, 147, 177
DFC, see Development Finance Corporation of New Zealand
discount swap 230
discounted replacement cost 215, 244–8
disintermediation 6, 13
Drexel Burnham Lambert 12, 16, 178, 240
Drysdale Government Securities 94
due bill repo 88, 90
due diligence 62, 148–152, 166–8
Duff & Phelphs 135
DVP, see delivery versus payment

EC, see European Community
ECP, see Eurocommercial paper
EII Holdings 11, 163
enhancement 20–21, 25, 48–51, 89, 102, 124, 162, 175, 204
Equitable Lomas Leasing 10
equity 46, 73
equity derivatives 16, 57
equity-linked 16
equity underwriting 5, 6
Escott v BarChris Construction Corp 168
ESM Companies 95
Eurobond 15, 155–6, 160–161
Eurocommercial paper (ECP) 7, 10, 15, 61, 134, 139–140, 146
Euronote 61, 139, 146
European Community (EC) 5
Exchange Act 138
external insurance 49

Fannie Mae, see Federal National Mortgage Association
FDIC 240
FE, see fractional exposure
Federal Banking Supervisory Office 14
Federal Home Loan Banks (FHLBs) 117–118
Federal Home Loan Mortgage Corporation (FHLMC) 115–118, 120–121, 123
Federal Housing Administration (FHA) 115, 117, 122
Federal National Mortgage Association (FNMA) 45, 97, 115–118, 120–123
Federal Reserve Bank 5, 13–15, 86, 99, 141, 231–2
Federated Department Stores 163
FHA, see Federal Housing Administration
FHLBs, see Federal Home Loan Banks
FHLMC, see Federal Home Loan Mortgage Corporation
Financial Institutions Reform, Recovery and Enhancement
Act 1989 (FIRREA) 95, 191, 233
Financial Services Act 15
FIRREA, see Financial Institutions Reform, Recovery and Enforcement Act
First Boston 135, 141
Fitch Investors' Services 135
Fleet Norstar 240
floor 196, 200–202, 204, 223–4
FNMA, see Federal National Mortgage Association
foreign bonds 156
foreign exchange (FX) 6, 15, 45–6, 48, 57, 74, 169–192
forward foreign exchange 4
forward GNMA securities 44–5, 74
forward rate agreements (FRAs) 8, 173–5, 187–190
forward swap 196, 202, 225–6
forward (extended settlement trades) 71, 99, 100, 104, 121
fractional exposure 209–217, 236
Franklin Savings 16
Franklin Savings Bank of NY v Levy 151
FRAs, see forward rate agreements
Freddie Mac, see Federal Home Loan Mortgage Corporation
Freddie Mae, see Federal National Mortgage Association
FRNs, see floating rate notes
futures 6, 16, 30, 44, 57
FX, see foreign exchange
FX settlement 174

generics 177
gilts 7
Ginnie Mae, see Government National Mortgage Association
Glass-Steagall Act of 1933 5, 15
GNMA, see Government National Mortgage Association
Goldman, Sachs 135, 141, 151
Government National Mortgage Association (GNMA) 74, 97, 115, 117–118, 120–121, 123
Government Securities Inc (GSI) 16
Group of 10 14, 17
GSI, see Government Securities Inc
guarantees 41, 62

haircut 69–70, 87, 91, 94, 232
Hazell v Hammersmith and Fulham London Borough Council 11
hedge 7–8, 16, 30, 34–5, 44–5, 47, 49, 241–3
hedging risk 56
Herman & MacLean v Huddleston 167–8
Herstatt Bank 177
high yield bonds 8, 162
historical volatility (HV) 36–7, 39, 69, 73–5, 77–81, 96–7, 114, 191–2, 211–213, 220, 236–7, 243
HUD, see Department of Housing and Urban Development
hurdle rate 34, 37–8
hurdle rate spread 34–5
HV, see historical volatility

index warrants 8
insider trading 16
insolvencies 16
Integrated Resources 10, 140, 147
interest only (IO) strips 87, 96, 121, 123
interest rate risk 17
interest rate swap (IRS) 8, 32–3, 39, 70, 196–8, 207, 219, 235
International Convergence of Capital Measurements and Capital Standards 17, 40, 231, 242
International Organisation of Securities Commissions (IOSCO) 17
International Swap Dealers' Association (ISDA) 234
inventory risk 30, 60–62, 65, 68, 73, 145–7, 163–4
IO, see interest only
IOSCO, see International Organisation of Securities Commissions
IRS, see interest rate swaps
ISDA, see International Swap Dealers' Association

Japanese Government Bonds (JGBs) 89
JGBs, see Japanese Government Bonds
JP Morgan 5, 120
junk bond 10, 11, 16, 44, 74, 156–7

Lamfalussy Report 190
lease financing 6
legal or documentary risk 55
Lehman Brothers 135, 141
letter of credit 41, 49, 62, 118, 135, 152–3, 205
letter of credit paper 137–9
leverage 28–9, 136
leveraged buyouts 10
LIBOR 70, 141, 173, 193–4, 197, 207-208, 217, 220, 225, 228–9, 241–2
LIFFE 171
Lion Capital Group 95
liquid repo 88
liquidity 17, 27–9, 37, 49, 56, 65, 89, 117, 137, 241
local authorities (UK) 11–12, 240
Lomas Financial 140, 147, 151
Lombard-Wall 94–5
Luxembourg Stock Exchange 15

management buyouts 10
Manville Corporation 10
market risk 8, 30, 57–9, 62, 64–8, 73, 90, 104, 163, 178–190, 195
market volatility 3, 7–8, 19
Markov model 210–211
mark-to-market 31–2, 42, 65, 68, 89–90, 92, 94, 96, 102, 105, 106, 123, 179, 199, 205–207, 209, 222, 237
mark-to-market exposure 11
matched book 86
material adverse change 136
maturity 20, 25, 36, 41–3, 65, 73, 77–81, 89, 92, 98, 102–103, 116, 123, 135, 142, 144, 162, 175, 179–180, 183, 195–6, 204, 206
Maxwell Communications 163
MBS, see mortgage-backed securities
MBS options 122–3
MBS products 118–123
medium-term notes (MTNs) 8, 134, 140–141, 144–7
Memorex Telex NV 11, 163
Merrill Lynch 120, 135, 140–141
Ministry for International Trade and Industry (MITI) 14

Ministry of Finance, Japan 14–16
MITI, see Ministry for International Trade and Industry
MOF, see multi-option facility
money market instruments 11, 47, 134–154, 163, 165
Monte Carlo simulation 212–213
Moody's Investor Service 135, 152
Morgan Stanley 135, 141
mortgage 44–5, 116–133
Mortgage and Realty Trust (MRT) 10, 32, 136, 151
mortgage backed securities (MBS) 5, 6, 46, 48, 86, 115–133
motivation 20, 25, 43, 47–9, 89, 102, 124, 142, 162, 172, 175, 193, 204
Mountleigh 32
MRT, see Mortgage and Realty Trust
MTN, see medium-term note
multi-option facility 140
municipal bonds 5–6

Nederlandsche Bank 14
netting foreign exchange 190–191, 197
netting swaps 233–5
New York Mercantile Exchange 44, 203
NIF, see note issuance facility
non-conforming residential mortgage 117
non-delivery limit 181–2
non-par swaps 229–230
note issuance facility (NIF) 40–41, 61, 63, 139–140, 147
notional principal swap 11, 70, 197–8, 230
NYMEX 226

OCC, see Office of the Comptroller of the Currency
OECD 14, 40, 49, 51, 161
OEM, see original exposure method
Office of the Comptroller of the Currency (OCC) 13, 15
off-balance sheet 6, 17, 39, 41, 152, 193, 231
off-market swap 33
Olympia & York 12, 32
on-balance sheet 14
open market paper 137
operational risk 55
option 6, 16, 30, 37, 57, 101, 108–112, 125–132, 185–7, 203
option to terminate 31, 42, 195, 200, 206
original exposure method (OEM) 231–2
OTC, see over-the counter
overcollateralisation 69, 87, 89, 91, 118
over-the-counter 100, 122 171, 203

PanAm 163
participation certificates 87
pass through securities 115–133
payment mismatches 227–9
payment netting 190–191, 233–5
Penn Central CP 151
Penn Central Transportation Company 150–151
Philadelphia Stock Exchange 171
PMR, see potential market risk
PO, see principal only
Polly Peck International 10, 32
position (inventory) risk 57, 60–61, 65, 68, 144–7, 163
potential market risk (PMR) 58, 65, 78, 181
potential risk equivalent exposure (PREE) 92
PREE, see potential risk equivalent exposure
premium 19, 33, 103, 200–201
premium swap 229
primary dealers 15, 115
principal only (PO) strip 87, 96, 123
private label pass-through 116, 118
privately placed paper 137–8
product risk 55–7, 73
provisional risk 30, 57, 61–5, 68, 73, 147–153, 163
PSA, see Public Securities Association
public sector bonds 6
public sector debt 15
Public Securities Association (PSA) 95, 117
pure risk 19
puttable swaps 196, 200–203, 222–3

rating agency 11, 26, 28, 118, 135
ratio analysis 26
REE, see risk equivalent exposure
registration requirements 153–4
Rendleman and Bartter model 210–212, 235–6
repurchase agreements 6, 41–2, 49, 57, 69, 85–97
Reserve Bank of Australia 14, 231
residential mortgages 115, 118
return 142
reverse repurchases 41, 90–97
reverse to maturity 88
reverse/repurchase agreements 47, 85–97
revolving bank line 62
revolving underwriting facility (RUF) 40–41, 51, 63, 139–140, 147
RF, see risk factor

risk adjusted exposure 67
risk adjusted loan equivalency 67
risk enhancement50–51, 89
risk equivalent exposure (REE) 63, 68–73, 91–7, 179, 218–219, 238
risk factor (RF) 35–7, 39, 41, 70–71, 73–4, 77–81, 91–97, 112–114, 123, 142, 153, 168, 180, 191–2, 214
risk quantification 104–112, 125–132, 143–153, 176–190, 206–243
risk weighting 17, 36, 38, 40–41, 50, 89, 102, 168, 174, 231–2
RTD Securities 95
RUF, see revolving underwriting facility

Salomon Brothers 135, 141
Sanders v John Nuveen & Co 151
savings and loan institutions 11, 44
SEC, see Securities and Exchange Commission
secured bonds 162, 165
secured swap 50–51, 205
Securities Act of 1933 134, 137–8, 147, 152–4, 161, 166–8
Securities Exchange Act of 1934 14, 62, 149, 166
Securities and Exchange Commission (SEC) 13, 14, 16, 136–7, 232
Securities & Exchange Law, Article 65 5
servicing 115
settlement risk 30, 58–9, 65, 68
Skopbank 16
Smithsonian Agreement 4
soft puts 63, 65
sovereign risk 56
speculating 45, 47–9, 124
speculative risk 19, 21
spot 4
spread 34, 36–8, 40, 50, 135, 169
square root rule 78
Standard & Poor's 135, 152
standby letter of credit 41, 152
sterling commercial paper 10
stock index futures 14
subordinated bonds 164
surety bonds 164
swap 6, 8. 11. 16, 30, 32–4, 37, 40–42, 44, 49, 57, 193–243
swap defaults 11, 240–241
swap derivative 8, 193–243
swap maturities 199, 221–2
swap options 199, 221–2
swap replacement costs 249–259

tax exempt commercial paper 137
TBA trades 121–3
third party guarantees 49, 205
third party insurance 50, 118
Tier 1 equity (core) 17
Tier 2 equity (supplementary) 17
time value of money 39
Toyo Shinkin 16
Treasury 38, 71, 94, 116, 121
Treasury bill 71, 81, 86–7, 92, 96–9, 101, 114
Treasury bond 73–4, 81, 86, 97–9, 114
Treasury derivatives 98–114
Treasury note 69, 76–7, 79–81, 85, 97–8, 114
Treasury option 73, 100–101, 103–4
Treasury security 70–71, 86, 98–114, 205
tri-party repo 88, 90
TWA 11, 163

underwriter's liability 62, 65, 147–152, 163, 165–8
universal banking 3, 5
University Hill v Goldman, Sachs 151
unsecured swap 50–51
US Bankruptcy Code 95, 191, 233
USCP, see US commercial paper
US commercial paper (USCP) 7, 9, 10, 15, 147, 151
US domestic bonds 156
US government bill 15
US government bond 15, 16
US government securities 15, 86–7, 89
US municipal bond 15
US Treasury instrument 85, 241

VA, see Veterans Administration
Veterans Administration (VA) 115, 117–118, 122
volatility 4, 7, 33, 73–6, 96, 191, 221

Wang Labs 10, 140, 147
Warburg, S. G. 140
warehousing 115
Welch Foods v Goldman, Sachs 151
West Texas Intermediate 44, 203
when issued (WI) 99–100, 102, 105, 121
WI, see when issued
Winter & Hirsch 151

yield enhancing 45, 47–51, 89, 102–103, 124, 199, 204

Zeller v Bogue Electric Manf. Corp 149
zero coupon bond 119, 157
zero coupon swap 33, 58, 206, 228